The Log Cabin in America

THE LOG CABIN IN AMERICA

From Pioneer Days to the Present

C. A. WESLAGER

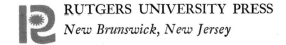
RUTGERS UNIVERSITY PRESS
New Brunswick, New Jersey

Copyright © 1969 by Rutgers University,
the State University of New Jersey
Library of Congress Catalogue Card Number: 69-13554
SBN: 8135-0596-8

Manufactured in the United States of America
by Quinn & Boden Company, Inc., Rahway, New Jersey

To the memory of my sister
Dolores Weslager Buente

Acknowledgments

Many people have assisted me over the years that this book was in preparation. Some of them are mentioned in the Foreword. Others to whom I am indebted are Mrs. Birgitta L. Wallace of Carnegie Museum, Pittsburgh, Pa.; Mrs. Marie Windell and Norman B. Wilkinson of the Hagley-Eleutherian Library, Greenville, Delaware; the Reference Department of the Wilmington Institute Free Library, especially Mrs. Sara B. Gere and Mrs. Andrew Nickolaus; Leon de Valinger, Jr., Delaware's state archivist; Dale Fields of the Historical Society of Delaware; the Morris Library of the University of Delaware; and the Chester County (Pennsylvania) Historical Society, especially Miss Dorothy Lapp.

Among the numerous individuals to whom I am particularly grateful for information or assistance, I would like to make separate acknowledgment to A. R. Dunlap, Ernest J. Moyne, Henry Glassie, Donald Hutslar, Wilbur Zelinsky, R. N. De Armond, Charles F. Gritzner, Peter O. Wacker, Hubert G. H. Wilhelm, Eugene M. Wilson, Estyn Evans, Toini-Inkeri Kaukonen, Mrs. Gail M. Gibson, Erik Forssman, Ingemar Liman, Fred B. Kniffen, Gordon and Ramelle Medaris, and William B. Marye.

C.A.W.

Contents

Foreword

In the years that have elapsed since America's pioneer days, the log cabin has become a sort of historical relic, an oddity like the flintlock rifle, the powder horn, or the spinning wheel, generally regarded as quaint artifacts of the past. The modern family is so far removed in its thoughts and surroundings from the homespun life of earlier generations of Americans that it is easy to overlook the reality and significance of the log cabin as a home.

Home means different things to different people depending upon the circumstances in which it is used. If an American tourist in a foreign country is asked about home, he usually answers that home is Arkansas; Ohio; California; or one of the other forty-seven states; or he sometimes identifies home in terms of a city. If he is a Bostonian, he will probably say, "Boston, Mass, is my home," using the name of the city and a contraction of the state in one breath. "Pittsburgh was my home," I usually reply to a question about my birthplace, "but Hockessin, Delaware, is now my home."

Home may also be designated in terms of a street address, in which case it refers to the specific location of a dwelling place. "My home," I would reply to a question raised by another Hockessin resident, "is on Old Public Road." The original Anglo-Saxon meaning of *ham* from which the word home is derived was limited to a fixed dwelling place, and for a long time home was used synonymously with house. A hamlet was a cluster of *hams*. Today, the expression, "I'm going home," may refer to returning to a specific country, a state, a city or town—or it may mean the house and the street address where the speaker lives. It may mean something more solemn, as in the scriptural line, "Man goeth to his long home."

Even when referring to a house, home has come to mean more than the dwelling place. Home is mother and father; brother and sisters; a baby in the cradle; accustomed pictures on the walls; a familiar arrangement of rugs and furniture; an alarm clock ringing at dawn; a cat purring on the hearth; a dog barking at the kitchen door; a television antenna on the roof, or it may mean a host of other things. It is a place of discipline and learning where prayers are said at bedtime by the younger children; current events and neighborhood affairs discussed; and a point of view developed on a variety of subjects irrespective of the nature or the location of the abode itself.

"Be it ever so humble, there's no place like home," is a memorable line, but the lyricist certainly had more in mind than a house. Although the family has long found common interests in a residence where the basic human need for shelter is satisfied, home has connotations that go far beyond the physical dwelling place. This was especially true of the log cabin, because home was not only the log shell of a primitive cabin, but the environment it encompassed where the dispositions of parents and children were combined and expressed in a behavior that might be called a family personality, involving among other things morality and manners. Home, in short, is a social institution that includes, among many other things, a house.

A characteristic of the modern American home is its mobility, because a mass restlessness has made us a foot-loose nation of movers. As Russell Lynes pointed out in *The Domesticated Americans* (Harper & Row, 1963), every year thousands of families gather together their household belongings and move to different houses or apartments. Expanding families move to seek larger living quarters; diminishing families move to smaller apartments; others move to a higher rung in the social ladder, to find new locations closer to schools and churches, to be near, or more distant from, relatives.

They move because they have had a tiff with the landlord about painting the kitchen or fixing the plumbing, because they don't like their neighbors, and for scores of other reasons. In no place in the world do moving vans loaded with furniture and household goods move back and forth with such regularity as in America. Moving is big business accomplished on a huge scale by companies who will do a complete job of packing and moving across the hall, across the town, across the city, or across the continent.

The usual pattern is that newlyweds begin their married life in a modest apartment, sometimes as tenants on the second floor of a dwelling whose first floor is occupied by the resident owners. When the couple start raising a family, they often buy or rent a small house in the suburbs, and as they prosper and their children get older, they sometimes move to a larger and more pretentious house. When the children grow up, and after the husband retires, many sell their homes and move back into small apartments, completing the cycle. Some retired couples may move to another part of the country where the climate is more to their liking, or to be near their grandchildren, whose father was moved by the corporation that employs him. This shuttling back and forth of families from city to city by American corporations gives modern business a nomadic quality, which is also a factor contributing significantly to home and family mobility. There is also the subject of military mobility—the movement of families from one military base to another, not only in America, but to foreign countries where our armed forces maintain installations. A certain segment of America's population actually lives on wheels, and their mobile homes can be seen in trailer parks built along our motor routes and on the outskirts of our cities. With or without wheels, home has become a moving sociological target, and the size, shape, and location of the dwelling place, the center of family activity, is only one of the factors making up the home complex.

"How did you become interested in log cabins?" I've been asked this question many times. The answer is that anyone who attempts to reconstruct the history of America's colonial period, with which I have been concerned for many years, cannot overlook this unique element in our traditions. It so happens, however, that my interest in log cabins predates my researches in the colonial period, having had its beginning when I was a boy in Allegheny County in western Pennsylvania. I once accompanied my father on a visit to relatives of his father's by a second marriage, the Hamels, who lived in a two-story log dwelling in what is now the suburbs of Pittsburgh, but fifty years ago was "out in the country in Fair Haven," a farm and mining community in Baldwin Township. My father explained the constructional features to me and showed me how the notching at the corners of the dwelling, and the clay daubing between the logs differed from conventional houses. Some time later when my teacher in the Mt. Oliver Borough Public School told the story of Abraham Lincoln's birth in a log cabin in Kentucky, I suddenly found myself basking in reflected glory when my classmates, who, like myself, lived in frame dwellings, learned that I had relatives living in a log cabin. It was almost as good as having been born in one myself. I didn't fully realize at the time that the Hamels, who initially rented the log dwelling for four dollars a month, depended on kerosene lamps for light, a coal stove for heat and cooking, an outhouse for sanitary facilities, and laboriously carried all their water from a cistern some distance from the house where roof rain water was collected (see Figures 1, 2). The Hamels lived there from 1909 until 1954, after which the house was removed to make way for a country club.

My father, a versatile man who had an acute awareness to his environment, never failed to point out old log cabins to me when on later occasions he took me on fishing trips on the Monongahela, Allegheny, and Ohio. I grew up with an alertness to these housing vestiges of the western Pennsylvania frontier, which were more numerous then than today. During the past twenty years this casual interest of my boyhood was renewed, and has evolved into a more serious study resulting in a large collection of notes, correspondence, photographs, color slides, newspaper clippings, and reprints of technical papers pertaining to American log housing.

My quest for representative examples of old log cabins before

Figure 1. Hamel Cabin, Fair Haven, Baldwin Township, Pennsylvania, where the writer first developed a boyhood interest in log cabins. Frame wing was a later addition to original one-room cabin with attic. Family's water supply was cistern supplied by rain spouts.

they were destroyed, and to learn something of their geographical distribution and the people who built them, has taken me to every state in the continental United States, and also beyond our borders. Like the long hours any researcher devotes to library or laboratory study, the time I have spent finding, examining, measuring, sketching corner notchings, and other features on log cabins may qualify me as an experienced observer, but is scarcely worthy of detailed treatment in a volume essentially intended as social history.

Perhaps I should make it crystal clear at the outset that I have not approached the subject of the log cabin as an architect, folklorist, or settlement geographer, although each has points of view that must not be disregarded if the log cabin is ever to be treated exhaustively by culturogeographic region. American geographers, with ample prece-

Figure 2. The author returned in 1952 to sketch V-notched hewn log corners on old Hamel House, which was removed in 1954.

dent set by their fellows in Europe, have in recent years turned their attention to housing as an integral part of settlement geography. The geographers have made notable contributions in their regional studies, which I will refer to in the text, but the number of geographers working in this specialized area is relatively small, and systematic treatment of the ingredients has not yet been carried very far, although an excellent beginning has been made and reported in the geographical literature.

Since I am dealing in the present volume with a broad expanse of land area—the Atlantic to the Pacific, including Alaska—and from a sociohistorical perspective—my principal aim is to give the general reader an understanding of the part played by the log cabin in early American family life, in the political arena, and in promoting Amer-

icanization and hastening democracy. My purpose has been to associate the log cabin with people, and although I will make references
to structural typology I will leave it to the settlement geographer for
a deeper analysis of forms and patterns, and to relate systematically
the several methods of log construction to specific areas of folk
housing.

I learned early in the game that the best places to find log cabins
are along the old routes which were originally Indian trails, and later
developed into horse paths, wagon roads, and finally, to modern automobile highways. Cabins are less numerous along the so-called "super
highways" which are usually new land routes. I have taken scores
of vacation, weekend, and holiday trips for the specific purpose of
looking for log cabins. I've motored from Boston to Bangor; from
Erie to Buffalo, Rochester, Syracuse, Utica, and Albany; from Chicago to Waukegan, Milwaukee, Port Washington, Barton, Addison,
Madison, and Marshfield; from Atlanta to Chattanooga, via Mur-
freesboro, to Nashville, Asheville, Charlotte, and Greensboro; from
Charleston to Savannah, St. Augustine, Orlando, Miami, and across
the Florida peninsula to Tampa and St. Petersburg. On the last leg of
the last mentioned jaunt, I was diverted by a roadside camp of Seminole Indians selling baubles to northern tourists, but I failed to find
one old log cabin. When an earlier tourist, John Bartram, the Pennsylvania botanist, visited Florida in 1769 he saw at Rollstown on the
St. John River "half a score of scattered houses in it built of round
logs," but to the best of my knowledge none of these old dwellings
has survived.

I left Dallas by car one Saturday morning, in company with Jack
Hale, a Texas informant, and we spent the remainder of the weekend
en route to Houston via Fort Worth, Waco, Austin, San Antonio,
Corpus Christi, and Galveston. I've driven from New Orleans to
Baton Rouge and thence to Jackson, Memphis, Little Rock, and
Tulsa; and from Columbia to Augusta, Raleigh, Charlotte, and Char-
lottesville. On a trip from Indianapolis to Cincinnati and Louisville
in 1956, I stopped to talk with an old gentleman along Route 2 near
Bedford, Kentucky, who told me his name was L. S. Ball. What made

me apply my brakes was that Mr. Ball was relaxing in a wicker chair on the front porch of a log house. He told me he helped his father raise the dwelling sixty-one years before when he was a boy of thirteen (see Figure 3).

A student of Kentucky folklore, with a broader interest than mine, could have spent many hours with this interesting patriarch recording all the details of the constructional process, including the tools that were used to build the cabin and the common names for them; measuring the logs; drawing floor plans to scale; and after finishing with that, examining roof, rafters, windows, doors, and fireplace, as well as taking a room-by-room inventory of some of the quaint furniture in the dwelling. I daresay that Mr. Ball could have supplied many other items of Kentucky folklore.

Figure 3. The late L. S. Ball, 74 years old when picture was taken in 1956, explains to author how, as a boy of 13, he helped his father erect this log house near Bedford, Kentucky.

Figure 4. Combination store and post office owned by George Shoemaker.

On a motor trip from Charleston to Savannah in 1967 along Route 17, I photographed the log post office at Switzerland, S.C., where George Shoemaker operated a general store and his wife was the postmaster (see Figure 4). He, too, as a boy helped his father notch the round logs and erect the store. Mr. Shoemaker was probably unaware that one of the earliest, if not the first, post office west of the Alleghenies at Danville, Kentucky, was built of logs, and there have been many others. Long before the U.S. Postal Service was institutionalized, pony express riders galloping the 2000-mile expanse of mountain and desert between St. Joseph, Missouri and Sacramento, California changed horses or riders at 190 stations along the route, many of which were built of logs.

My log cabin travels have included the rural areas of Pennsylvania, Ohio, Indiana, Illinois, and Minnesota, and my longest drive, which took three weeks, was from Phoenix (where I had flown from Philadelphia) to Flagstaff, Las Vegas, Riverside, Los Angeles, San Francisco, Portland, Seattle, and then to Spokane, from whence I returned east by train with many photographs and my notebook brimming. Some years later, I returned to Arizona to drive south to Tucson and into northern Mexico, an area that has few trees, and fewer log houses. I've explored the forested Olympic Peninsula in northwest Washington, and the rural sections of the Provinces of Quebec and Ontario, always returning from my jaunts to my home in the Delaware Valley where the log cabin made its American debut and where I have resided for the last thirty-one years.

There have also been some disappointments. I traveled with anticipation to Cazadero, California, hoping to find the log house which had been reported to me as the last dwelling surviving from the Russian occupation. I found it, only to learn that it was built about 1890 by an Anglo-American, one C. Christopher, according to Mrs. John Bei, a local historian who had an old snapshot of the cabin bearing a sign over the door, "The Log Cabin Resort." This disappointment was overshadowed by the thrill of seeing the original log walls of the commandant's house at nearby Fort Ross, a true vestige of the Russian occupation, which is described further in the last chapter of this volume.

After these—and many other excursions—I learned that certain areas were of importance in the distribution and diffusion of the log cabin whereas others were of lesser significance. For example, in the bayou country of Louisiana, where Henry Guidroz and I examined the houses of the shrimp fishermen, I saw many frame cottages, but in this section of the state, log cabins are as rare as they are in southern California and the desert areas of Nevada. On the other hand there are still so many log houses standing in Pennsylvania between Philadelphia and Pittsburgh that I have made a number of profitable trips back and forth over the Lincoln Highway (Route 30), portions of which were laid out by General John Forbes in the autumn of 1758. I have also made many sallies on the secondary roads, marking on a map all the log cabins seen en route.

I have also gone back and forth many times between Uniontown and Hagerstown over the old road that General Braddock built as he marched to his defeat on Fort Duquesne. Originally a path laid out

Figure 5. Photographed from moving car, old log house along roadside on Polish Mountain, Maryland, is covered with clapboards, but boards have rotted away at extreme left, exposing hewn logs.

by the Indian Nemacolin and Thomas Cresap, now Route 40, there
are still many log cabins that can be photographed from the window
of an automobile, like the boarded house on Polish Mountain whose
log walls are concealed beneath the clapboards (see Figure 5). I have
also driven many times into the Shenandoah Valley via Frederick,
Harpers Ferry, and Winchester to Hot Springs and White Sulphur
Springs, and from thence to Charleston, West Virginia, Parkersburg,
and Wheeling, dotting a road map with the locations of the dozens of
cabins on the route.

I have been fortunate in having the invaluable assistance of a number of local informants who guided me to log cabins which were so
remote that I could never have found them unaided. Once, over a
long weekend, Hugh Johns of Uniontown took me deep into the
mountains of Fayette County, Pennsylvania, where my windfall consisted of twenty-three log houses, five log barns, a memorial log church
(Jacobs Evangelical Church at Smithfield) and a deserted log blacksmith shop at Leckrone, which regrettably has since been destroyed.
This blacksmith's shop was no less an oddity than the eight-sided log
barn on the Hiwan Ranch near Morrison, Colorado, and the eight-
sided log building near Evergreen, now used as a clubhouse, which
my Colorado informant, M. J. Feller, turned up for my inspection
when I was combing that state.

Dr. George B. Scriven, an Episcopal priest of Baltimore, who has a
special interest in the history of Maryland's Harford and Baltimore
Counties, took me in 1956 to see many log cabins off the beaten track
in Harford County, including the old Amos Mill of logs near Carea,
a water-powered grist mill then operated by John Amos (see Figure 6).

Charles F. Kier, Jr., who has explored almost every foot of New
Jersey in search of Indian artifacts, trotted me over the southern
stretches of the state to show me the old cabins extant there, as did
Joseph S. Sickler on another occasion. Some time after my trip, Mr.
Kier decided to buy a log house where he and his wife now reside
(see Figure 7). My late uncle, Kenneth Lowe, and his wife Leah, who
lived in Moberly, Missouri, took me to see several typical pioneer

Figure 6. Amos grist mill, near Carea, Maryland, still in operation when photographed by author in 1956.

cabins still standing in the rural area between Moberly and Jefferson City.

The late Dr. J. Alden Mason, curator emeritus of the American Section of the University of Pennsylvania Museum, guided me to seven old cabins in Tredyffrin Township, Chester County, Pennsylvania, in an area settled by the early Welsh. The example I most fondly remember was a log dwelling with a stone addition on Irish Road near Daylesford, which Conrad Wilson, the owner-occupant was restoring as his family residence, with sensitivity for the traditions of the past.

Mrs. Josephine Albrecht showed me several cabins in the Darby Creek area of Chester County built under Swede-Finn influences,

Figure 7. Modern log dwelling, Weymouth Road, Hammonton, New Jersey, owned and occupied by Charles F. Kier, Jr., illustrative of contemporary log structures built along lines of old log cabins.

and the late Mrs. Olive C. Cadbury of Glen Moore listed for my inspection more than a dozen old cabins in the upper Brandywine drainage. My good friend and associate Arthur G. Volkman, who accompanied me on many log cabin jaunts, added a number of others to my list.

I also learned that the American pride in preserving historical structures has found expression in "log cabin memorials." Such is the Kemper Log House, built in 1804, and re-erected in Cincinnati's Zoological Gardens where it is maintained by the National Society of Colonial Dames of America. The replica of the log cabin birthplace of the author of the McGuffey Reader is preserved in Ford's Greenfield village in Detroit, a duplication of the original cabin that stood in Washington County, Pennsylvania, where William Holmes McGuffey was born in 1800.

The one-room cabin in Temple Square, Salt Lake City, with its protective canopy, is an original dwelling renovated and moved from the farm of an early Mormon pioneer to its present city location. In Tabernacle Park in Ogden is the Miles Goodyear Cabin, erected in 1845, and said to be the first white man-made structure built in Utah.

The John Neely Bryan Cabin, built in 1843 by the founder of Dallas for his bride, was moved downtown in recent years to the courthouse lawn where thousands of visitors to Texas have seen and photographed it.

The Newcom Log Tavern in Dayton, Ohio, erected by a pioneer settler, Colonel George Newcom in 1796, has been successively used as a tavern, dwelling, court house, school, church, and post office (see Figure 8).

Figure 8. Dayton, Ohio's, best-known log memorial, one of many hundreds of American log structures that have been converted into tourist attractions.

In a secluded valley of the Great Smokies at Cades Cove stands the restored log house of John Oliver, veteran of the War of 1812, the first permanent settler in the cove. Near Weaversville, N.C., is a restored pine log home, birthplace of Zebulon B. Vance, Congressman, Senator, Civil War officer, and former governor of the state. Erected after the close of the Revolution, the Vance log house is about three times as large as the typical one-room mountain cabin and was considered something of a showplace in its day. Near Knoxville, Tennessee, on the Marble Springs Farm is a restored log house, home of John Sevier, Tennessee's first governor.

The "Home on the Range" Cabin near Smith Center, Kansas, was restored by the local Rotary Club, and it was here that the pioneer physician, Dr. Brewster Highley, composed the words to the familiar tune adopted by the Kansas Legislature in 1947 as the state's official song.

In the Black Hills of South Dakota near the town of Custer is a log cabin, built in 1875, now called the Way Museum, which houses General George Custer memorabilia, although that valiant officer was actually born in a frame house in New Rumley, Ohio, and is buried at West Point.

In Arkansas, at the White County Farm Museum, the nucleus of a planned pioneer homestead, is the restored Gordon House built of logs a century ago. Near Branson, Missouri, is "Old Matt's Cabin," one of the Ozark's famous landmarks, and the home of the Matthew family who figure in Harold Bell Wright's, *The Shepherd Of The Hills*.

I could cite many other memorial log cabins which I have seen, and the reader will find mention of some of them in the text because of their relevance to the subject matter. However, my listings are far from all-inclusive, and if the reader finds me negligent in failing to make reference to a log cabin memorial in his state, city, or town I hope I will be forgiven. It would take a lifetime to get around to all of them, and a separate book to describe the circumstances leading to their preservation, all part of America's log cabin lore. There seems to be an increasing number of old cabins that are being renovated, rebuilt, and preserved each year as historical memorials, and I believe the reason for this will become readily apparent before one finishes the present volume.

New structures of logs continue to be built in America—we have really never stopped building log cabins, although the motives prompting the builders are different today than they were in the colonial period. Whereas the first log cabins were a cheap form of residential housing, the cost of virgin logs today is prohibitive for log house construction on a large scale. Nevertheless, log cabins are still being built as mountain lodges, summer camps, and fishing and hunting retreats; the log cabin motif continues also to be used in roadside inns and restaurants. Today's sophisticated builders have refined the building techniques by using modern tools, including the electric saw and power drill, and the logs are made smooth and coated with varnish, sometimes embellished on the cut ends with red or white paint.

But, despite these modern innovations, the basic form and structure remain the same. The log cabin has survived and indeed flourishes as an expression of indigenous American architecture.

I

LOG CABINS ON THE AMERICAN FRONTIER

1 Pioneers Go West

America was settled by restless people. Some came to the New World because Europe didn't want them any longer; some to avoid political or social repression; some to Christianize the heathen Indians; others to exploit them; some came seeking land and wealth; some came for other reasons. Whatever their motives, and no matter whence they came, they brought with them their own concepts of the house and the home, of husband and wife relationships, and of child-raising as rooted in Old World sociology. The houses they built when they arrived in America were constructed under the strong cultural influences of their differing European environments, modified by prevailing conditions of the New World climate, the availability of building materials, and social organization.

Englishmen, Dutch, Swedes, Finns, Germans, Swiss, Welsh, and Scotch-Irish carried to the American seaboard individual concepts of their own domestic housing which varied by nationality. As time went on, there was a melding of these nationalities, creating a new social fabric having its own cultural traits in which there persisted strong threads of the past. By the time of the great expansion westward across the continent from the eastern seaboard a century or more later, a recognizable American character was beginning to take shape, and a specialized kind of dwelling ultimately made its appearance—the American log cabin.

In the days of America's expanding frontier, when hundreds of pioneer families left their eastern homes and pushed westward, they faced a hard living without conveniences of any kind. Life was full of danger from hostile Indians, wild animals, scarcity of food, and exposure to devastating rains, drouths, sleet, ice, and deep, enveloping snows. The family, homeless and on the move for weeks, sometimes months, faced countless difficulties, but father, mother, and children were drawn closer together in meeting the adversity of their common problems.

In the beginning, overland travel was on foot, with the family belongings tied to the backs of one or two plow horses. If there were extra horses, the women and children rode, and the men walked; otherwise, mother and children walked behind the pack horse led by the father. This was during the period when people from the seaboard pressed only as far west as the first range of the Alleghenies. It was not safe to go farther, and transportation limitations and the threat of Indian attack did not permit taking women and children through the mountains. At first the migrating families veered southward, shunted between the western fringe of the Blue Ridge Mountains, populating Virginia in the 1730's and the Carolinas in the 1740's and 1750's.

River systems like the Susquehanna, James, Potomac, Tennessee, Cumberland, etc., directed the pattern of America's earliest internal migrations. The French and Indian War, a wilderness conflict, which began with General Braddock's march, followed by his ultimate defeat in 1755, and ended after Wolfe's capture of Quebec, opened the way for westward expansion over the land routes. In particular, it was the success of the army that Forbes, Bouquet, and Washington led across Pennsylvania in 1758 that unlocked the gateway to the Ohio and Mississippi. Forbes seized the ruins of the French-built Fort Duquesne at the forks of the Ohio, and founded there a village called "Pittsbourgh," which he informed William Pitt he had named in his honor. Along with the British regulars in Forbes' army there were five thousand men from North Carolina, Virginia, Maryland, and Pennsylvania, and they helped build the road across the Alleghenies that bore Forbes' name, and the log blockhouses that guarded it. They carried back to their homes the news that the Appalachians were passable—a barrier that had been formidable not because of its height, but due to the series of parallel ridges constituting its breadth, in whose secluded valleys hostile Shawnee and Delaware war parties sought the scalps of the white intruders.

With the defeat of the French and their Indian allies, the era of the American frontiersman really had its beginning, and two-wheeled and three-wheeled carts, known as horse barrows, took the place of foot travel over the narrow road built by Forbes' troops. The family rode part of the way, alighting to walk up the steep mountain slopes, assisting when necessary to push the carts over the rocky summits when the horses faltered. Women and children helped sprag the wheels with tree limbs thrust between the spokes on the downgrades, and assisted in building log rafts to float the wagons across the streams in the mountain valleys. Although horses and mules were used to pull the wagons, slower-moving oxen were also harnessed, and frequently household goods and bedding were tied to the backs of cows, sometimes followed by their bawling calves.

In time, after the mountain roads were widened and improved by use, canvas-covered wagons transported the migrating families, as well as their pots, kettles, flour, bacon, sugar, salt, yeast, vinegar, bedding, farm implements, seed corn, and oats to feed the horses en route. Often several families would travel together so they could lend a helping hand to each other in the event a wagon was mired or broke down in the mountains and needed repair. At first, Pittsburgh was the most westerly destination that the pioneer families aspired to reach—at least a thirty-day trip from Philadelphia over the Forbes Road, and several days longer from Baltimore over the Cumberland Road, which the Virginians and Marylanders used to migrate westward. Prior to the Revolution, the main stream of settlers flowed from Virginia, with lesser numbers coming from eastern Pennsylvania, and they settled in the coves and valleys east of Pittsburgh and penetrated the heart of the Monongahela Valley.

Southwestern Pennsylvania was settled mainly in the five-year period from 1769 to 1774, and with adjacent parts of West Virginia, it became the first English-speaking trans-Appalachian frontier. At the opening of the Revolution there were probably fifty thousand people living west of the Allegheny Ridge and south of the Allegheny and Kiskiminetas in what is now Pennsylvania. These settlements lured others to move west from eastern Pennsylvania and New Jersey, and after the Erie Canal was opened connecting the Atlantic Ocean with the Great Lakes, many New York and New England families loaded their household goods on barges for the first leg of their westward journey.

The western frontier continued to advance, and it was not long before the land beyond the Ohio became the destination, and after reaching the forks of the Allegheny and Monongahela, many of the mobile families made their way down the Ohio on open rafts, flatboats, or "arks." No matter by what route, in what manner, or into what part of the country the migrating families went, their first task after arriving at the promised land they had long discussed and dreamed about, was to pick a site where they wanted to live, and next to clear the trees and build a house. It was impractical to carry building supplies with them, and they were thrown on the mercy of the land for their materials.

Where woods and trees were plentiful, and this was true in Western Pennsylvania, Maryland, the Virginia and Carolina Piedmont, Ohio, Indiana, Kentucky, Tennessee, Illinois, and elsewhere in the timber-rich areas constituting more than three million square miles of the North American continent, the log cabin became a typical pioneer dwelling. It was young America's answer to the mobile family's gravest problem—a safe and durable haven that an ordinary family man could build with few tools, minimum skills, and little money. It was simple and practical, a direct outgrowth of urgent practical necessity. Log cabins were literally built by the thousands. "The dwelling of the pioneers of the Western Reserve outside of the rude bark and brush shack consisted *solely* of the log cabin," wrote an Ohio historian. Thomas Dillon said in 1796 of Tennessee "the truth is, that there are no Buildings in this State, a very few excepted but Log Cabins," and J. F. D. Smyth in his account written in 1784 describing a trip to Kentucky wrote, "Almost every house in the whole settlement was built of logs." [1] Log cabins were so important in the frontier settlements of Pennsylvania, dominating all other kinds of housing, that an entire chapter will later be devoted to this subject.

Defense was of primary consideration to the earliest cabin builders, taking precedence over convenience and comfort, especially in territory where hostile Indians resented the invasive white families. A well-built log dwelling provided a secure family shelter, and neither flint-tipped arrows nor lead bullets could penetrate the log walls. When, for example, the log fort at Boonesboro, Kentucky, was attacked by Indians in 1778, resulting in the death of two of the white defenders, and the wounding of four others (with thirty-seven of the attacking Indians killed), the white survivors "picked up one hundred and twenty-five pounds weight of bullets, besides what stuck in the logs of our fort . . ." [2] The lead balls shot at defenders in a log cabin stood a good chance of being salvaged, remelted, remolded, and later used against the attacker!

Nevertheless, a family living in an isolated cabin stood little chance against a large and determined force of whooping Indians who could drive out the occupants by setting the structure on fire. Therefore, at numerous frontier posts, the cabins were built in a cluster and protected by log palisades surrounding them. A typical example was Fort Nashborough overlooking the Cumberland River at Nashville, Tennessee where four cabins of chestnut logs were surrounded by a stockade of locust logs built in 1779 by James Robertson and his party (see Figure 9). In some of the forts the log dwellings were not constructed separately within an enclosure, but were built as an integral part of the stockade line, a house-fence combination. These so-called forts were not military establishments in the modern connotation of the term, but were residential structures built and occupied by hunters, woodchoppers, and farmers who were obliged to provide for their own defense. These frontier forts were miniaturized replicas of European walled cities, not of stone, but of wood hacked from the virgin timber of the American forests, defended

Figure 9. Replica of Fort Nashborough, Nashville, Tennessee. Within stock-aded areas are reconstructions of four cabins built in 1779. Stick-and-mud chimney and "roof timbers" accurately represent features found on many early pioneer cabins.

by the civilian population. The true military forts, garrisoned by professional soldiers for the protection of towns and villages, came later.

The availability of trees was the principal factor contributing to the widespread distribution of log housing, but the fact that no nails or spikes were needed to build a log cabin, or to erect a log stockade, was an advantage of the utmost importance. Until the latter part of the nineteenth century, nails were hand-wrought by American blacksmiths, and they were relatively high-priced and too heavy to transport in quantity in wagons already overburdened with family necessities. A snug, reasonably tight log cabin could be built without nails, and if necessary, with only one tool—an axe. No pioneer family could long survive without an axe; it was a vital tool

A PIONEER WOMAN MAKES DESPERATE WORK.

Figure 10. Mrs. John Merrill of Nelson County, Kentucky, protects her injured husband after killing or wounding four Indians with an axe when they tried to force door of the log cabin. (Reproduced from *Our Western Border*, by Charles McKnight, Phila., 1875)

used to fell the trees and notch the logs for the cabin. It cleared the land for cornfields and pastures; it was used to sever the spidery roots that held the tree stumps in the earth; to cut wood to size for the fireplace; and to split the rails and posts needed in building fences "horse-high, bull-proof, and pig-tight." In extreme circumstances the axe could become a deadly weapon in the hands of a man or woman protecting the family against human or animal trespassers when the rifle was beyond reach (Figure 10).

The axe is one of man's most ancient tools, having a continuous history for at least ten thousand years dating back to the stone age, with modifications made during the bronze and iron ages. During the Middle Ages in Europe the axe became an essential carpenter's tool, and this craftsman's axe that the colonists brought from Europe was basically patterned after an old Roman design, influenced perhaps by later European war axes. It had a long straight handle, a small poll, and a flaring bit about eight inches long. It weighed

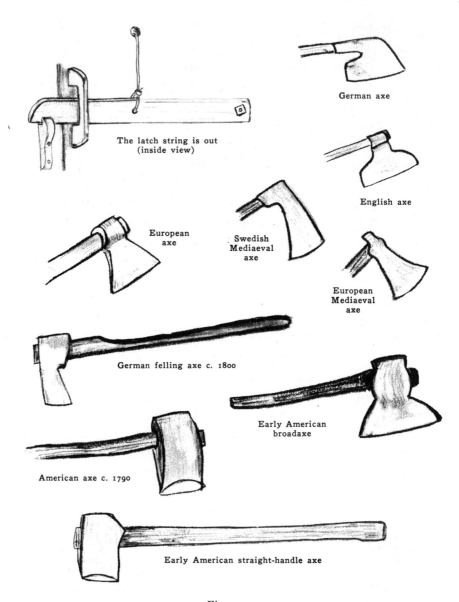

The latch string is out
(inside view)

German axe

English axe

European
axe

Swedish
Mediaeval
axe

European
Mediaeval
axe

German felling axe c. 1800

Early American
broadaxe

American axe c. 1790

Early American straight-handle axe

Figure 11

about three pounds and was not thickened opposite the blade to provide a pounding surface. These products of seventeenth century European factories, of which there were several types (see Figures 11, 12), were useful to the first colonists on the Atlantic seaboard, but they proved inadequate to meet the needs of the cabin builders on the American southern and western frontiers. Around 1740, an improved tool that the English called the "American axe," designed specifically for felling trees and building log cabins, made its appearance.

The forged iron head created by American axe makers weighed up to seven pounds or more; the steel blade welded to the iron bit could be honed on a whetstone to knife-like sharpness; the poll

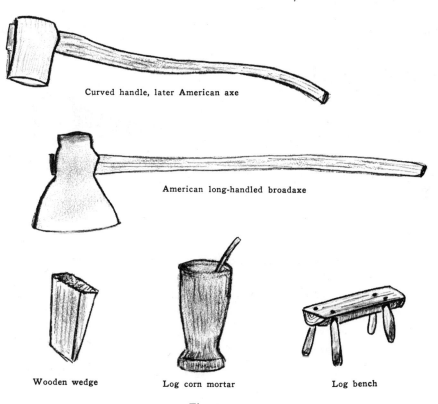

Curved handle, later American axe

American long-handled broadaxe

Wooden wedge   Log corn mortar   Log bench

Figure 12

opposite the blade was thick, flat, and square, and could, if necessary, be used as a sledge to pound fence posts into the ground, to
split a boulder, to sever a log that had been cut partially through
by dealing it a final, solid blow, or to kill an ox or bull by battering
the center of the animal's forehead. An experienced frontiersman,
with respect for his tools, did not, however, abuse his axe by using
the poll as a hammer, but made a wooden maul to pound his posts
and wedges.

The long hickory handle of the American axe was smooth and
well-balanced, and designed to fit the grasp of a man's hands. The
axe in the grip of a master, as Richard Lillard wrote in *The Great
Forest* (Alfred Knopf, N.Y., 1948) was "equivalent in artistry
to a bow in the hands of a great violinist." It was not easy for those
Europeans who seldom saw a tree in their tight little towns to con-
ceive of how an axe was used to fell a tree, cut it up, and split it,
using wooden wedges, into rails and posts. The backwoods expert
learned how to evaluate the tree, or the fallen log, down to every
detail, getting the best of the hardened knot, placing his wedges in
the right places, holding his axe handle just so, allowing his right
hand to slide down and meet the left at the split second of impact.

The practiced axeman, seldom stopping for breath, developed a
rhythm as he swung his axe overhead in an arc, striking his blows
rapidly and gracefully, the blade glittering as it slashed the air and
bit the wood. He hurled the steel blade into the trunk of a tree with
vigor and deadly aim, and working on either side, made one cut
lower than the other, so that the tree fell exactly where he wanted
it. When he spit on his bare hands and notched the fallen logs, his
left foot holding each member firm on the ground, it was with precise blows delivered alternately left and right, the chips flying neat
and clean, later to be gathered up for kindling, leaving the sides of
the notch smooth as though wrought with a steel chisel. When he
paused it was not to waste time resting, but to gulp down cold
spring water from a gourd dipper, and to splash the residue on his
sweaty face and neck.

Some builders preferred a site for their cabins facing east to get

the benefit of the warmth of the morning sun at the front door, or
in a sheltered nook at the bottom of a hill to escape the cold winds
and winter snowdrifts. Others located their cabins with regard to the
nearness of springs, running streams, rivers, or land trails. A member
of the John S. Williams family, who erected a log cabin in Harrison
County, Ohio, in 1800 wrote, "In building our cabin it was set to
front north and south, my brother using my father's pocket compass . . . we had no idea of living in a home that did not stand
square with the earth itself." [3] The notion that a log cabin should
square with the compass was shared by many builders, whereas
others gave this no thought.

William Brown of Montgomery County, Missouri, built his cabin
under the high bluffs along the Missouri River so that he could cut
his firewood on the bluff and roll it down to his front door. When
the wood gave out, rather than haul it from a distance, he deserted
his cabin and built another at the foot of the next wooded bluff!

Occasionally a builder made an unfortunate choice of a cabin site
—a log dwelling built near Brownsville, Pennsylvania, was inadver-
tently placed over a den of rattlesnakes. When the snakes came forth
during the first summer the owner and his wife were forced to abandon their house and build another.

In constructing his cabin, the settler first selected trees with
straight smooth trunks of approximately the same diameters. The
trees were then felled, cut into logs of the desired length, then
pulled by horse, or dragged by hand, to the site of the cabin where
the notching was done. The first settler in a new area had to build
his cabin alone, or assisted by his wife and children, but as the settlements grew, "raising" a log dwelling was a sort of neighborhood
social event. The log cabin became a product of community cooper-
ation with the work carefully divided so that the various materials
were ready as needed. A group of choppers felled the trees and cut
them to their proper lengths, and a man with a team hauled the logs
to the site of the dwelling. There the "corner men" notched and
fitted the timbers, and when everything was ready the walls were
raised, with all hands assisting in this heavy work. While the roof

members were fitted into place, others were wetting down the mud and kneading it with bare hands into the gaps between the logs.

The smaller cabins were usually about twelve to fifteen feet long, sometimes sixteen by eighteen feet, or larger, the axe handle used as a measuring stick. In building a cabin of round logs it was not necessary, or even desirable, to strip off the bark, which, left in place, served to protect the log walls from decay. The logs were laid out and notched at each end to make them fit securely one over the other. Sometimes the top and bottom surfaces of the round logs were axed off to provide a surface for a better fit. The builder had no formal plans or blueprints—he improvised as the cabin took shape. He used whatever trees were nearest to his cabin site—hickory, oak, pine, walnut, chestnut, poplar, and others—but once he had made his choice he preferred to use logs for all four walls of the cabin cut from the same species of tree.

The first four logs were laid in place horizontally flat on the earth, or if the builder intended to install flooring, he placed the four foundation logs on a base of fieldstones or sections of logs set vertically in the earth at each of the four corners. Then he laid other logs across these members to serve as joists, each notched into place. The sidewalls were heightened by laying successive logs one upon the other to a height of seven or eight feet, or sometimes higher. Each log was held in place by its own weight, reinforced by the weight of the log above and supported by the log below. In actuality, the structural technique, although appearing primitive today, was a unique development representing a notable advance in human technology.

If the builder had an auger to make dowel holes, a drawing knife, a frow, a broadaxe, or a crosscut saw he could build a neater cabin than if an axe were his only tool. Most builders allowed the ends of the logs to extend beyond the corners of the dwelling, but a more exacting builder or one adhering to group cultural practice, evened up the ends of the logs and made flush corners if he had the time and tools.

Two limbs at either end of the cabin walls were erected diagonally above the logs to hold the ridgepole, and additional straight limbs were ribbed into place to form the skeleton of the roof, which was covered with tree limbs, or thinner slabs of wood. Shingles or "shakes" held down by "weight timbers" were the preferred roof covering, but their manufacture required skill and riving tools, which many builders did not possess, and so they often covered their roofs with pieces of bark or thatch. The spaces between the logs forming the walls were filled with smaller pieces of wood, or stones wedged tightly, and then caulked with moss, or wet clay, sometimes tempered with animal hair or straw, in the process known as "daubing" or "chinking." Animal skins were sometimes hung on the inside walls to insulate the house in the winter.

After felling the trees, if time permitted—and the builder were sufficiently experienced—he could hew the logs with a short-handled broadaxe or adz before notching and setting them in place. Logs were sometimes hewn only on two surfaces, top and bottom or front and back, but often the complete log was squared by hewing all four sides. Although I have used the term "squared," and will continue to do so, the hewn log seen in cross section was moderately rectangular. Typical of cabins in Pennsylvania are hewn logs measuring six by nine or seven by eleven inches in section. A log can properly be called a "whole timber," and if the log is halved and each half squared, the term "half timber" is applicable. Strictly speaking, therefore, a whole log hewn square, or its halves similarly squared, should be termed a timber, but when used in horizontal, notched construction it was always called a log. In the 1828 edition of his dictionary, Noah Webster said that a piece of timber hewed square was not called a log "unless perhaps in the constructing of log huts," and thus a log could be round or square in its log cabin context. If in the hewing process the logs were reduced in width even smaller than a half timber, the resultant board might properly be termed a plank, and the term "plank house" is sometimes used to describe a structure of logs so hewn. This is a nonspecific term, which I try to avoid, because a house built of unnotched planks conventionally nailed to studding can also be termed a plank house.

The flat surfaces of hewn logs could be made to fit closer together than round logs permitted, and, if carefully notched, there
was a minimum of open spaces between the timbers to be chinked.
However, no generalizations can be made, because in most American cabins, either of round or hewn logs, interstices were present
in the walls; some hewn log dwellings had gaping spaces between
the logs equal to, if not wider, than those found in some round-
log cabins. It all depended upon the preference, skill, and cultural
background of the builder. Usually a different method of corner
notching is found on hewn log houses from that on round logs, and
the most common methods of corner notchings characterizing
American log construction will be briefly discussed in the concluding chapter of this volume.

The front door, which usually opened outward to allow more
room inside the cabin, was made of heavy wood slabs fastened with
wood pegs before nails were available. The door swung on wood
hinges or strips of animal skin, and was usually mounted on the inside with a wood latch and crossbar. Attached to the latch, and
threaded through a hole whittled in the door, was a string of buckskin which hung outside the door (Figure 11). When the string was
pulled from the outside the latch was lifted from its bracket on the
inside and the door could be opened. At night the string was drawn
in through the hole, and the door securely barred on the inside.
The latchstring hanging outside the door became a symbol of pioneer hospitality and an open invitation for the friendly stranger to
enter and share the family table and the warmth of the fireside. The
hospitality of the frontiersman was a characteristic trait without
precedent in Europe and was commented on by many early writers.
John James Audubon wrote of the American south ". . . the hospitality received from an inhabitant of the forest, who can offer only
the shelter of his humble roof and the refreshment of his homely
fair, remains more deeply impressed on the memory of the be-
wildered traveller than any other."

Audubon was doubtless thinking of the hospitality shown to him
and his fourteen-year-old son when they were on foot in 1823, trav-

eling from the mouth of the Ohio River to Louisville, Kentucky, stopping enroute to share the hospitality of the log cabin dwellers. He described one experience in detail in his journal when he and his son were welcomed by a young married couple in their twenties who lived in a log cabin in the Kentucky backwoods, which the bridegroom's father had helped his son build.

"The cabin was new," Audubon wrote, "the logs of which it was formed were all of the tulip-tree, and were nicely pared. Every part was beautifully clean. Even the coarse slabs of wood that formed the floor looked as if newly washed and dried. Sundry gowns and petticoats of substantial homespun hung from the logs that formed one of the sides of the cabin, while the other was covered with articles of male attire. A large spinning-wheel, with rolls of wool and cotton, occupied one corner. In another was a small cupboard, containing the little stock of new dishes, cups, plates, and tin pans. The table was small also, but quite new, and as bright as polished walnut could be. The only bed that I saw was of domestic manufacture, and the counterpane proved how expert the young wife was at spinning and weaving. A fine rifle ornamented the chimney piece. The fireplace was of such dimensions that it looked as if it had been purposely constructed for holding the numerous progeny expected to result from the happy union." [4]

Audubon's youthful host, who had no whiskey or other beverages in his cabin, rode on horseback in a driving rainstorm to bring back a keg of cider to entertain his guests before they ate supper and retired for the night.

To continue with a generalized description of the log cabin, and the reader must realize that there were structural differences varying by area, many of the earliest American cabins were built without windows, and in those having window openings, animal skins or sliding boards were used as coverings. Later, paper greased with animal fat to make it waterproof and translucent was used as a substitute for crown glass, which was not widely manufactured in America until the 1800's. Even when glass was commonly used in city and town dwellings, it was still too expensive for poor cabin builders to buy, and too fragile to transport long distances over rough roads. In 1827, an English naval officer, Captain Basil Hall, who was visiting in Georgia, questioned a log cabin owner, who had recently built a new log cabin, about the absence of windows in the structure.

"Oh said he," according to Captain Hall, "we never make the windows in the first instance, but build up the walls with logs, and then cut out the windows. Now, I have not yet money enough to enable me to go into that matter; but I hope in the course of the year to put in a couple of glazed windows." [5]

Often an open-shelf loft was built in the cabin as sleeping quarters for the children, and it was reached by a crude ladder made of tree limbs or by pegs placed in the log walls. The loft was also a sort of larder, and peppers, strips of apples, pumpkins, seed corn still on the cob, as well as sassafras, hepatica, ginseng, pipsissewa, tansy, and other medicinal herbs were strung up to dry under the roof. By no means did all one-room log cabins have lofts, the floor of the single room often consisting of the entire living and sleeping space. Although the floors in many primitive cabins were of dirt pounded hard by the feet of the members of the family, some had floorings of puncheons—logs that had been split lengthwise and laid close together with their flat sides up on the log joists.

The most familiar type of pioneer cabin had an outside chimney attached to one of the end walls built of mud wattled with tree limbs or small logs, referred to as a "catted" chimney. These inflammable stick-and-mud appendages were later supplanted with stone or brick chimneys, and are now only a vague memory in most parts of the country except on memorial cabins. Stone or clay was used to construct the hearth and to form the interior walls of the fireplace, but after kilns were in operation, brick was used for constructing chimneys and fireplaces by many cabin builders. Back bars forged from iron, cranes from which pothooks were suspended, or other makeshift contrivances, held the iron or brass kettles in which the food was cooked.

Winters were long and severe in many parts of the country and the fireplace came to be an integral part of log cabin living, not only for cooking, but for warmth. As William M. Kephart stated in *The Family, Society and the Individual* (Houghton Mifflin, 1961), the fireplace somehow captured the spirit of the early American family, and even today, when its utilitarian value has been largely destroyed by modern heating methods, the open fireplace remains in many city homes "as a vestigial culture trait, emblematic of the family of an earlier day." Although some cooking was done in outdoor ovens in log cabin days, especially in the summer, the fireplace was used to prepare the food in most American houses until about 1840, when it was replaced by cast-iron ranges that burned coal or wood.

The interior furnishings of the frontier log cabin were simple and practical, and the family's most prized possessions were the articles or utensils brought from the East—dishes, wood or pewter spoons and porringers, a clock, spinning wheel, candlesticks, wooden wash tub, a Bible, and the tinder box with its flint and steel so necessary to start a fire. On the log walls hung firearms, hunting knives, powder horn, gourd dipper, and other domestic utensils. The unpainted benches, stools, tables, and low beds were made of wood, their quality depending on the proficiency of the builder. If there were no candles the cabin was lighted by the knots of the fat pitch pine, sometimes called "candlewood," if it was available, but, if not, the open fireplace provided the only illumination.

The building of a log cabin required very little time in comparison with modern residential construction, and most cabins were raised in a hurry. There is record of three men felling and trimming the trees, dragging the logs to the nearby house site, notching them, and erecting a one-room cabin complete with chimney and fireplace in two days. Even a solitary builder could construct a cabin alone in a matter of a week or two, although it necessarily had to be small, because one man, unaided, had difficulty lifting heavy logs to a wall position above his head. Six or eight tiers of short logs was about as high as one man could go. Assisted by a second man, or strong boys, he could cut longer logs and raise the walls higher by using skids consisting of two logs placed at an angle against the wall to serve as an inclined plane, and forked sticks or ropes to guide the logs into place.

While their cabin was being built, the members of the family slept in a lean-to of boughs, makeshift tents, or either in or under their wagon, depending upon the season of the year. Sometimes in areas where other families had arrived first and had completed their cabins, the newcomers shared a neighbor's dwelling until their own was raised. When Joseph Hawes brought his wife and four little daughters in a wagon train from Ohio to Kansas in 1865, they were taken in by a couple who had a family of six children. While Hawes was building his own cabin, assisted by his hospitable neighbors, he lived in the neighbor's one-room cabin which temporarily housed two families of four adults and ten children! [6]

In situations like this some privacy could be afforded by hanging up blankets or cotton sheets to make partitions for undressing, but parents, children, and visitors all lodged together in log cabin homes, some sleeping in crude beds, others on the floor, and still others in the hay in the loft. A log cabin was no place for shyness or modesty.

"In almost all these rural Cots," wrote Philip Fithian in 1775, "I am under the Necessity of sleeping in the same Room with all the Family—It seems indelicate, at least new, to strip, surrounded by different Ages & Sexes, & rise in the Morning, in the Blaze of Day, with the Eyes of, at least, one blinking Irish Female, searching out Subjects for Remark." [7]

Exposing his undressed person to strange female eyes was a new and embarrassing experience for the young Presbyterian circuit rider, who slept in many one-room cabins in the Shenandoah and Susquehanna Valleys, but his hosts and their families thought nothing of it.

The pioneer cabin containing a single room was never intended as a permanent house. It was considered only as a stepping-stone, a temporary shelter where the family could live in safety and reasonable comfort until such a time as someone dug a saw pit or erected a sawmill, and lumber could be obtained to build a larger residence with wooden sides, oak floors, and glazed windows. Alexis de Tocqueville on his American trip in 1831–1832 fully recognized the provisional nature of the log cabin when he wrote,

And in fact the log cabin is only a temporary shelter for the American, a concession circumstances have forced on him for the moment. When the fields that surround him are in full production, and the new owner has time to concern himself with the amenities of life, a more spacious dwelling and one better adapted to his needs will replace the log-house and make a home for those numerous children who will also go out one day to make themselves a dwelling place in the wilderness.[8]

What frequently happened as the years rolled by, was that the women bore more babies—the family tended to be large because many hands were required for the ceaseless labor—the men struggled harder to support their growing families, and their housing dreams were never fully realized. Many families, in conflict with circumstances, continued to occupy their original one-room cabins, never able to afford the luxury of larger and better houses, and in some areas newcomers continued to build log dwellings well into the nineteenth century.

Family bonds were cemented tightly together in the log cabin home in the wild freedom of the forests because the rigors of life demanded the best from everyone for the good of all—and here I am referring specifically to the western frontier, not to the South where Negro field hands were put to work to help support the cabin residents. The efforts of father, mother, and children in the closely-knit kinship group were combined to meet their common needs as they worked together in the daily tasks, and at the end of a hard day, shared dreams of a better future as they huddled around the flickering light of the open fire. In those days of unbroken families, with divorce practically unknown, survival depended upon this mutuality of effort, and a fundamental family concept; namely, a group of kinsmen living together to protect one another, was paramount in log cabin life.

A factor contributing significantly to the preservation of strong family ties, was that the occupants of the log cabin constituted a *producing* unit. Almost everything in the agriculturally-based, non-industrial society was homemade, the family creating its own fuel, drink, food, light, heat, medicine, and clothing. There was work for both young and old, and a division of labor was clearly understood by everyone, although necessity at times required a certain flexibility. If circumstances required, the female was expected to chop wood, carry water, hoe corn, and undertake other chores that normally belonged to the male, and if she fell ill her husband took over the cooking and the care of the children. The family tended to become a complete, self-subsistent, *producing and consuming* social unit. Log cabin life was contributory to the strong family-mindedness that accompanied the labor of calloused hands working for the common good, in sharp contrast to today's crowded urban neighborhoods where children are often economic and social liabilities, and the family, eroded through the growth of technology and urbanization, is plagued by a host of social problems.

Authority in the log cabin home was generally lodged in the male head of the family, with the female playing a dominant role in household affairs. Father and sons in their tanned deerskin breeches and fringed hunting shirts cultivated the land with the plow, hoe, and harrow, planted the seeds, and harvested the crops. They cared for the livestock; laid traps in the woods for wild animals; shot turkeys, ducks, geese, and pigeons; caught fish in the streams; gathered hickory nuts, chestnuts, walnuts, pawpaws, persimmons, berries, and wild grapes; and chiefly concerned themselves with providing food, shelter, and protection for the family. Let de Tocqueville, who met many log cabin dwellers, characterize the father of the family:

His angular muscles and thin limbs make one recognize at first glance the inhabitant of New England. This man has not been born in the solitude where he lives. His temperament alone makes that clear. His first years were passed in a society used to thought and argument. It is the strength of his will that has taken him to do work in the wilds to which he seems little adapted. But if his physical powers seem too slight for this undertaking, his features lined by the cares of life bespeak a practical intelligence, and a cold, persevering energy that strike one at first sight. His movements are slow and stiff, his words measured and his appearance austere. Habit and still more pride have given his features that Stoic stiffness that his deeds belie: it is true that the pioneer scorns things that often move men's hearts most violently; his goods and life will never depend on the chance of a throw of dice, or the fate of a woman; but to win affluence he has braved exile, the solitude and innumerable wretchednesses of life in the wilds, he has slept on the bare ground and risked fever in the forest and the Indian's tomahawk. He has one day made that effort, and renewed it through the years: perhaps he will carry on with it for twenty years more without discouragement or complaint. Can a man capable of such sacrifices be a cold, unfeeling being? Should one not rather recognize that he is consumed by some burning, tenacious, implacable passion of the mind? Concentrating on the single object of making his fortune, the emigrant has ended by making an altogether exceptional mode of existence.[9]

The mother, assisted by her daughters, managed the household, did the cooking, churning, washing, spinning, sewing and weaving. She knitted stockings, scarves and mittens, and made moccasins of deer or buffalo skin. Indian influence was strong, especially in the clothing styles of the men—the deerskin leggings worn in the winter and laced well up to the thigh, and the breeches and jackets were copied from the natives.

Both parents shared the responsibility for training their offspring for the society and culture into which they were born. The parents were educators before the first schools were built, and religious training took place in the cabin by Bible reading and prayer before there were churches. Emphasis was on teaching the children the skills of everyday life in an educational process within the home. The role of the mother as the guardian of the family morals was generally recognized and accepted.

She had to be able to organize her household efficiently, a difficult accomplishment in the cramped and cluttered quarters of a dwelling with a single room, and plan for the months when deep snows would isolate the family for days on end. She had to do everything by hand from salting pork and curing bacon to making jellies and preserves from fruits and wild berries. She had to know how to grind the corn kernels into meal; what herbs should be picked and dried for use as seasoning and medicine, and which ones were poisonous. She used Indian recipes to prepare corn meal, corn pone, corn dodgers, as well as mush, hominy, suppawn, and succotash. She saved the meat fats and grease and mixed wood ashes or lye with it to make crude yellow soap, and she collected honey combs from "bee trees," and wax from the bayberry leaves for use in making candles. She stuffed the mattresses and pillows with feathers, corn husks, and barley straw. She kept the hearth clean with a turkey-wing brush, and swept the floor with an Indian broom of her making—birch or spruce splints tied together on the end of a stick.

As part of her unremitting toil, the mother of the family also had to know how to treat the children's ailments, dress burns and cuts, apply a spider web to stop blood, set a broken limb, cauterize a snake bite, or prescribe for worms and prepare poultices for croup. Above all she had to be able to deliver, with the assistance of her husband, the infant born to her without the assistance of doctor or midwife.

For her it was a hard, isolated life, a struggle to keep alive, with living standards low, and unending work from sunup to sundown. To the young woman bred in an eastern town, who came west with her husband, it was particularly lonely because she was separated by hundreds of miles from her family and friends. There were few amusements for her to enjoy, and even fewer amenities to lessen her drudgery. Yet her dedication may well have brought the American family to its most closely knit state, as its members responded to exigent circumstances far removed from the comparative comforts of the older coastal settlements.

The [log] dwelling in which the emigrants live [wrote de Tocqueville] has no internal division and no storehouse. The whole family comes to seek shelter of an evening in the single room which it contains. This dwelling forms as it were a little world of its own. It is an ark of civilisation lost in the middle of an ocean of leaves, it is a sort of oasis in the desert. A hundred paces beyond it the everlasting forest stretches its shades around it and solitude begins again.

Survival of living things depends upon meeting such environmental challenges as the "everlasting forest," as well as heat, cold, humidity, drought, and the competition of other living things. Whereas the nonhuman species of the animal kingdom usually adapt to change through an evolution in their genetic makeup, man has survived due to his rapid adaptability to environmental change. He has done so despite the fact that the offspring of his species remain incapable of self-support much longer than the lower animals. Families on the American frontier faced physical change by insulating themselves against the effects of a new environment and protecting themselves against predators through the utilization of the native trees. The log cabin which they built was as important in the survival process as the thin layer of top soil in which they planted the precious seeds from which would grow the crops to sustain them.

In those instances where the crops flourished and the livestock multiplied, some log cabin families enjoyed a modicum of prosperity, and they could afford to enlarge their cabins by adding frame wings. As the danger of Indian attack lessened with the arrival of more settlers, the owner was able to give more attention to comfort, and the defensive character of the log cabin became second to its domiciliary function. Frequently a log cabin family sold their first cabin and farm after two or three years of residence, and moved to another location, usually farther west, there to erect a new cabin and clear the land for a larger farm. Abraham Lincoln's father moved from Kentucky to Indiana and thence to Illinois building a new log cabin at each location.

Some families who prospered were able to build larger houses of frame or stone, often butting the larger house against the original cabin and using it as a kitchen. In areas where planks and clapboards continued to be scarce some families erected new one and one-half or two-story houses of hewn logs, intended as permanent dwellings, and they had advantages over frame houses. They were less flammable, warmer in winter, drier in rainy seasons, needed no paint, and did not fall into disrepair as readily as a frame build-

Figure 13. Old log cabin near Bedford, Kentucky, was turned into a barn by adding frame addition, and strips of wood were nailed to logs and weatherboarding attached. Not until it was abandoned and began to fall apart were the logs exposed.

ing. Various uses were then made of the original cabins—they became barns, tool sheds, and I know of one example where the log cabin still survives as the nucleus of a modern garage (see Figures 13, 14, 15).

However, there was often a sentimental interest in preserving the original one-story cabin as a souvenir of the past, and it was allowed to stand vacant and unused. A folk versifier expressed the sentiment in the following lines:

> The ol' log cabin lef' alone deserted now an' still
> Nobody 'pears to care fur it an' reckon never will
> An' so I keep it fur myse'f, same way it wuz when we
> Moved over in to our brand new house, like fine sassiety.

When less prosperous families were forced by circumstances to continue to reside in their original cabins, they sometimes modernized their houses by nailing boards to the exterior of the weatherbeaten logs, installing glass windows and larger doors, covering the roof with shingles or shakes, and later with corrugated tin, and lathing or plastering the rough interior walls.

There were many instances where the original cabin remained essentially in the state in which it was built, and it continued to be occupied down to the present century by successive families unwilling, or financially unable, to make improvements. When Ed Bumgarner bought an old cabin made of poplar logs in 1960 on the headwaters of Barker Creek in western North Carolina it had been occupied by four generations of the Wikle family, and prior to that,

Figure 14. The author examines cedar-shingled roof on old one-room log cabin near Gum Tree, Chester County, Pennsylvania, which was used as a farm shed after the original occupants erected a larger dwelling.

Figure 15. At Eagle, Pennsylvania, old log cabin, lengthened and heightened with modern lumber, is still in use as a garage.

by others only vaguely remembered. Hix Wikle and his family of nine were living in the cabin when Bumgarner purchased it, and when Hix was asked when he thought the structure was built he drawled, "I can't date it back exactly to the year it was built, but I can tell you this: old man Stance Jones helped build the cabin when he was 16. He's the great-grandfather of Early Jones who lives on the left-hand prong of the creek, and Early is fifty-six." [10]

Where the original logs have not been boarded over, a surviving log cabin can be readily recognized for what it is, but such is not the case when the logs have been covered with siding or otherwise concealed (see Figure 16). Hundreds of cabins built in the late eighteenth and early nineteenth centuries, their log walls hidden from view, are still standing in many parts of the country. Some of these modified dwellings at first glance appear to be modern bungalows often neatly painted, some with flower boxes on the window sills, trellised front and back porches, often with television antennae on the roofs, and electric and telephone wires running to roadside poles. The deep window and door frames, and other clues, may suggest to the practiced eye that a log cabin is hidden beneath a modern exterior of clapboards or wood siding, although additions and renovations may make such detection next to impossible unless the building is carefully examined.

I know of many examples of old log cabins having been incorporated as part of a larger frame or stone house, and these are the most

Figure 16. Along Route 30 at St. Thomas, Pennsylvania, thousands of tourists driving past this two and one-half story dwelling were unaware it was built of logs until siding was torn off one end to make repairs.

difficult to recognize, because the old logs may be deeply buried in partitions installed when the newer house was built (see Figure 17). There are numerous instances on record in recent times where houses were remodeled or torn down, and the residents were astonished to find, as the partitions were removed, that, unknown to them,

Figure 17. The walls of an original one-room log cabin were concealed in the partitions of one of the rooms of a large frame house near Unionville, Pennsylvania.

a log cabin of indeterminate age was the nucleus of the home in which they had been living. This phenomenon is by no means confined to rural areas—log cabins have survived in large cities, such as the hewn log house at 16th near Arch Street in downtown Philadelphia, still standing as I write, but destined to be removed to the grounds of the Stenton Mansion; and the Neal Log House on Pittsburgh's Schenley Park golf course which had been boarded over and used as a haven by the golfers.

Two other examples are typical of a score or more that have come to my attention:

In 1940, a general store on the main street of Newark, Delaware, was torn down and replaced by a larger building. As the contractor removed the weatherboards and studding he surprised himself by laying bare the four walls of a one-room log cabin still intact with some of the original chinking in place. An appreciative Newark architect, the late Harry Clark Boden IV, purchased the logs and re-erected the cabin on his own residential property as a memorial to the past. Deed searches of the property on which the cabin was located indicated that it may have been the first home of the parents of Captain Robert Kirkwood of Revolutionary fame.

In 1964, a Kansas City, Missouri, contractor acquired four small dwellings in the 4400 block on Jarboe Street as a site for a new apartment building. When he began the work of demolition he encountered an unusual discovery—beneath the siding of one of the houses were the hand-hewn walls of a log cabin which the residents never knew was there.

In the eighteenth and early nineteenth centuries, young America dreamed of the future and looked into the west as the frontier moved south and west from the forks of the Ohio. Actually there were a number of frontiers, each a physiographic province created by mobile families. There are a number of books and essays available describing these American frontiers, the land speculations, and other phases of the subject which cannot be detailed here.[11] By 1800 the western frontier has been described as assuming the shape of a triangle, with its point thrusting into the Mississippi Valley, its two sides sloping backwards to the north and south. America's thoughts crossed the Mississippi in 1803 when Congress purchased the Louisiana Territory from France, and the way for southwest expansion was opened in 1845 when the plains of Texas were acquired. The next year, ending a long dispute with Great Britain over the western fur trade, Oregon was added, taking American enterprise to the Pacific northwest as far as the 49th parallel. In 1848, by secession from Mexico, came the fertile fields of California, and in 1853, with the Gadsden Purchase of a stretch of Mexican desert, now the southern parts of Arizona and New Mexico, American territory became continuous from the population centers of the Atlantic coast across the mountains and plains to the Pacific. In this expansion the frontier disappeared.

This, too, has been fully treated in American histories and many books relate how the fever of adventure took the caravans of covered wagons across the Santa Fe, the Oregon, and other land trails. Mobile families pressed westward, economically motivated as they had been when they settled the western slopes of the Alleghenies and the valleys of the Ohio and its tributaries. Although driven by an inherent desire to better themselves in material respects the pioneer families did not expect an immediate life of ease and comfort. Their hope was that while enduring hardship and inconvenience they could improve the land and own more of it, and become masters of their own destiny. As the nation expanded—and wherever the moving families settled—trees were felled, fields cleared, crops planted, fences built, and log cabins erected to house a hardy generation of Americans. In this process of wresting a living from the land they conquered nature, surmounted the physical obstacles, and left a memorable legacy in the traditions that have become part of the settlement folklore. In the midwest and the "wild and wooly" far west there is a legion of stories about pioneer days, and how the log cabin was prominent in an era when traders, trappers, miners, prospectors, and Indian fighters were the first actors in a drama before permanent settlers appeared. State and local histories are rich with such accounts, and I cite only a few examples to indicate that America's pioneering families carried the log cabin wherever they settled.

The Eleazer Williams Log House, about twelve miles south of Green Bay, Wisconsin, on the west bank of the Fox River, constructed in the 1820's, has an unusual romantic background. It seems that its builder was not only conversant in the Indian tongues, and of considerable influence among the local tribes, but he claimed to be Louis XVII, the "lost Dauphin" of France. The renovated cabin of this would-be heir to the French throne is now in the custody of the Wisconsin Historical Society.

In the outdoor section of the Norwegian-American Historical Museum at Luther College, Decorah, Iowa, there are a number of original cabins erected by early immigrants from Norway. Prominent among the builders was Erik Egge who constructed a log dwelling in 1851–1852 in Winneshiek County shortly after the Norwegian colony was founded. Built of squared logs, measuring fourteen by sixteen feet, it was later moved to its present location.

Bellevue on the Missouri River, six miles below Omaha, Nebraska is said to be the state's oldest existing town, and it was here that John Dougherty, an Indian agent, built a cluster of log cabins in 1831 where the Indians came to barter their furs. If one looks elsewhere in Nebraska he will find that in 1868 Daniel Freeman settled four miles northwest of Beatrice where he "built a house thereon, part log and part frame fourteen by twenty feet one story with two doors two windows shingle roof board floor and is comfortable to live in."

The pioneers who settled the northeastern border of Kansas in the 1850's found both timber and stone available to them, and they built both log cabins and simple one-room stone houses. The Old Settler's Memorial Cabin at Gage Park in Topeka built of walnut logs, with an exterior stone chimney, was moved here from the Adams Bauer farm and is a good example of an early Kansas log dwelling. After the treaties with the Delaware and Shawnee in 1854, some two million acres of reserved lands became available to the whites and the race for Kansas was on, with log cabin builders pouring in from Ohio, West Virginia, Indiana, Pennsylvania, and especially Missouri.

Missouri had not only felt the influence at an early date of the westward-moving log cabin builders, but with a later tide of German immigration in the nineteenth century the hewn-log house had a fresh introduction into the state. At Altenburg in Perry County there is still standing a one-story log building built in 1839, the first home of Concordia Seminary, erected by Lutheran emigrants from Saxony who settled in Missouri. There are, of course, other surviving log cabins in the Ozarks and elsewhere in the state, although the numbers have greatly diminished (see Figure 18).

The first house built by white settlers at Mormon Station in Ne-

Figure 18. Most surviving log cabins in Missouri are off the beaten paths of commerce, and this hewn cabin, with attic, but no windows or chimney, was found in backwoods country near Ashland. Residents told author it was built in 1810.

vada in 1851 was made of logs. It has since been memorialized in a log museum reconstructed on the original site. In a later chapter I will have more to say about Mormons and log houses.

The oldest building in Helena, Montana at 208 S. Park Avenue is a low, two-room log cabin built about 1865, further evidence that log cabins continued to be built in some of the western states well into the Civil War period, and even later.

Wyoming's first trading post on the Middle Fork of Powder River consisted of hewn log houses. Although Fort Laramie, as it appeared in the early 1840's, was built of adobe in Mexican style, Fort Bridger was described in an 1847 account as consisting of "two adjoining log houses, dirt roofs, and a small picket yard of logs set in the ground, about eight feet high." Later military forts along the Bozeman, the Oregon, and Overland trails followed the same general pattern—a row of attached log houses forming barracks for the soldiers and officers, surrounded by a stockade of pointed logs. In Muskogee County, Oklahoma, Fort Gibson, built in 1824, consisted of log houses surrounded by a log stockade. The state of Oklahoma reconstructed the fort in 1936 as a historic memorial. Most of the log dwellings built in or near the Army posts by the civilians had roofs made of small poles, brush, or rough slabs of wood, and they were often covered with a layer of six inches of dirt in which plants or weeds took root and an occasional wild flower opened its petals in season.

Towns did not become established in Wyoming until after the Union Pacific Railroad came through the state in 1867–1868, bringing much needed goods and supplies, including cast-iron stoves. The stoves were cheaper and easier to install than stone fireplaces and chimneys, and the stovepipe, collared by a piece of sheet iron or tin, was a roof fixture even on the earliest log cabins built by Wyoming's settlers. As time passed, many of the ranchmen prospered as their herds increased, and they were able to build larger and better houses, converting their original log cabins into storehouses or bunkhouses for the hired hands. Today in Wyoming, as well as in other western cattle states, one often sees groups of log cabins of various sizes and shapes bunched together near the main ranch house. Perhaps the best known log cabin in the state is the Jim Barker Cabin in Frontier Park in Cheyenne, originally built in 1873 by the noted Indian scout and frontiersman, which originally stood near Snake River in Carbon County before it was moved to its present location as a memorial.

Prescott, Arizona's, first boarding house for itinerant miners, a two-room log building, was presided over by "Virgin Mary," whose establishment was christened "Old Fort Misery." The proprietor's nickname was not designative of her chastity, but of her charitable and benevolent disposition toward the poor and needy miners. Arizona's log cabins were principally found in the northern parts of the state which are wooded. In the south, where trees were scarce, adobe was the most common building material, reflecting influences from Mexico. Although log cabins are found in Mexico, the concept did not appear there until a late date when people from other European countries settled among the Spanish-Mexican descendants.

In parts of the Dakotas—and in other areas of the western grasslands, where the plains were practically treeless—many of the pioneer settlers built sod houses, crude shelters made with rectangular blocks of hardened sods roofed with poles which were also covered with a thick layer of sods. But in the river valleys and in the Black Hills, where trees were readily available, cabins were built of both round and hewn logs. The softness of the cottonwood was especially adaptable to hewing as illustrated by the squared logs used in the building of Fort Rice on the west bank of the Missouri in 1864. The gold rush to the Black Hills in 1876 brought a resurgence in the building of log cabins, mostly of Ponderosa pine logs. The use of logs was by no means confined to Army forts and pioneer residences—the first schoolhouse in South Dakota built in Bon Homme County in 1860 was made of logs, and another school of round logs built in Oliver County, North Dakota, was still in use as late as 1888.

The land bordering the Pacific was the last to be settled, and the Oregon Territory, at first occupied only by Indians, wandering white trappers, and fur traders, experienced an influx of eastern and midwestern cabin builders in the 1830's and 1840's who were to become the first permanent settlers. They came in wagon trains which followed the Oregon Trail to its western terminus in the Willamette Valley, and then they crossed the Columbia River and pushed farther north seeking suitable lands to settle.

In 1834, after several individuals in New York and Boston formed the Columbia River Fishing and Trading Company, Captain Nathaniel Jarvis Wyeth set forth with a party headed for the Oregon Territory. A Philadelphia naturalist, John K. Townsend, was a member of this caravan, and his journal provides a vivid contemporary description of the first houses built along the Columbia River. In the vicinity of Fort Vancouver on the north bank of the river Townsend wrote there were "30 to 40 log huts" placed in rows with broad lanes or streets between them. He noted further that at Fort Williams on "Wappatoo Island," eight miles from Vancouver, the settlers had built "several comfortable log houses." [12] The Job Carr Log Cabin preserved as a memorial in Point Defiance Park in Tacoma, Washington, is purported to typify the early log structures of the Oregon Territory. Built in 1865 of round logs for use as a residence it was also used as a post office. The Richard Covington Cabin in Vancouver's Loverich Park, built of squared and dovetailed logs in 1845–1849, originally stood northeast of the city where it was used as a residence, and later as a school, prior to its removal to its present location as a memorial structure.

Starting in the decade before the Civil War, the bright lure of southwestern land brought another movement of people from the southern states to Texas, which had been admitted to the union in 1845. A Mississippi or Louisiana planter's son might head for the southwest determined to prove to his doubting family that he could make a fortune on his own; a taciturn hill man from Tennessee or the restless sons of North Carolina or Georgia tobacco farmers might set out to shape new lives for themselves as cattlemen or homesteaders. Someone else was a fugitive from the law; another had deserted a faithless wife; and still another had been rejected by the girl he loved. Some were family men, who brought their wives and children with them, seeking to improve their economic status, but it was a migration of a slower pace than had characterized the movement across the Alleghenies or the mass rush to the California gold fields.

Sam Houston and Davy Crockett were from Tennessee, and Jim Bowie was born in Georgia and raised in Louisiana. Colonel William Barrett Travis, who died a hero's death with his command at the Alamo, was a South Carolina lawyer, and Stephen F. Austin was born in Virginia. Scores of other southerners became adopted Texans and practically all of them had knowledge of log cabins; some had lived in log dwellings in their youths; others had attended log churches or log schools. Sam Houston was a teacher in a log school before he left for Texas, and near Maryville, Tennessee, the visitor can see the restored log structure where he is supposed to have taught before he was elected governor of Tennessee (Figure 19).

In the wide open spaces of Texas where angered and resentful war parties of Comanches and Apaches sought revenge, there began to appear white men's houses of native stone, and in areas where there were trees, log cabins constructed by the new settlers added color to the Spanish and Mexican adobe architecture. San Felipe de Austin, at the old Atacosito Crossing on the Brazo River some forty-five miles west of Houston, the cradle of Anglo-American settlements in the Lone Star State, had about twenty log cabins as early as 1828. But in the 1850's when there converged into the wooded parts of Texas the log building techniques of the Carolinas, Alabama, Mississippi, and Tennessee, scores of log houses were built. One of the migrant sons of Tennessee, T. J. Shaw, proficient in log work, built his own cabin on Shaw Creek, and then built, or helped to build, cabins for his neighbors.

It would be an oversimplification to give sole credit to Anglo-American immigrants from the southeast for the existence of log cabins in a state that covers more territory than Michigan, Wisconsin, Iowa, Illinois, and Indiana put together, and one whose history

Figure 19. Restored log building near Maryville, Tennessee, where Sam Houston taught school.

includes Comanche and Apache Indians, Spanish conquistadors, missionaries, cowboys, cattle kings, homesteaders, cotton planters, miners, lumberjacks, oil drillers, and others. In fact, immigrants from Germany, as well as those from other European countries, were attracted to Texas's rich farming lands, and the German influence on log housing in certain parts of the state has been assessed by Hubert Wilhelm in a doctoral dissertation.[13] In the northern mountainous sections of neighboring New Mexico, there is also a wealth of log house traditions dating from the nineteenth century, although in the southern parts of the state log structures are rare. Various types of corner notchings are found, including the double-notch joint, and adobe is commonly used as a caulking between the logs and in some instances the entire building is covered with adobe. Both

Figure 20. Spanish-American dwelling, approximately 120 years old, in Lower Colonias, east of Pecos, New Mexico. Posts supporting roof are recent additions. (Courtesy Charles F. Gritzner, Louisiana State University)

round and hewn logs were used in these dwellings (see Figures 20, 21). Log housing in New Mexico is the subject of another doctoral dissertation by Charles F. Gritzner.[14]

Texas log cabins were constructed in varied styles and shapes usually of rough pine, gum, or oak, with different methods of corner notchings, depending on where the builder formerly lived and his cultural background. Texas natural resources also influenced certain features of the cabin; grass or broomweed was often used as a binder in the clay daubing, and where clay was scarce, burnt limestone mixed with sand made a substitute for mud daubing, often held in place by riven post oak shakes nailed to the edge of each log. Native limestone or sandstone was frequently used to build chimneys, although the stick-and-clay chimneys found on pioneer dwellings in the Southeast were not uncommon in Texas. Handmade boards covered the roof, and where nails were unavailable, the roof was held down by poles or rocks. Wood shutters opened and closed from the inside with a thin piece of rawhide stretched over the window to admit light but exclude flies and mosquitoes.

The era of pioneer log cabin building in Texas was relatively short, coming to an end when east Texas lumber mills began to ship by ox train. With the advent of the railroads in the 1880's bringing supplies of all kinds, including weatherboards, many ranchers living in log dwellings tended to board them over, and to add porches, frame additions, and attic rooms. But during the short period of the log cabin many dramatic incidents occurred involving Indian attack, forays by cattle thieves, kidnapping, and horse rustling, all of which are now part of Texas lore.

In 1958, a Texas Pioneer Heritage Committee laid plans for suitably commemorating the state's log cabin days, which was executed

Figure 21. Round log dwelling, in contrast to hewn logs shown in Figure 20, in Sangre de Cristo Mountains of northern New Mexico, approximately 80 years old. Tin roof, metal stovepipe, and adobe plaster are typical of these mountain dwellings. (Courtesy Charles F. Gritzner, Louisiana State University)

several years later by the Tarrant County Historical Society in the establishing of a Log Cabin Village at Forest Park in Fort Worth, now operated by the city's Park and Recreation Department. Of all the log cabin memorials in the United States, the restoration and furnishing of the Isaac Seela Cabin, the Pickard Cabin, the T. J. Shaw Cabin, the Isaac Parker Cabin, the Captain Howard Cabin, and the Tompkins Cabin, all originally built in the nineteenth century, provide one of the richest regional legacies for the citizens of the state and their visitors.

Like the trains of prairie schooners rumbling toward the setting sun, the frontier log cabin, a concrete expression of the life and structure of pioneer society, not only strengthened the family and the home, but played a dominant role in contributing to the nation's expansion. In the aftermath of the French and Indian Wars, and the Revolution, an American way of life found a beginning, entirely different from the Old World pattern that molded colonial life along the eastern seaboard.

The gradual transition from log cabin, hand churn, long rifle, home-produced foods, and furrowed fields to modern steam-heated homes and apartments, electric lights, telephones, packaged and frozen foods, ready-made clothing, and automobiles has been accomplished by the changing roles of all ages of both sexes, and it has brought about a change in the structure and function of the American family. All this, and much more, has been discussed pro and con in modern sociological literature where the subject of family mobility and internal migration has come prominently to the front in recent years. In examining the ebb and flow of migrating families and their influences on modern society, sociologists have not yet arrived at a definitive answer to the question of the effect that a change in housing has had on family stability. Is the family strengthened or weakened by frequent changes in the place of residence which characterizes our times? Conversely, is family integrity, in terms of divorce, desertion, separation, and other factors, influenced

if successive generations of nonmigrating families continue to occupy an old family homestead which the original owner erected
not only for himself, but sentimentally intended it to accommodate
his children and his children's children. What part, in fact, does a
house play in sustaining the structure of the family? In terms of the
residential mobility of the twentieth century these questions still
remain unanswered and beg for thoughtful statistical analysis and
interpretation.

As one re-examines the events of log cabin days on the western
frontier through the eyes of contemporary observers, even without
unavailable supporting statistics, he arrives at the impression that a
transitory dwelling place in a sparsely settled country gave new
strengths to mobile families. Under the circumstances then prevailing, moving from an eastern dwelling to a primitive log cabin
on the frontier did not attenuate the American family, but apparently contributed to its vitality and integrity.

Another interesting hypothesis arises from an examination of log
cabin life: it would seem that the log cabin was an extremely important element *per se* in facilitating the internal migrations of the
eighteenth and nineteenth centuries. If the techniques of log cabin
construction had remained unknown in America, it is quite possible
that the prospective migratory families may have been fewer in
number, despite the strong economic incentives to go south or west.
In support of this hypothesis is a basic consideration which entered
into an individual's decision whether or not to migrate, which sociologists have termed "intervening obstacles." [15] What this means is
that between the point where migration begins and the intended
destination a variety of obstacles are encountered, including the distance factors, physical barriers to be surmounted such as mountains,
rivers, lakes, deserts, and others, to say nothing of the bands of
hostile Indians who resented white migrations as a threat to their
way of life. If these barriers had proved to be insurmountable, the
migration would have been deterred. If there had been no sailing
vessels, the Atlantic Ocean would not have been crossed in the first

place by European families, and the settlement of America would have been delayed until this barrier was conquered. Man has feared the Atlantic, he has died in it, caught food in it, relaxed on its sandy beaches, and dumped his refuse in it—but above all he learned he could travel on it. It actually became less of a barrier and more of an artery of commerce, and contributed to the peopling of the New World. When the settlers began to move westward, new obstacles blocked their way, and after the formidable barrier of the Appalachian ranges was conquered, the migratory flow to the Ohio was accelerated. When Americans learned that traveling together in the security of wagon trains they could move farther west despite Indian warriors, and conquer the wide deterring expanse of prairies and mountains, those intervening obstacles were also eliminated and mobile families were able to continue on to the Oregon Territory.

There existed from the very beginning, even after means were found to surmount the geographical obstacles, the problem of finding suitable housing at a new location in untamed territory. The pioneer knew that he could not transport sufficient building materials to erect a dwelling house, and even if he could, he lacked skills in carpentry. This obstacle must have been of major concern to a man with a wife and young children who considered abandoning a reasonably comfortable home on the Atlantic seaboard for unsettled and unknown territory. Unless he had confidence in his ability to provide a protective shelter, on which the very survival of himself and his family depended, even after surmounting the physical barriers en route, he would never have left his eastern home in the first place.

The knowledge that no matter where he settled, as long as trees were within easy reach, he could obtain wood to build a cabin minimized this "intervening obstacle." The one-room log cabin which he could build, unaided if necessary, using only an axe, gave him the assurance he needed to guarantee the security of himself and his family. To this extent, therefore, it would appear that the log cabin, like the sod house, were factors that facilitated the process of internal migration in colonial America.[16]

Notes—Chapter i

1. P. P. Cherry, *The Western Reserve and Early Ohio* (Akron, 1921), 76; *Virginia Magazine of History and Biography*, XII, 1904–1905, 260; J. F. D. Smyth, *A Tour of the United States of America* (London, 1784), II, 327.

2. *Filson's Kentucke*, ed. Willard Rouse Jillson (Louisville, Ky., 1929), 70.

3. Charles A. Hanna, *Historical Collections of Harrison County* (New York, 1900), 67.

4. *Audubon's America*, ed. Donald Culross Peattie (Boston, 1940), 107.

5. Captain Basil Hall, *Travels in North America in The Years 1827 and 1828* (Philadelphia, 1829), II, 257.

6. Hanna, 27.

7. *Philip Vickers Fithian Journal, 1775–1776*, ed. Robert G. Albion and Leonidas Dodas (Princeton, 1934), 67.

8. Alexis de Tocqueville, *Journey to America*, trans. George Lawrence, ed. J. P. Mayer (New Haven, 1960), 334.

9. *Ibid.*, 339.

10. A. Clark Medford, *Mountain People, Mountain Times* (Waynesville, N.C., 1963), 36.

11. See Ray Allen Billington, *Westward Expansion* (New York, 1967, third ed.) for a comprehensive account of the various frontiers. Excellent bibliographical material appears in Jack M. Sosin, *The Revolutionary Frontier* (New York, 1967).

12. "Narrative of A Journey Across the Rocky Mountains to the Columbia River," *Early Western Travels, 1748–1846*, ed. Reuben Gold Thwaites (Cleveland, 1904), XXI, 297, 319.

13. Titled "Organized German Settlement and Its Effect on the Frontier of South Central Texas," this dissertation was submitted in 1968 to the faculty of the Louisiana State University in partial fulfillment of the requirements for the doctoral degree. Dr. Wilhelm kindly permitted me to read portions of the dissertation while he was in process of writing it.

14. This dissertation, tentatively titled "Spanish American Folk Log Construction in Northern New Mexico," has not yet been completed, but will be submitted to the Louisiana State University in partial fulfillment of the requirements for the doctoral degree. I have had considerable correspondence with Mr. Gritzner on the subject of log housing in New Mexico.

15. Everett S. Lee, "A Theory of Migration," *Demography*, III, No. 1, 1966, 47–57. For thorough discussions of the family, see William F.

Kenkel, *The Family in Perspective*, 2nd ed. (New York, 1966); Arthur
W. Calhoun, *A Social History of The American Family*, I: *Colonial
Period* (New York, 1960 [reprint]).

16. In the holdings of the Prints and Photographs Division of the
Library of Congress is the Historic American Buildings Survey Collection containing more than 26,000 sheets of drawings, 30,000 exterior and
interior photographs, and 7000 typed pages of historical and architectural
data pertaining to American dwellings, churches, public buildings, shops,
mills, etc., from the seventeenth to the late nineteenth century. Included
in this mass of data are several hundred photographs of log structures
which, with the kind assistance of Virginia Daiker, Head of the Reference
Section, I spent two days examining. It was a coincidence that I had per-
sonally photographed many of these log buildings at a different point in
time.

2 Red Men and Log Cabins

The European axe, like the steel knife, the garden hoe, and the iron cooking pot, was an object of wonderment to the Indian tribes of the eastern woodlands who had no knowledge of metal weapons and utensils before the coming of the white man to their shores. Thomas Harriot said of the coastal Algonkian peoples that they had "no edge tool or weapons of iron or steel to offend us withal, neither know they how to make any . . ."

The eastern Algonkians applied their grooved stone axes and stone celts, in combination with fire, to cut down trees for use in making their sturdy dugout log canoes. After cutting the log to size "they set fire into it, and when it hath burnt it hollow, they cut out the coal with their shells."

The Five Nations Iroquois, further advanced in their social and material culture than their Algonkian-speaking neighbors, were also using stone axes and stone knives as weapons, along with spears and chalcedony-tipped arrows, when Champlain, with his Huron and Algonkian allies attacked and subdued their villages with guns and iron swords. The Iroquois people were no match for the Frenchman, even though they used their stone tools effectively to fell trees to make clearings for their corn fields, to hoe the earth, to construct log palisades around their villages, and for many other nonmilitary purposes. They even used sinkers of stone to hold down their fish nets in the beds of streams, stone anchors to keep their canoes from drifting, and they smoked tobacco in stone pipes.

The fine birchbark canoes of the Iroquois and other northern

tribes, and the ornate totem poles of the Tlingit, Haida, and Tsim-
shian tribes of the Pacific Northwest exhibited more mature wood-
working techniques than those of the coastal Algonkian, but none
of the historic American Indian tribes from Maine to California,
even those most advanced in woodcarving technology, constructed
cabins of notched logs laid horizontally.

In the far northwestern corner of the American continent the
prehistoric ancestors of the Eskimo learned to place logs horizontally, one on the other, to construct the walls of their winter houses.
These houses, consisting of separate rooms, with kitchen and storage
sheds detached from the living room, were built in the earth and
covered with earthen mounds. Access to the rooms of the composite
dwelling was via underground tunnels through which the residents
crawled to huddle together in the warmth of the living room heated
by whale-oil lamps. In his 1958 archeological expedition at Cape
Krusenstern in Alaska, the late Dr. J. Louis Giddings, professor of
anthropology at Brown University, identified what he called a Western Thule phase of early Eskimo culture. As he excavated on the
old beaches Dr. Giddings uncovered the rooms of composite subterranean dwellings, the walls made of "driftwood poles laid
horizontally and dovetailed as in a modern log cabin." [1] The Western Thule occupation extended back as early as 3000 B.C., and like
other Eskimoan cultures, probably had its deepest roots in the
Mesolithic cultures of northern Eurasia, which are dated from 10,000
to 8000 B.C.

Henry B. Collins of the Smithsonian Institution also uncovered
the remains of underground houses of horizontal logs of driftwood
on the Punuk Islands off the tip of St. Lawrence Island which lies
in the Bering Sea between Alaska and Siberia. This culture was
full-blown about 1000 A.D., having its origin much earlier. [2] This
technique of notched log housing apparently did not survive among
the historic Eskimo nor did it diffuse southward to the American
Indian tribes.

To see the white colonist felling trees with his axe, and then to
watch the sharp blade biting notches into the logs as the chips flew

must have amazed the American Indian. Most astonishing of all was the cabin itself, which took shape as the felled logs were welded one on the other to form walls as durable as the trunks of the tall oaks standing in the forest. Like the sailing vessels having the wings of a giant *cohunk*, which glided over the water without oars or poles, and the deck cannons which boomed with the voice of an evil Manito and belched smoke from their bellies, the log cabin probably appeared to the unsophisticated red man as another example of the white man's magic.

When Captain Zebulon Montgomery Pike sailed up the Mississippi from St. Louis in 1805 with twenty men in a keel boat, he reached Indian territory where no white man had yet penetrated. One can imagine the interest of the Indians when Captain Pike and his men cut down sixty trees in one day to build log cabins for their winter shelters. "This, considering we had only two falling axes and three hatchets," he wrote in his journal, "was pretty good work."

Why the Indian, living in a sylvan environment surrounded by many species of trees, didn't apply log cabin building techniques is one of the cultural mysteries to which an ethnologist cannot give a ready answer. Although the process would have been slow, the Indian was capable of notching logs with his stone tools, in combination with fire, the same technique the Algonkians used to fell the trees and hollow out dugout canoes. But the log structure held together by corner notching was simply not a trait in the Indian craft culture.

After the Indian cultures were modified by European influences, which brought a myriad of new things from the Old World, including guns, ammunition, metal tools and weapons, glass, and alcoholic beverages, the Indians did, indeed, learn how to build dwellings of notched logs. This did not occur until long after the Indians were thrown into contact with Europeans, and as native institutions crumbled under the successive waves of newcomers who spread a new culture across the North American continent. The white man also borrowed from the Indian cultures, because the influences were reciprocal. When peoples differing in cultural heritage are suddenly thrown into intimate association, the more advanced groups give more than they receive, but, nevertheless, it is a matter of give and take for each.

To cite one example, the most important indigenous food product, Indian corn, had not previously been seen by the European colonists, and without it the pioneer log cabin families could not have survived. It has been said that some of the American Indian tribes constructed corn cribs of logs prior to white contact, but there is yet no archeological evidence to support that contention. But the cultivation, preparation, and consumption of corn was accompanied by such practices as planting seeds in hills fertilized with fish; periodic suckering and hoeing; and finally the harvesting, usually followed by a corn dance or other social festival. The corn was husked with a bone or wood husking peg; the husks were plaited to make mats and baskets; and the kernels were pounded into corn meal in a log mortar with a stone pestle. The corn flour was used to make mush, pone, ash cake, and what the pioneers called "journey cake," later corrupted to "Johnny cake." The preparation of these and many other corn-derived dishes required stirring paddles, mixing bowls, shell spoons, and other specialized utensils made by the Indians. The manufacture of these utensils, in turn, necessitated other tools and implements. All were part of a vast, wonderful corn complex, which was taken over in totality by white settlers as an integral part of log cabin life. The whites, in fact, found new uses for corn, one of which was the distillation of whiskey from the grain, and the innumerable stills on the frontier led to the widespread consumption of "corn likker." Other practices, which need not detain us, were also borrowed from the Indians by Europeans as they adapted to the new environment. Insufficient credit has been given the Indians whose trails guided the white settlers; whose clothing was adopted by the pioneer; whose hunting and fishing customs were borrowed by frontiersmen; and whose cultivation of beans, tobacco, pumpkins, gourds, and squash was soon imitated by white farmers.

Prior to building log cabins, many of the European settlers in the New World (as will shortly be discussed) had no hesitation in imitating the house styles of neighboring Indians. Some even lived in the crude Indian wigwams before building their own houses. The Indians built many different kinds of family shelters in aboriginal America and housing forms varied by area and by tribe. The most familiar family dwelling, pictured in many storybooks, was the simple *tepee* of the Plains Indians, a pointed or conical tent made of a tripod of poles covered with bark or skin. But this was only one of at least thirty identifiable house types found among North American tribes, including the pueblos and cliff dwellings of stone and adobe of the southwest; the earth lodges (such as the Navaho *hogan*); the bee-hive shaped grass homes of the Caddoan peoples; the palmetto huts found among the Louisiana tribes; the brush shelters of the Apache called *wickiup*; the caribou-skin tents of the Naskapi in Labrador; the plank houses of the Puget Sound Indians,[3] the igloos of the Eskimo, and many others.

The wigwam of the Algonkian-speaking tribes was found throughout the coastal area from Canada as far south as the Carolinas. The term was applied either to a rectangular house having an arched roof or a round house with a dome-shaped roof. Both dwellings were made of a framework of saplings anchored in the ground, and then bent and tied together with twisted reeds, rushes, or strips of inner tree bark. Smaller tree limbs were threaded cross-wise through this framework, and the outside walls and roof were then covered with rectangular sections of bark, or mats made of dry grass or corn husks. A separate family usually occupied each wigwam.

"Their houses," wrote Captain John Smith of the wigwams of the Powhatan tribes in his well-known *Travels and Works*, "are built like our Arbors of small young sprigs bowed and tyed, and so closely covered with mats or the barkes of trees very handsomely, that notwithstanding either winde, raine or weather, they are as warme as stooves, but very smoaky, yet at the toppe of the house there is a hole made for the smoake to goe into right over the fire."

When the Pilgrim landing party from the *Mayflower* went ashore that cold December morning in 1620 to explore the Cape Cod area, the first human signs they saw were two deserted wigwams covered with mats, the typical residences of the Algonkian-speaking Nauset Indians, similar to those Smith described in Virginia.

The Long House of the Five Nations was a rectangular structure larger than a single-family wigwam, consisting of tall, strong saplings set in the earth in two rows to form the two sides of the house, bent until they met and lashed together at their tops with strips of inner bark or sinews. Tree limbs were bound transversely into this frame and covered with sheets of bark from the oak, elm, spruce or white cedar. Large mats were hung to close the openings at either end of the structure. Inside, on both sides of the Long House were wide scaffolds of tree limbs about four feet from the floor and extending the full length of the dwelling. They were covered with skins and used both as beds and seats. As in the Algonkian wigwam, the fire was built on the earthen floor, the smoke escaping through a hole cut in the center of the roof. In the winter the cooking was done over this fire, but in the summer the family prepared and ate its food outdoors over an open fire. A number of families related by kinship ties occupied each Long House under the general superintendency of an elderly matron of the same lineage.

Both the wigwams and Long Houses of the Algonkian and Iroquois peoples were grouped together in small, semipermanent communities, often on or near the banks of a running stream, where the land had been cleared for gardens, and where the Indian women planted corn, tobacco, beans, squashes, pumpkins, and other vegetables. Prior to the planting season, and after the harvest, the Indians frequently left their villages to go into the woods to hunt and trap, or in the case of coastal Indians, to visit the seaside to fish and gather oysters, conches, and clams. During the periods they were absent from their villages, some of the eastern Indians camped in temporary lean-tos or in rock shelters. The young Swedish engineer, Peter Lindeström, writing in 1654 said of the Delaware Indians, "During the summer they have no certain dwellings, but move about here and there around the country."

Some of the Indian villages, but not all, were palisaded by logs set together in the earth vertically, usually sharpened at the top. The palisade formed a protective fence around the town or village, and early English explorers called such complexes "Indian forts" or "castles."

In contrast to the houses in Europe, the wigwams of the Eastern Algonkian and the Iroquois Long Houses were regarded by the white men as crude, primitive, impermanent structures, and a contemporary English word that aptly described an Indian dwelling was "cabin." When the founder of Quakerism, George Fox, noted in his journal during a trip to the Province of Maryland in 1672, that he visited "an Indian-King's Cabbin," he meant one of the typical Algonkian bark wigwams occupied by a town chief and his family. The dwelling bore no resemblance to a log cabin.

"The smallest sort of these *cabins*," wrote Robert Beverley of the houses built by the Virginia Indians, "are conical like a bee-hive, but the larger are built in oblong form, and both are covered with the bark of trees, which they rive off into great flakes."

The use of the word "cabin" by Fox, Beverley, John Lawson, and many other seventeenth century English writers to describe Indian wigwams, still continues to be misconstrued by some readers to mean a log cabin. Yet, it is well known to students of early English that during Elizabethan times in England, the word cabin had two principal meanings, either an enclosed room on a sailing vessel, or a frail hut of boughs. When Viola said in *Twelfth Night* (I, v.267), "Make me a willow Cabine at your gate," she meant a hut of twigs and boughs, not a cabin of notched logs set horizontally to form the walls.

The log cabin, as we know it in America, did not exist in England at the time America was being explored and settled, but if it had, it is unlikely the English would have called it a cabin. Even a small one-room dwelling of logs was far too sturdy and durable a structure to be so designated, and the English colonists probably would have termed it a log "house."

The word cabin, as applied to a dwelling of logs, was strictly an American use of an old English word given a new meaning, and a comparatively late one at that. In 1769, Botetourt County in Virginia came into existence when Augusta County was divided, and the following reference to two log structures by the specific use of the term "log cabin", which I have italicized, occurs in the court records of the new county on April 11, 1770:

> The court doth appoint Is. [Israel] Christian & Stephen Trigg to agree with a workman to build a *log cabbin* twenty four feet long and twenty wide for a Court House with a clapboard roof with two small sheads, one at each end for jury rooms.
>
> The Court doth give leave to James McGavock to build a *log cabin* twenty feet long and sixteen feet wide, with an addition at the end of it the same width and twenty feet long for a prison and the Goaler's house, the expense of which to be repaid by the County.[4]

The following August the court records refer to the prison, and in October to the courthouse, leaving no doubt that both structures were built as planned.[5] Whether the logs used in the two buildings were round or squared is not clarified in the court records, but the reference has been previously quoted as the first example of the use of the term "log cabin" in American documents as recorded by a Scotch-Irish scribe.

I have found an earlier reference in the Minutes of the Pennsylvania Provincial Council. On July 31, 1750, there was introduced into the official record a report written by Richard Peters, Secretary of the Province, dealing with white settlers unlawfully seated on lands beyond the "Kittochtinny Mountains" not purchased from the Indians. A paragraph in the report reads as follows, to which I have added the italic:

> On Tuesday the twenty-second of May [1750] Matthew Dill, George Croghan, Benjamin Chambers, Thomas Wilson, John Finley, and James Galbreth, Esquires, Justices of the said County of Cumberland, attended by the Under Sheriff, came to Big Juniata situate at the Distance of twenty-five miles from the mouth thereof and about ten Miles North from the Blue Hills, a Place much esteemed by the Indians for some of their best hunting Ground [apparently in present Juniata County near Mexico or between there and Thompsontown] and there they found *five Cabbins or Log Houses* one possessed by William White, another George

Cohoon, another not quite finished in Possession of David Hiddleston, another possessed by George and William Galloway, and another by Andrew Lycon; of these Persons William White, George and William Galloway, David Hiddleston and George Cohoon appeared before the Magistrates, and being asked by what Right or authority they possessed themselves of those Lands and erected Cabbins thereon, they replied by no Right or Authority but that the Land belonged to the Proprietaries of Pennsylvania.[6]

Since the Pennsylvania authorities were apprehensive of antagonizing the Six Nations, who then held the balance of power between them and the French, the settlers were dispossessed and some of the log cabins were burned.

In the same report, to which I have also supplied the italic, Peters stated that on "Sheerman's Creek or Little Juniata, situate about six miles over the Blue Mountains they found white settlers living in 11 *Cabbins or Log Houses*," and these, too, were burned to appease the Indians. "It may be proper to add," Peters reported, "that the Cabbins or Log Houses which were burnt were of no considerable Value, being such as the Country People erect in a Day or two, and cost only the Charge of an Entertainment."[7] No doubt the entertainment referred to included a jug of "corn likker," which the potential resident made available to those who helped him raise his cabin. Burnt Cabins, a drowsy village of frame houses in Fulton County at the foot of Cove Mountain near Fort Littleton was evidently the site of this incident commemorated in the town's name.

Thus, it was the English-born Peters, educated at Oxford, an Anglican clergyman in Philadelphia, appointed by Thomas Penn as Secretary of the Province of Pennsylvania, who associated the word cabin with a dwelling of logs twenty years before the term appeared in the court records of Botetourt County, Virginia.

Peters did not attempt to differentiate between a log cabin and a log house, as did another clergyman, Thaddeus Mason Harris, a New Englander, who visited the Pennsylvania frontier in 1803. At the time of Harris's visit he saw not only one-room cabins but larger and more commodious dwellings of logs. Harris was very specific in his description of a log cabin; it was, he said, a temporary structure built of round, unhewn logs, caulked with moss, straw or mud, having no windows, and a hole in the roof in lieu of a chimney.[8]

A log *house*, he said, was a dwelling built of hewn logs, the interstices stopped with stones and neatly plastered, having glass windows, a chimney, and a shingled roof (see Figure 22).

Figure 22. Dwelling in Allegheny Mountains near Masontown, Fayette County, Pennsylvania, having glass windows, chimney, shingled roof, and its hewn logs caulked with stones and plaster meets Thaddeus Mason Harris's definition of "a log house."

The presence of windows, chimney, and whether or not the logs were left in the round or hewn were, in his judgment, the distinguishing characteristics between a log house and a log cabin. Needless to say, Harris's definitions represented a personal judgment of an individual with only superficial knowledge of log housing, and cannot be reconciled with popular usage. The term log cabin has long been used throughout the United States to describe structures of either round or hewn logs, irrespective of whether or not they have chimneys, windows or shingled roofs. In fact, I have often heard a two-story log dwelling referred to as a log cabin. Both terms have, to some extent, been interchangeable in popular usage throughout the years, although to most Americans a log cabin is a small dwelling of logs, either round or hewn, usually having a single floor and one room, which may or may not have a loft. If the room is partitioned to make two rooms on the ground floor, or if a shed or lean-to has been attached, it would still be called a log cabin. On the other hand, if a second room, or rooms, is built on top of the first making an additional story, popular usage would accept it being termed a log house and many Americans would be inclined to call it that. The modern dictionary definition of a log cabin is a "small, rough log house."

Strictly speaking, a one-room cabin built of logs is one mode of construction whereas a multiroom log house with more than one story, is another, especially if the former is roughly built and the latter is constructed for permanence. Size rather than differing architectural features seems to be the point of departure between a cabin and a house, and this has been reinforced by the inclusion of a relatively new word in the American vocabulary, i.e., tourist cabin. The latter is almost always a small structure, usually having only one room, although it may or may not be constructed of logs, the usual material consisting of brick, cinder blocks, or wood.

In the present volume I have inclined to use the words log cabin to mean a small log structure, either of round or hewn logs, built on one level, and, in general to use the words log house for larger residences, particularly those with floors above the ground level.

When I refer to a log *dwelling* it usually means I have some doubt about the size of the structure, although the reader will probably find that I am not very finical about these terms and have no inflexible rules. There is, however, one technical point that I have tried to observe in my terminology: a house or cabin built of logs is not an architectural *type*, but rather a method of construction, since a house type can be executed in log, frame, stone, brick, or other materials.

To return to the American Indian, the native was quick to adopt many of the white man's ways, particularly in his use of guns and ammunition, liquor, and duffel cloth obtained from the traders, which he used to cover his body instead of the animal pelts that constituted the clothing of men and women alike in the prehistoric period. The Indian learned to covet these European articles and no price seemed too high to pay for them, although initially he clung steadfastly to his own native house-building customs. After the Indians and whites established a commercial rapport and were thrown into close contact, the natives were soon using copper and iron kettles, metal knives, hatchets, and hoes, glass beads, and the rest of a long list of trader's goods obtained in exchange for furs.

Native pottery, the bow and arrow, utensils of stone, wood, and bone, and ornaments of stone and shell gradually fell into disuse in favor of European artifacts. Long after it was too late, the Indian realized that the European materials he sought so eagerly from the fur traders contributed to a dissolution of his own culture, resulting in a growing dependence on the whites. As the old Cherokee chieftain Skiagunsta said, "The clothes we wear we cannot make ourselves. They are made for us. We use their ammunition with which to kill deer. We cannot make our guns. Every necessary of life we have from the white people." [9]

Skiagunsta might have added that the Indians, who usually bore a single personal name, also began adopting the white man's naming habits along with other European customs. In the records of the Eastern Shore of Maryland as of 1704, I have found Choptank Indians named Betty Caco, George Attowcase, William Ahconepatokack, John Quash, etc., the Christian name affixed to their former Indian names.

In this process of acculturation it was inevitable that the native dwellings would eventually give way to white men's houses, although this came about more slowly than the adoption of European names, guns and ammunition, white men's clothing, and alcohol. There were some few exceptions, such as the frame cottage built after the English style which Francis Yardley erected in 1653 in North Carolina for "the great emperor of *Rhaanoke*," and the frame house the English of Virginia built for the chieftain, Opechanca-nough,[10] but so long as the Indian families were able to move with the seasons and follow the wild game in pursuit of ancient food-gathering processes, their tepees, hogans, wigwams and wickiups continued to satisfy their need for shelter. As the white intruders encroached on their hunting territories, and built towns along the fishing streams, and as the wild animals grew scarce, the Indians were forced to adopt different modes of living, and build new kinds of houses in order to survive. In doing so, they found it necessary to lean more and more on the white settlers.

During the middle of the eighteenth century, the concept of the log cabin spread to the eastern and southern Indian tribes, who by then were already partially Europeanized. During the negotiation of a treaty with the provincial authorities at Easton, Pennsylvania, in 1757, Teedyuscung, the pretended "king" of the Delawares, whose people had been widely scattered by the incursions of the whites on their lands, made the following request to which I have added the italic:

And as we intend to make a Settlement at Wyoming [near present Wilkes-Barre] and to build different Houses from what we have done heretofore, such as may last not only for a little Time, but for our children after us; *we desire you will assist us in making our Settlements, and send us Persons to instruct us in building Houses*, and in making such Necessaries as shall be needful.[11]

The Pennsylvania authorities responded to Teedyuscung's request by sending workmen to erect ten log cabins for his people each measuring ten by fourteen feet, with a larger one for the chieftain, measuring sixteen by twenty-four feet, all made of squared logs dovetailed at the corners. Teedyuscung later burned to death in his hewn log dwelling when it was set afire by his enemies while he was sleeping off a stupor brought on by drinking white man's whiskey.

Logstown, an important settlement of the wasted Delaware, Seneca, and Shawnee tribes, between 1725 and 1727, was situated on the right bank of the Ohio River about eighteen miles below Pittsburgh at present Ambridge. Straggling bands of Wyandotte, Mohawk, and Miami Indians also settled there temporarily with their red brethren, all of whom had been forced from their native villages by an expanding white man's civilization. Many brought with them the acquired skills of log cabin construction, and perhaps the settlement derived its name from the log dwellings within its perimeter. Father Bonnecamp, who was with Celeron de Bienville when he deposited the lead plates at the mouths of the tributaries of the Ohio on behalf of France, wrote in his journal that there were "80 cabins" in the Indian settlement at Logstown although he did not specify how many of these cabins were built of logs. By 1807, after most of the Indians had been pressed farther westward, Logstown was reported to have declined to "a scattering hamlet of four or five log cabins."

Traders also played a part in teaching the natives log cabin skills. During the early part of the seventeenth century the traders were constantly on the move, traveling long distances to reach the Indian villages where they bartered European merchandise for furs, and then returned to the coastal towns to make shipments of the pelts to Europe. The first Dutch and Swedish traders living in New Amsterdam or New Sweden often made long trips inland to obtain the prized beaver pelts from the Indians. As time went on, and bartering became more competitive, the traders erected log cabins as combination residences and trading posts in closer proximity to the Indian villages. On October 17, 1770, George Washington noted in his journal that there were twenty log dwellings along the Monongahela River near Fort Pitt all occupied by Indian traders. The traders living nearest to the source of the furs were in a preferred position in the competition that developed. The enterprising George Croghan, "king of the traders," moved his headquarters to the mouth of Pine Creek on the Allegheny River at present Etna, Pennsylvania, where he erected a number of log cabins. Croghan also maintained similar log trading posts near Sewickley Creek on the Youghiogheny; also at Logstown; and after 1748, at *Pickawillanee* on the Miami River. During the peak of his commercial activities Croghan employed twenty-five men and owned over one hundred pack horses used in the fur trade with the Indians. The example of the log cabins built by the traders had a strong influence in making the Indians aware of the advantage of this method of house construction in contrast to their own frail huts. There can be little question that some of the traders taught the Indians to build log cabins and even assisted them.

In 1772–1773, David Jones visited the wasted Indian tribes then living in Ohio, and there are several references in his journal to the Indians living in log cabins. For example, the town of *Pickaweeke*, known to the whites as "Blue Jackets Town," was occupied by a mixture of Shawnee and other Indians, and Jones described it as containing "12 log huts." *Chillicaathee*, then the principal town in Ohio of the Shawnee, also contained log dwellings, and the Delaware Indian towns on the Muskingum had a number of log cabins, with the Delaware and Shawnee in one of the towns living together "in pretty good log houses well shingled with nails." [12]

When the Moravian preacher, David Zeisberger, settled a band of "Christian" Indians near present New Philadelphia, Ohio, in 1772, at a place called Schoenbrunn ("beautiful spring"), red men and white men worked together and erected sixty cabins of hewn logs, and a log church and school.

In the fall of 1775, the twenty five-year old Englishman, Nicholas Cresswell visited this Indian settlement on the banks of the Muskingum and he described the church as "built of logs sixty foot square covered with Shingles, Glass in the windows and a Bell, a good plank floor with two rows of forms." [13] Today in the reconstructed Schoenbrunn village the visitor can see restored log cabins, the trading post, church, and schoolhouse built to resemble the original structures. Gnadenhuetten ("tents of grace") established by the "Moravian Indians" in 1772 also contained log cabins, as did Goshen, another Ohio settlement established by Zeisberger in 1798 as part of the Moravian missionary effort among the Indians. The log housing at these settlements followed the same patterns as the Moravian-built log houses at Nazareth and Bethlehem; see pp. 219–22.

William Bartram in 1776 wrote that the southern Cherokee were living in log dwellings roofed either with shingles or chestnut bark.

One of the best documentary evidences of how the log cabin had diffused to the Indian tribes can be found in the account of the famous expedition led by Major General John Sullivan who invaded the New York state area in 1779. The avowed purpose of Sullivan's expedition was to lay waste the entire territory of the Iroquois, an act of vengeance against the Indian confederacy which had allied itself with the British against the Americans during the Revolution. Sullivan's troops sacked and burned forty Iroquois towns, destroying an estimated 200,000 bushels of corn and thousands of fruit trees, depriving the Indians of their food supply. This mission of destruction was the final blow that broke the strength of the Five Nations (then called the Six Nations, for the Tuscarora had earlier joined forces with the original five confederated Iroquois tribes). The diaries and journals of Sullivan's officers contain many entries describing the numbers of log cabins, in the towns then occupied by the Iroquois, and the hundreds of cabins, built of both round and hewn logs which were set afire and destroyed by the troops. Some of these cabins seem to have been exceptionally well constructed; for example, the Mohawk village called *Onoquaga* was "built on each side of the River with good Log Houses with Stone Chimneys and glass windows." [14]

By the early 1800's, migrant Indians settled in the area between the Susquehanna and Ohio Rivers had become proficient in erecting log cabins, felling the trees and notching the logs with the metal hatchets they obtained from white traders for their furs. As the incursions of white families pushed the red men farther west the acquired knowledge of how to build log cabins went with them. Marietta, Ohio's oldest white settlement, built at the confluence of the Ohio and Muskingum in 1788, consisted of log dwellings and a log stockade, and as the reader has seen from the passages in David Jones' and Nicholas Cresswell's journals, the Indians living along the Muskingum were already living in log cabins before the white settlers arrived.

A newly-arrived observer from Europe, unfamiliar with the diverse types of shelters built by the American Indian tribes in the precontact period, could have readily concluded that the log cabin was an ancient and universal type of native dwelling on the North American continent. From superficial observations at Marietta he might easily, yet erroneously, have assumed that the white man borrowed log cabin techniques from the Indian, whereas the opposite was true.

Once the Indians became proficient in log cabin construction, successive generations of natives continued to build this kind of house on their reservations, and elsewhere, long after the whites had given up log dwellings for houses of frame, brick, or stone. During the late nineteenth century, white scribes told of how the remnant tribes were housed in log cabins in various parts of the South and West. De Tocqueville in 1831, en route from Detroit to Saginaw, the last outpost of the white man on the Michigan peninsula, saw in Chippewa hunting territory "two cabins very much like log houses," although the Indians across the river from the white settlement at Saginaw were still clinging conservatively to their conical tepees.[15] Captain Basil Hall in 1827 visited a Creek Indian village in the South which consisted of twenty log cabins, and many other references could be introduced to show how the Indian housing patterns included log cabins even in the latter part of the century.

In 1907, an ethnologist on the staff of New York's Museum of the American Indian, Mark R. Harrington, reported that surviving

members of the Delaware Indian tribe then living near Dewey, Oklahoma, were still conducting their annual non-Christian religious
festival, the so-called Big House Ceremony, in an ancient log building covered with hand-split shingles. At this late date the Delawares
spoke the English language, normally dressed like their white neighbors with whom some of their young people had intermarried, were
becoming integrated in white communities, and had given up their
former log cabin dwellings for frame residences containing modern
improvements. It was of particular interest to Harrington that log
house techniques had survived in a structure where, once a year,
the Delawares danced and sang in the ceremonial pattern of their
forefathers observing ancient religious rites.

A similar situation was reported as late as 1944 by the University
of Pennsylvania ethnologist, Frank G. Speck, who found that surviving members of the Cayuga tribe (one of the affiliates of the
Six Nation Iroquois) had preserved a Long House of squared,
notched logs on their reservation in Ontario, Canada, known to them
as the "Sour Spring Long House." There, they, too, on occasion,
conducted ancient tribal ceremonial rites and dances. At this time
the Cayuga families lived in frame houses, dressed like white people,
normally spoke the English language, and many of them attended
Protestant churches on the reservation. It would seem that when
a primitive culture is invaded by a superior and more complex one
its technology is the first aspect to change, sociological practices
and concepts are more resistant, and the spiritual life is the last to
be affected.

In 1940, I visited at Wewoka, Oklahoma, the Council House of
notched logs built prior to 1900 by the expatriated Seminole who
settled there. In their native habitat in Florida before their contact
with white people, the Seminole built their council houses of leaves
and grass on a wooden framework—never of logs. Obviously they
borrowed log building techniques from the whites.

When I was doing ethnological research among the mixed-blood
Nanticoke Indian descendants in Indian River Hundred, Sussex
County, Delaware, in 1942 and 1943, I found no surviving religious
structures or council houses, because the native ceremonial patterns,

like the Algonkian dialect, had been obliterated. However, there were still in use on some of the Nanticoke farms a few old corn cribs built of round logs, vestiges of an earlier day when the Nanticoke advanced from the traditional bark wigwams of their ancestors to adopt the white man's log housing methods. The Nanticoke themselves were then, as today, living in neat frame bungalows and comfortable farmhouses indistinguishable from dwellings occupied by their white neighbors.[16]

Visitors today to Indian reservations, such as the 50,000-acre Qualla Reserve at the entrance to the Great Smokies at Cherokee, North Carolina, are not surprised to see log cabins in the recreated Oconaluftee Indian community. It is well known by almost every American that Indians like the Cherokee and Catawba; the Delawares, Shawnee, Six Nation Iroquois; and many other Indian tribes once lived in crude log dwellings (see Figure 23). But the visitor

Figure 23. Cherokee cabin on Qualla Reservation, North Carolina, photographed either in 1888 or 1893 by the ethnologist James Mooney on one of his investigatory trips. (Courtesy Bureau of American Ethnology)

will be mistaken if he concludes that the log cabin was a native type of Indian dwelling, although some Americans still have this impression.

NOTES—CHAPTER 2

1. J. Louis Giddings, *Ancient Men of The Arctic* (New York, 1967), 83.

2. *Ibid.*, 155.

3. It has often been said that the Indians of Washington and Oregon built log cabins, but I can find no support of this contention as applied to the prehistoric period; see Ronald L. Olson, "Adze, Canoe and House Types of the Northwest Coast," *University of Washington Publications in Anthropology*, II, No. 1, Nov. 1927; T. T. Waterman and Ruth Greiner, *Indian Houses of Puget Sound*, Heye Foundation, Museum of the American Indian (New York, 1921); Philip Drucker, *Cultures of the North Pacific Coast* (San Francisco, 1965).

4. Lewis Preston Summers, *Annals of Southwest Virginia, 1769–1800* (Abingdon, Va., 1929), 77.

5. *Ibid.*, 90, 93.

6. *Minutes of the Provincial Council of Pennsylvania* (Philadelphia, n.d.), V, 441–442.

7. *Ibid.*, 449.

8. Thaddeus Mason Harris, "The Journal of a Tour into the Territory Northwest of the Allegheny Mountains, 1803," *Early Western Travels, 1748–1846*, ed. Reuben G. Thwaites (Cleveland, 1904), III, 322. Hawley, observing log dwellings in Ohio in 1820–1821 for the first time, had his own definitions of a blockhouse in contrast to a log house, Zerah Hawley, *A Journal Tour Through Conn., Mass., N.Y. and the North Parts of Pa. and Ohio* (microfilm, Univ. of Delaware), 52–53.

9. David H. Corkran, *The Cherokee Frontier* (Norman, Okla., 1962), 14.

10. *Narratives of Early Carolina*, ed. Alexander S. Salley, Jr. (New York, 1911), 27; *Hakluytus Posthumus, or Purchas His Pilgrims*, Samuel Purchas (Glasgow, 1906), XIX, 160.

11. Anthony F. C. Wallace, *King of the Delawares—Teedyuskung* (Philadelphia, 1949), 176.

12. David Jones, *A Journal of Two Visits Made to some Nations of Indians*, etc. (Sabin reprint) (New York, 1865), 52, 56, 88, 92.

13. *The Journal of Nicholas Cresswell 1774–1777* (New York, 1924), 106. Cresswell's dimensions of the church were exaggerated, since we learn

authoritatively from Heckewelder that it was built of squared timbers, measuring 40 x 36, and had a shingled roof with cupola and bell, *cf.* John Heckewelder, *A Narrative of A Mission, etc.* (Philadelphia, 1820), 128.

14. *General John Sullivan's Indian Expedition, 1779,* ed. Frederick Cook (Auburn, N.Y.), 23.

15. Alexis de Tocqueville, *Journey to America,* trans. George Lawrence, ed. J. P. Mayer (New Haven, 1960), 359.

16. C. A. Weslager, *Delaware's Forgotten Folk* (Philadelphia, 1943), 51.

3   Log Houses in Europe

Long before the outbreak of the Civil War, innumerable log houses, log schools, log churches, log barns, log post offices, log inns and taverns, log smokehouses, log tobacco sheds, and log corn cribs were found from New York to Florida, and as far west as pioneering families had reached. Contrary to the popular concept of the log cabin as an isolated dwelling seen only in the mountains or backwoods, houses built of logs were the characteristic residences in the growing towns on the expanding American frontier. In 1777 Samuel Doak founded a log cabin college, Martin Academy, the first school of higher education in Tennessee; in Pittsburgh an old log cabin that stood at Third and Cherry Streets was chartered as the Pittsburgh Academy in 1799, the inception of the University of Pittsburgh; at South Bend, Indiana, Father Stephen Theodore Badin in 1834 built a log residence which was used as a chapel, the forerunner of Notre Dame University.

Log houses were an interesting novelty to visitors from England and other European countries, preoccupied as they were with those external features of American life that differed from their own institutions. Like the widespread use of ice, the ice houses so common in both town and country, and the heavy American breakfasts of fried eggs, bacon, coffee, and what visiting Mrs. Trollope called the "sempiternal ham" and the "horrible half-baked rolls," the log cabin stood out in sharp contrast to Europe's frame cottages and brick houses. I have quoted extracts from several contemporary

European journals, but there are other observations worthy of attention.

Fortescue Cuming, a well-traveled Englishman of culture and refinement, was astonished at the numbers of log cabins he saw on his American trip in 1807–1809, but the courthouse of squared logs in the center of the town of Steubenville, Ohio was to him an oddity worthy of special entry in his journal.[1] In actuality, log courthouses were not uncommon in America, although Cuming didn't know it; the early courts in Charlotte, North Carolina, Decatur, Illinois, and in Nashville, Tennessee, were held in log buildings, and there were numerous others. Had Cuming lived long enough he would have learned that Colorado's first capitol building, following its admission as a state one hundred years after the signing of the Declaration of Independence, was of logs. If he were living today he could see in Prescott, Arizona, the reproduction of a two-room cabin built in 1863–1864, originally used as a courthouse and judge's residence; as well as the two-story governor's mansion, also built of logs in 1864, where early sessions of the Arizona legislature were held before the capitol of the forty-eighth state was moved to Phoenix.

The British actor, John Bernard, observed in 1799 that the primitive ordinaries he visited in the South, identified by a brown jug suspended over the door, were "mostly log-huts."[2] Bernard had frequent occasion to seek overnight shelter in these backwoods taverns, sleeping on a blanket laid on the floor in front of the fireplace, his saddle cradling a weary head. A breakfast of fried eggs, ham, and "half-baked rolls," washed down with hot tea or strong black coffee was, in these circumstances, fare for a king, and even a French nobleman, the Marquis de Chastellux, noted that he became "perfectly accustomed to the American habit of drinking coffee as a beverage with meat, vegetables or other food."[3]

Captain Basil Hall said of the poor rural dwellings in upper New York state in 1827 that " . . . trees are laid prostrate on the earth, one on top of another, and a miserable log hut is the only symptom of a man's residence."

Hall's English readers were indebted to him for this further description of upper New York's log dwellings:

Most of the houses are built of rough, unbarked logs, nicked at the ends so as to fit closely and firmly and roofed with planks. The better sort of dwellings, however, are made of squared timbers framed together neatly enough, and boarded over at the sides and ends; and then roofed with shingles, which are a sort of oblong wooden slates. The houses are generally left unpainted, and being scattered about without order look more like a collection of great packing boxes, than the human residences which the eye is accustomed to see in old countries.[4]

In the early nineteenth century several aggressive Englishmen promoted an agricultural colony in Edwards County, southeastern Illinois, known afterwards as English Prairie. In 1820, a well-to-do English farmer, John Woods, seeking a home at English Prairie, made a two-month journey from Baltimore to Wanborough, Illinois. His journal contains references to the hundreds of log cabins he saw as he followed a winding wagon trail through the valleys and over mountain trails, and down the Ohio River on an ark through the "western country."

Such Maryland and Virginia settlements as Pew's Town and Trap Town were "mostly log houses." Frankfort and Springfield each had "near 40 log houses," and Cresapburg was a "very small place of log houses." Smithfield on the Youghiogheny River in western Pennsylvania had "20 houses mostly of logs." Monroe at the foot of the Alleghenies near present Uniontown also had twenty log houses, and Pittsburgh had "a great number of log and frame houses." Mechanicsburg, Ohio, was a small place "mostly of log houses," and in Fredericksburg, Kentucky, the residents lived in forty log houses, and Northampton, Indiana, had twenty-five or thirty houses built of logs. One could go on and on citing other examples from Woods' journal of the log cabins in the towns, as well as in the country, along his route where he sought overnight shelter or was supplied with corn pone, bacon, roasting ears, and potatoes by hospitable occupants who had their latchstrings out.

Some miles north of the route Woods followed lay the young

towns of Ohio where log cabins were also the prevailing dwellings. Zerah Hawley, who was visiting in Ohio at the same time Woods was en route to Illinois, although the two never saw each other, wrote that the four hundred inhabitants at Geneva "lived mostly in log houses," and the fifteen families at Denmark were "all living in log houses."

When Woods arrived at his destination he found that Wanborough was a settlement of twenty-five log cabins and Albion had twenty cabins, which probably came as no great surprise in view of his experiences en route, but finding his conservative countrymen housed in them must have given him pause. They had no other alternative—nor did he; so he purchased a 160-acre tract from a settler on which there stood a cabin different from many of the others—two log structures interconnected to form one house. In addition to writing a detailed description of the typical one-room log cabin for the edification of curious English readers, which I

Figure 24. Double-pen house of hewn logs with modern porch, Wilson, Arkansas. (Reproduced from the collections of the Library of Congress)

have quoted verbatim in the Appendix, he made special mention of the two-unit structure as follows:

"Cabins are frequently made double; that is, two are built from 10 to 20 feet a-part with a roof laid over the space between them." A double cabin of this type, he added, with a twenty-foot porch connecting the two residential units could be built for approximately $150.[5]

While Woods was looking with wonderment at the two-unit cabin, Zerah Hawley, in 1820, was also viewing this identical style of dwelling in Ohio. He wrote that in the space between the two log units were "placed the swill barrel, tubs, pots, kettles, etc. Here the hogs almost every night dance a hornpipe to a swinish tune, which some one or more musicians of their own number play upon the pots and kettles, while others regale themselves at the swill-barrel . . ."[6] Mc Intire's Hotel, built in Zanesville about 1800, and the town's first hostelry, was a two-unit log building of the type described by Hawley.

The specialized double-cabin log dwelling was common in southeastern Tennessee and in southern Georgia where it was variously known as a "double-pen," "dog-trot house," "dog-run house," "possum-trot house," or as "two-pens-and-a-passage." Its basic form, as described by both Woods and Hawley, was two single rooms separated by an open passage, prototype of the modern breezeway, with both units covered by a common roof (see Figure 24). One unit usually served as a kitchen and living room, and the other as a bedroom. The covered passage formed an area for household activities in the summer and a cool veranda where the family could sit on hot nights. In one variant of the two-unit log dwelling, the "saddlebag," the two cabins were built close together with a common chimney between them (see Figure 25g). This eliminated the need to build two chimneys and two fireplaces, but there was no breezeway. The saddlebag house was often two stories high, and sometimes had one, two, or even three front doors. It was generally only one room deep, and its central chimney is its diagnostic feature. The saddlebag house is still found in substantial numbers in West Virginia and Kentucky.

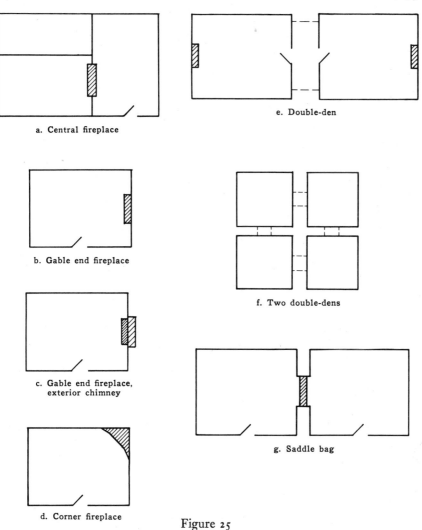

a. Central fireplace

e. Double-den

b. Gable end fireplace

f. Two double-dens

c. Gable end fireplace,
   exterior chimney

g. Saddle bag

d. Corner fireplace

Figure 25

When Captain Basil Hall visited the South—seven years after Woods and Hawley had written their descriptions—he wrote that the double-unit type of log dwelling was common in Georgia. Some opinions have been expressed that this type of structure came into being in southeastern Tennessee as a dominant form, but it was obviously widely distributed in the early American settlements and at a later date found its way to Texas and other western states.

One student of southern log house construction has suggested that the double-unit cabin, or double-unit barn, was built because the size of a conventional one-room cabin was limited by the length of the logs which could be conveniently handled by pioneer craftsmen, and the corner-timbering of a one-room cabin resisted the lengthwise addition of logs to make it larger. Obviously where two logs were notched together at the corner it was difficult to bring two more notched logs together and splice them at the point of juncture of the first two. Unable to erect a cabin longer than the maximum length of the single logs, rarely longer than twenty-four to thirty feet, beyond which the log began to taper, the builder simply erected two one-room units side by side, then connected them by means of the breezeway and built a common roof that covered both units.[7] This type of construction is not confined to log houses and log barns, but is also frequently found on old frame dwellings.

Pioneer physicians who "purged, bled, blistered, puked and salivated" their patients utilized the breezeway of the double-unit cabin to bring on the shakes believed to cure a patient suffering from ague. "Carry then your patient into the passage between the cabins," one old-time doctor wrote, "and strip off all his clothes that he may lie naked in the cold air and upon the bare sacking—and then and there pour over and upon him successive buckets of cold spring water and continue until he has a decided and pretty powerful smart chance of a shake."

Another geographer, who has made a special study of Tennessee rural housing, holds to the opinion that the double-unit house was a natural development from the original one-room log cabin. Furthermore, this observer advances the interesting hypothesis that the life history of an individual house often illustrates the series of developmental steps that characterized the general evolutionary process of *all* houses. For example, there are specific examples where a one-room log dwelling was enlarged to a double-pen stage, and later became a two-story structure to which various wings, lean-tos and porches were added at different times, and often of different materials. In Tennessee, houses were observed that were built partly of round or hewn logs, partly of weatherboards, and partly of bricks, a phenomenon no means unique to this state, which illustrates the evolutionary process in the same structure. Houses, according to this authority, have undergone a process of development and modification from simple to more complicated structures, just as a species of plant or animal organism evolved from a simpler form.[8] The two-unit type of construction is commonly found in log barns in many parts of the country, and this form is particularly abundant along the Tennessee River. Four-unit log barns have also been recorded, consisting of two double units facing each other under a common roof (see Figure 25f).

One of John Woods' countrymen, Richard Flower, was settled at Albion, Illinois, before Woods arrived, and he had a disdain for the crude American log dwellings, both one-room and two-unit forms, for very practical reasons. He made his distaste clear in the following passage extracted from a letter he wrote on August 16, 1819:

But to return to our settlement and its infant capital Albion. Log houses, those cabins, unpleasant to the cleanly habits of Englishmen, the receptacles of the insect tribe, are no longer erected. I have had the pleasure of laying the first brick foundation in Albion; it is for an inn where travellers I hope may find rest without disturbance from insects.[9]

There can be no question that flying and crawling insects buried themselves in the cracks between the logs in the walls of the cabins and were next to impossible to expel. In an era before biological spraying, the extermination of insects called for swatting, stepping on them, or trying to smoke them out. Roaches, beetles, crickets, and bedbugs were comparatively safe in the deep crevices between the logs, finding a haven not available in clapboard, brick, or stone dwellings. Mud daubers and hornets often nested under the overhang of the log cabin roof, and carpenter ants and termites attacked the foundation logs and puncheons resting on or close to the earth.

When Harriet Beecher Stowe described the log cabin where

Uncle Tom and Aunt Chloe lived in domestic bliss (before Simon Legree appeared to blight their lives) she drew a pretty word picture of the front of the dwelling covered with scarlet bignonia and how the multiflora rose twisted and interlaced which "left scarce a vestige of the rough logs to be seen." But Mrs. Stowe said nothing about the spiders, daddy-long legs, and black and red ants, which probably crawled in the dark corners, and the mosquitoes and houseflies that buzzed in the cabin during the summer when the door stood open and there were no screens.

When he traveled through the pre-Civil War South, the northern journalist, Frederick Law Olmsted, who was gathering material for a series of articles later published in the *New York Daily Times*, had a succession of annoying experiences during the nights he spent sleeping in log cabins. In the following passage he describes how one of his log cabin hostesses in the backwoods cotton country of Alabama took measures to protect the occupants from insects:

Then taking a deep tin pan, she filled it with alternate layers of corn-cobs and hot embers from the fire. This she placed upon a large block, which was evidently used habitually for the purpose, in the centre of the cabin. A furious smoke arose from it, and we soon began to cough. " 'Most *too* much smoke," observed the man. "Hope 'twill drive out all the gnats, then," replied the woman. (There is a very minute flying insect here, the bite of which is excessively sharp.)

The woman suddenly dropped off her outer garment and stepped from the midst of its folds, in her petticoat; then, taking the baby from the place where she had deposited it, lay down and covered herself with quilts upon the floor. The man told me that I could take the bed which remained on one of the bedsteads, and kicking off his shoes, rolled himself into a blanket by the side of his wife. I ventured to take off my cravat and stockings, as well as my boots, but almost immediately put my stockings on again, drawing their tops over my pantaloons. The advantage of this arrangement was that, although my face, ears, neck, and hands were immediately attacked, the vermin did not reach my legs for two or three hours.[10]

There were two doors in the cabin, but no windows, and both doors were allowed to stand open all night because of the stifling heat. This was a welcome invitation to the mosquitoes and other night bugs to join the insect intruders who infested the dwelling by day.

Olmsted also introduces a note in his journal about a Lafayette, Mississippi, Negro, who occupied a cabin with his wife and three children. To rid the dwelling of fleas, while his wife and children were sleeping, he scattered corn shucks in the crawl space under the floor of the cabin, and lighted them to smoke out the insects. The cabin was consumed by the fire, and his wife and children burned to death.[11]

Olmsted learned a simple and practical way of coping with the bedbug situation. "I adopted the habit," he wrote, "of passing the night on the floor of the cabins, rather than in their beds."

After spending many nights in log cabins in the Shenandoah and Susquehanna Valleys during his journey in 1775, Philip Fithian wrote, "But o the Fleas! Some mornings at some Houses, I rise spotted & purple like a Person in the Measles!"

Another Englishman, who visited America between 1798 and 1802, John Davis, and who was pro-American in his sympathies, offered an interesting rationalization on the subject of insects. He wrote:

> I eat my dinner in a log house on the road. It was kept by a small planter of the name of Homer. Such a tavern would have raised the thunder and lightning of anger in the page of my brother travellers in America. But the lamented scarcity of American inns is easily accounted for. In a country where every private house is a temple dedicated to hospitality, and open alike to Travellers of every description, ought it to excite surprize that so few good taverns are to be found? When, therefore, the Travellers through the United States, curse in their pages of calamity the musquitoes and fleas, the bugs, and ticks that interrupt their slumbers, they make the eulogium of American hospitality.[12]

There were disadvantages to cabin life, other than annoying insects, which will be cited in a later chapter of this volume, but Richard Flower's statement that log houses were no longer being erected in the English settlement expressed a hope rather than a reality; log cabins continued to be built, not only in Illinois, but elsewhere in the United States for many years to follow.

Charles Dickens on his first American visit in 1842—twenty-three years after Flower's letter was written—saw log cabins still being erected in the West. Dickens was not impressed with the crude American dwellings, so unlike the picturesque stone houses and frame cottages on the English landscape. On one leg of his journey, from Harrisburg to Pittsburgh, partly by canal boat, he saw hundreds of log cabins in the Allegheny mountain settlements and he wrote that they had an "utterly forlorn and miserable appearance," because the windows were stuffed with old clothes, boards, and paper. The log cabins Dickens saw in Virginia "with external chimneys made of clay or wood" were, he wrote, "squalid to the last degree."

In his *American Notes*, which stirred up resentment in the United States after it was published, the novelist described his overnight experiences in a log tavern at Lower Sandusky, Ohio. There were no locks on the doors, and Dickens was apprehensive of thieves breaking in because he was carrying £250 in gold in his dressing case. He piled his baggage against the doors to bar intruders. His secretary, a young man he had hired in Boston, tried to sleep in an upper room in the cabin, but was so beset by bedbugs that he was compelled to go outside to finish the night in the coach. There he was so annoyed by the grunting of the pigs who gathered around the coach seeking food that he spent a sleepless night. Although the pioneer families in the South and West raised cattle and sheep, they soon learned that tough-skinned pigs required less care and provided excellent meat. Almost every log cabin dweller had his herd of swine that foraged in the woods.

Both Dickens and Flower would have been astonished and perhaps mortified to learn that log cabins continued to be built as family residences well into the next century. Sigfus Olafson told me that his paternal grandfather who emigrated from Iceland to Canada in 1876, settled on the west shore of Lake Winnipeg with others of his countrymen, sharing a one room cabin, fourteen by twenty feet with another family. Sigfus's grandfather built a two-story house, the lower of logs and the upper of frame, and Sigfus's father, who was nine years old during the family's first winter in Canada, later moved to Indian lands in northern Minnesota in 1890, building a log house where Sigfus spent his boyhood.

It was built in the prevailing style, [according to Sigfus] logs notched at the corners and flattened top and bottom to lessen the size of the cracks between them. They were daubed or chinked with clay, but as the driving rains had a way of making it disintegrate, it was later replaced with a lime or cement mixture, which was much more permanent. Nearly all of our neighbors had similar houses, but as soon as they had the means, most of the settlers built frame houses. In our community this took quite a while, because everybody was terribly poor, not because the land was not fertile, but because we were 80 miles from a railroad, and it was a five day round trip with a team of horses and wagon to take a load of grain to market at such rare times as the roads were passable. . . . .

About the same time there was quite an influx of Swede-Finns and Finns into the iron mining section of Minnesota, particularly in St. Louis and Itasca Counties, and many of them homesteaded in the surrounding areas. That section was quite heavily wooded and these people usually built log houses, the best I have ever seen. Some of them are works of art, with the outside walls nearly as smooth as those of a frame house and the logs fitted together so closely that you can hardly stick a knife blade between them. One of these people can take an axe and square a log nearly as well as can be done with a saw. I don't think they used an adze much as an ordinary axe seemed to be all they needed. Many of these houses are still standing.[13]

Not all Englishmen were as critical of log cabin life as Richard Flower, Captain Hall, and Charles Dickens. John Bradbury, representing the Botanical Society of Liverpool, made a journey in 1809 to Missouri, Ohio, Kentucky, and Indiana, where he was impressed with the "Good neighbourship" which he said he found in great perfection among log cabin dwellers. He describes in his journal how a day was appointed for the residents on the frontier to assist a newcomer to build his log cabin, and then he goes on to say:

On the morning of the appointed day they assemble, and divide themselves into parties, to each of which is assigned its respective duty; one
party cuts down the trees, another loops and cuts them to proper lengths,
a third is furnished with horses and oxen, and drags them to the spot
designed for the scite of the house; another party is employed making
shingles to cover the roof, and at night all the materials are ready upon
the spot, and on the night of the next day, he and his family sleep in their
new habitation. No remuneration is expected, nor would it be received.
It is considered the performance of duty, and only lays him under the
obligation to discharge the debt by doing the same to subsequent settlers.[14]

The journals and diaries of other European travelers in the late
eighteenth and early nineteenth centuries describe how the log
cabin was spreading beyond the Ohio River to constitute the architectural nucleus of new towns along the rivers and smaller streams
of the western country. One wonders how a reputable modern writer
could have been so misled into making the statement that, "There
were so few log cabins built before 1800 that the number is hardly
worth considering." [15]

Even in the town of Gallipolis ("city of Gauls") on the left
bank of the Ohio, which was settled by Frenchmen, *all* of the original residences were built of logs. Before the arrival of the French
emigrants in 1790, the Scioto Company, who had transported them
to America, built sixty to eighty log cabins to house them. When
the French botanist André Michaux visited the town in 1793, he
noted, "The houses are all built of squared logs merely notched at
the ends instead of being Mortised." [16] His son, F. A. Michaux, nine
years later, made an 1800-mile trip from Charleston, South Carolina,
to Ohio, Tennessee, and Kentucky, and he wrote that one-third of
the inhabitants west of the Alleghenies then resided in log cabins.

The younger Michaux was also eager to visit his countrymen at
Gallipolis, but he found that most of the French settlers had departed
the town, unable to endure the hardships of log cabin life. The dwellings then consisted "of about sixty log-houses, most of which being uninhabited are falling into ruins; the rest are occupied by
Frenchmen, who breathe out a miserable existence." [17] Michaux was
unaware that before many years would pass, influences from the

East would bring to *La Belle Rivière* frame houses and other architectural refinements transmitted westward to take the place of the rudimentary log cabins, which the French, like the English, found so unlike the dwellings they knew in their homelands.

At Vincennes, Indiana (named for a French officer, François Morgane de Vincennes) the French were the first white settlers in a community that became the center of French midwestern colonial life. Catholic families, many who came from Canada, lived in comfortable whitewashed, one-story log houses, some with four rooms, dormer windows, and porches. But these dwellings, called *poteaux en terre* or *pieux en terre*, did not meet the definition of true log cabins, because the logs were placed close together in an upright position instead of being notched and laid in horizontal tiers parallel with the ground. Numerous examples of this mode of vertical log construction have been recorded in France, especially in Normandy, where horizontal notched log housing was uncommon. Vertical post construction is a very old architectural form which was a dominant method of construction in the late Neolithic period in many parts of Europe. It was largely vestigial in France in the eighteenth century, but was rejuvenated in forest-rich North America by French settlers thrown on the mercy of the land. It was found in French colonial settlements extending from Acadia westward to the Great Lakes and southward to the lower Mississippi Valley, and in Canada it gave way to horizontal timber construction or stone.

The adaptability of the frontier settler in building log cabins seems to have created a resourcefulness that became characteristic of Americans, especially in times of dire need. When Martha Washington arrived at Valley Forge on a cold February day to be near her soldier husband she saw from the window of her coach row upon row of snowcapped log huts facing each other in streets laid out like a little town. A shivering sentry, feet bound in rags, head tied up in a tattered muffler over his hat and under his chin to keep his ears from freezing, directed her to General Washington's headquarters. The coachman whipped the horses across the snow-covered road between the log stumps which were all that remained of the trees recently felled to build the cabins. The General was headquartered in a small stone farmhouse, to which his men had added a log wing used as an orderly room and dining room. It was in this dwelling that Martha lived while she was in Valley Forge, and from here wrote deprecatingly to a friend that the General "had a logg cabin to dine in."

Next to these one-thousand miserable log huts where Washington's troops spent a terrible winter and where some three-thousand died of disease and privation (see Figure 26), there has probably never been a larger aggregation of log cabins than those built by the Mormons in Illinois and Nebraska prior to their migration to Salt Lake City. Brought together by their prophet-evangelist Joseph Smith, they were Vermonters, Pennsylvanians, upstate New York-

Figure 26. One of the reconstructed log cabins at Valley Forge, typical of the makeshift shelters where the Continental troops spent the terrible winter of 1777.

ers, and midwesterners from Kentucky, Ohio, and Illinois who had joined the movement. At Nauvoo, Illinois, they transformed a malarial swamp into a thriving city. When they were driven away in 1846, they left behind 1500 to 2000 vacant houses, 80 percent of which were built of logs. The two-story, hewn-log house (with a later frame addition) which Joseph Smith occupied from 1839 to 1843, is still standing as one of Nauvoo's oldest residential structures, if not the oldest.[18]   At their "Winter Quarters," now Florence, Nebraska, near Omaha, in December of 1846, 3483 Mormons were living in 458 temporary log cabins and eighty-three sod houses, which they later deserted when Brigham Young led them on what must have seemed an endless trek across prairie and mountain, terminating in their long-sought Zion near the great salt lake in Utah. At their destination many also erected temporary log dwellings.

Small wonder that popular writers and careless historians reading the journals of European travelers, and noting in other American literary sources of the widespread distribution of the log cabin in the eighteenth and nineteenth centuries, were led astray. They jumped to the conclusion that the log cabin was characteristically the first type of dwelling built by the colonists who settled along the Atlantic seaboard in the seventeenth century. With no factual basis they mistakenly projected the log cabin back from American frontier days to the English cavaliers at Jamestown, the planters in Maryland, the Dutch burghers in New Netherland, the Pilgrim fathers at Cape Cod, and the Puritans on Massachusetts Bay. In colorful language, but with no foundation in history, writers described how the first Europeans to arrive on the shores of the New World, regardless of the country of their origin, immediately set to work to fell the trees and erect cabins of horizontally-laid notched logs to house their families. Although Harold R. Shurtleff, posthumously through his editor, Samuel Eliot Morison, laid this notion to rest thirty years ago in the volume *The Log Cabin Myth* (Cambridge, 1939), now out of print and extremely scarce, the myth keeps coming back to life in books of fiction and undocumented articles written for popular consumption. There are still teachers in the elementary grades who persist in introducing log cabins to their pupils in their stories of the Pilgrims' first Thanksgiving.

Since the American Indians did not live in log cabins when the Europeans arrived, as I have shown in the previous chapter, it would seem reasonable to assume that white colonists—or black Africans—must have transplanted the log cabin to America as an offshoot of their Old World cultures. This generalization is not entirely correct, because the log house was unknown among African tribes, where the thatched hut was the typical shelter built as a protection from the equatorial heat, nor was it a trait in the material culture of many Europeans in the seventeenth century. The concept was brought to America by some Europeans, but not by others. To arrive at the facts, therefore, one must first examine the distribution of log house architecture in Europe at the time America was being explored and settled.

To begin at the beginning, the origin of dwellings built of logs still remains a mystery for the archeologist to solve as he studies and learns more about the evolution of house types among primitive peoples. Early man sought protection under spreading trees, below overhanging ledges, and in caves like La Madeleine in the Dordogne, although cave-dwelling was by no means universal. Even the most primitive human being was able to make some artificial shelter of mud, stone, bones, skin, dung, leaves, grass, tree limbs, or a combination of these materials, just as the animals built their nests. As man learned to make simple tools, first of wood and stone, and later of metal, he became superior to the animals in developing the means to modify and improve his shelters.

With the aid of a stone knife he learned how to skin animals and then to make tents of their pelts. With a stone pick he found he could dig a hole in the earth and cover it with tree limbs hacked to a suitable size with his stone axe or celt. He learned to make a tent of logs by cutting or burning them to size and setting them vertically with the top ends together in the shape of a tepee, and he found he could use smaller tree limbs to fabricate the same type of shelter. Perhaps the earliest evidence of man-made shelters so far known to the archeologist are the tent-standings at Molovova in south Russia marked by rings of mammoth bones to hold down the animal skin tents, which may date back as far as 40,000 B.C.[19]

Through trial and error man underwent centuries of primitive experimentation before he found the means to build houses that gave his family adequate protection from the weather, wild animals, and his human enemies, although extreme weather conditions—floods, storms, and hurricanes, as well as fire—continued to be constant threats to his security, as they are today. Where stone and wood were scarce, as in the frozen north, he modified his architecture in response to climatic conditions by building igloos of snow. In tropical zones where tightly built wooden houses would have been insufferable, he used the palm and other broad leaves to construct his shelters.

During the evolution of house building, which varied by area, crude shelters of horizontally-laid round logs made their appearance. The logs were not notched at first to make interlocking corner joints, but were merely placed one on top of another. Some scientists believe that the first true corner notching originated with log structures in the Mesolithic with the Maglemosian culture, centered in Denmark, southern Sweden, and northern Germany. The continuing work of the archeologist, with new discoveries making old theories obsolete, reminds one to be cautious in interpreting prehistory, because much still remains to be discovered, and today's tentative conclusions may be changed tomorrow.

One thing is certain: notched log dwellings were built in several parts of Europe during the Bronze Age; for example, archeologists have found the remains of log houses in southern Germany in the Persazig-See, on the "Wasserburg," an island settlement on the Federsee-Moor, and in other locations. Yet it seems extremely unlikely that the warlike German tribes known to the Romans as the *Usipetes*, the *Tencteri*, and the *Suebi* were building houses of logs in 53–58 B.C. when Julius Caesar and his legions marched through Gaul and crossed the Rhine. These uncivilized German tribes, who lived on milk, cheese, and meat, practiced agriculture on a very limited scale, and covered their bodies with animal skins, apparently spent most of their time hunting and in military pursuits. Their magistrates and chiefs, who allotted pieces of land to the clan groups, compelled the tenants to move to new holdings each year, discouraging their building permanent houses and becoming attached to specific home sites. Like the Gauls, whose dwellings Caesar described as straw-thatched huts, the houses of the German tribes were doubtless frail and flimsy hutches built for temporary occupancy. Log houses came later when the German tribes settled down to practice agriculture and established permanent farming villages.

By mediaeval times, in the forested parts of Germany, the log house was a common type of peasant dwelling, and when America was being settled there were hundreds of log houses in parts of the Rhine Palatinate, Saxony, Bohemia, Moravia, Silesia, and elsewhere, occupied by farm and mountain folk. Here, the basic unit of economic and social organization was the agricultural village, and except in rare cases, the residences, stables, hay sheds, and storehouses of the peasants, some built of logs, were clustered in the village proper under the shadow of the church tower, with the farm fields and pastures laying round about. Different styles of corner notchings had been developed for log structures to which the Germans gave such colorful terms as *schwalbenschwänzen* (swallow tail), *weyaschwanz-strick* (falcon tail) and others. There were, of course, other types of houses in Germany in the Middle Ages, some half-timbered, others of stone, and peasant housing varied by region to suit the climate, soil, and the available building materials.

One difficulty the archeologist faces in interpreting ancient cultures is that wood is perishable, and only under certain favorable climatic conditions can he expect to find log dwellings *in situ*. When a Polish schoolmaster in 1933, walking with his class along a peninsula jutting into Lake Biskupin fifty miles northeast of Poznan, spotted the tops of logs sticking out of the mud flats, it was a discovery of unusual significance. Later investigation by scientists of the Poznan Museum indicated that the area had once been an island covered by a prehistoric walled village. Within the walls the area was packed with the preserved remains of houses of horizontal logs, built wall to wall in thirteen straight rows almost exactly alike. The village flourished about 550 B.C. which dates the log house to the Iron Age in Poland long before it became an independent kingdom and at a time when the more advanced peoples of the Mediterranean countries considered northern Europe a primeval hunting ground for uncivilized Slavic tribes.[20]

In the Scandinavian countries log house architecture has been traced back to the age of the Vikings, 800 A.D. to 1000 A.D., representing a significant advancement from the turf huts of the reindeer-pursuing Laps. The Vikings were skilled woodworkers, building longboats and fashioning oars to propel them; they also sectioned logs to make chairs and benches for eating and sleeping, and even constructed plows and household articles of wood. The Viking cabin, known as the *eldus* or *kokus*, was a crude rectangular structure of horizontally-laid logs containing a central hearth and a hole in the roof to vent the smoke from the fire built on the earthen floor. This type of dwelling was an early form of the diverse log structures found in Sweden, Norway, and Finland in mediaeval times, replacing the Finnish portable skin tent and the Norwegian turf hut or *gammijord*. Remains of log houses dating from the ninth to the eleventh century A.D. have been unearthed in archeological work at Birka, Sigtuna, and Lund in Sweden, and some archeologists hold to the theory that the log house diffused to Sweden from Russia and central Europe, whereas theories have been advanced that it was the Scandinavians who influenced Russian log architecture.

In the Middle Ages a mature log complex characterized Swedish rural architecture, including not only residences and farmhouses, but churches, stables, barns, storage sheds, and other types of buildings. Even the double log cabin described by Woods in Illinois, Hawley in Ohio, and Hall in Georgia in the early nineteenth century had its antecedents in Sweden, and examples of the wide variety of log structures may be seen today in the numerous reconstructions in the open air museum at Skansen near Stockholm, and the Zorn Museum at Mora. At Lillehamer in Norway, an open air museum founded by Anders Sandvig, there are also examples of various types of old Norwegian log construction.

Although I am unable to add information to the question relative to the prehistoric cultural exchange between Russia and the Scandinavian countries, there is ample documentary evidence that log dwellings were prevalent in Russia, as well as in Scandinavia, in the sixteenth century. In 1553, an English schoolmaster, Clement Adams, recorded the details of a trip to Russia, "Enterprised by Sir Hugh Willoughbie Knight, and perfourmed by Richard Chancelor[,] Pilot major of the voyage." He described what to him were unusual Russian peasant dwellings in the following terms:

> The common houses of the countrey are every where built of beames of Firre tree: the lower beames doe so receive the round holownesse of the uppermost, that by the meanes of the building thereupon, they resist, and expell all winds that blow, and where the timber is joined together, there they stop the chinks with mosse. The forme & fashion of their houses in al places is foure square with streit and narrow windowes, whereby with a transparent casement made or covered with skinnes like to parchment, they receive the light. The roofes of their houses are made of boords covered without with ye barke of trees: within their houses they have benches of griezes hard by their wals, which commonly they sleepe upon, for the common people knowe not the use of beds. . . .[21]

There can be little question that Adams was describing a prototype of the dwelling place, complete with glassless windows, that two centuries later would evolve into the American log cabin.

Should there be any doubt about the early appearance of the log cabin in Russia, the following note from the journal of Doctor Giles Fletcher, who represented England at the court of Emperor Theodore in 1588, should settle the issue:

> Their houses are of wood [he wrote], without any lime or stone, built very close and warme with Firre trees plained and piled one upon another. They are fastened together with dents or notches at every corner and so clasped fast together. Betwixt the trees or timber they thrust in mosse (whereof they gather plenty in their Woods) to keep out the aire.[22]

Fletcher was as much surprised to see, for the first time, houses built of hewn pine logs planed smooth, and laid one on the other and interlocked with notches, as he was to observe that the streets of Moscow were planked with the boards of the fir tree. He was familiar with neither practice in his native England and we can imagine his astonishment at this prodigality with wood which might have been used to build hundreds of ships!

Log houses continued to be built in Moscow, as well as in the rural areas of Russia, and there has been preserved an engraving of a residential district of Moscow made in 1647 by Adam Olearius (see Figure 27). The reader will note that these dwellings were all built of round logs with *vertical boards* under the eave ends, a trait, as the reader will learn from a later chapter, often associated with the Germans. Investigation by Russian archeologists indicates that

Figure 27. Residential section of Moscow in the seventeenth century, with men in foreground carrying bows and arrows, and houses with roofs and walls of round logs, from an engraving made in 1647 by Adam Olearius.

round log dwellings date back to the fortified towns as early as the eleventh and twelfth centuries A.D. For instance, a twelfth century cobbler's hut uncovered at Novgorod had pine log walls.[23]

Log dwellings continued to be built in Russia in succeeding centuries, and when Raphael Pumpelly made a trip in the 1860's from California to Japan, and from thence to Peking, and across Siberia to Moscow and St. Petersburg, he noted in his journal that the Russian peasant villages "consist altogether of log houses, generally not more than one story high." [24] Despite the razing of old wooden houses in recent times in favor of modern apartments, there are still many log dwellings remaining in Russia as far east as Irkutsk in Siberia. Nikita Khrushchev, recently deposed Communist party leader, was born in a log cabin.

The Buriats, a Mongol group living on Lake Baikal in southern Siberia were using both round and hewn logs in their housing when Jeremiah Curtin visited them in the early 1900's.[25]

South of Russia's borders at the eastern end of the Black Sea lay the ancient country of Colchis, which was described in the writings of Vitruvius in the first century A.D. Henry C. Mercer, an American archeologist and an authority on colonial handicraft tools, who wrote one of the first accounts of log cabins in the United States, interpreted Vitruvius's descriptions to mean that houses of horizontal logs were built in ancient Colchis.[26] It has also been reported that log cabins were built in parts of the islands of Japan before 1000 A.D.,[27] and their existence in Korea has also been corroborated.

The accompanying drawing by the German scholar, Herman Phleps, attempts to delineate the general distribution of log structures in Europe (see Figure 28). An American geographer, Wilbur Zelinsky, has gone even further and he says that the log house trait

reaches across Eurasia in two broad bands: the first extends through the sub-Arctic forests of Sweden, Finland, and central and northern Russia, and, since the seventeenth century, across Siberia to the Pacific, then, later to Russian America; the second—and the more relevant here—begins in

Figure 28. Translation: Territorial expansion of the wood-style house construction in Europe. The block-construction [squared or round logs] forms a continuous chain in Scandinavia, by-passing at the east the *Fachwerk* and *Standerwerk* [architectural styles] and extending all the way to Switzerland and into the Balkan countries. (From Herman Phleps, *Der Blockbau*)

the French Savoy, with a possible minor outlier in northern Spain, and reaches through the mountainous spine of Eurasia at least as far eastward as Iran and possibly Kashmir. Included within it are the rugged areas of southern Germany, Switzerland, Austria, Bohemia, the Carpathians, Transylvania, and perhaps Turkey.[28]

The reader can conclude without reservation that the American log cabin is not an innovative form of domestic architecture, but its origins go back to the dawn of written history, and much still remains to be learned about its beginning and distribution in the Old World.

As I have already emphasized, the first requirement for a residence of logs was an abundance of trees near at hand. In a country where there were no woods or forests, or where the land had been denuded of its trees, one would not expect to find log dwellings. Even where trees were available, it does not necessarily mean that log houses were built, because a log house was considered by many builders to be wasteful of wood. The same number of logs needed to build a one-room cabin could be sawed into planks to construct two or more dwellings, and economic considerations discouraged the wasteful use of the whole log to construct house walls.

During the period of settlement in America, Europe was a panorama of different architectural representations from the Arctic Circle, as it crossed Scandinavia, through England, Germany, Russia, France, Belgium, Holland, Switzerland, and Spain to the heel of Italy. Some of the differences were national or ethnic; others resulted from the physical environment of mountains, forests, lakes, and lowlands. From the architecture of logs in the Scandinavian countries, southern Germany, Switzerland, Poland, and Russia (and other house types were also present in the residential housing in these countries), one passed to house styles of brick, tile, framed timber, wattle and daub; houses built on crucks; huts of sod and turf, to an architecture of stone in the wide-spanning arches, domes, and vaults of ancient Rome as it survived in mediaeval Italy. In some areas, roofs were steeply pitched to shed the snows; in others, the roof was flattened. Windows and doors were often small in the colder countries to exclude winds and snows, whereas porches, verandas, and piazzas were seen in southern countries where the sun shone and the days were bright.

Without going into further detail in a subject which is thoroughly treated in architectural histories, suffice it to say that when America was being explored by Italian, Portuguese, French, Spanish, Dutch, and English mariners, the European continent was a conglomeration of widely diverse architectural forms ranging from Swiss châlets, Gothic arches, Greek temples, Breton villages, brick patterns in the Doge's Palace, and in the commercial establishments and dwellings of Amsterdam, to the buttress scrolls of Venice, the gargoyles of Notre Dame and the cruck houses built by the Saxons.

Regardless of its form or style, size or shape, a house was designed to provide living space for the residents, to protect them while they slept, to keep them sheltered from the weather and intruders, and to permit them to prepare their food where cooking out of doors was impractical or inconvenient. Houses in the beginning consisted of only one room with man and his family sleeping on one side and his domesticated animals on the other. Then he partitioned his room to separate the animals from the people, and he finally moved the animals out to a stable, partitioning his house into rooms for his own use.

As people from the various European countries came to the New World they brought with them as part of their cultural ethnocentricity the traits of their native lands, and those from Scandinavia, Germany, and Switzerland built log cabins when they arrived. Those living in countries where log dwellings did not then exist built the types of houses with which they were familiar when they planted their roots in American soil. This can best be brought into sharp focus by turning back the pages of history to see exactly what kind of shelters the first settlers in the original colonies built when they were thrown on the resources of the New World.

In *The Log Cabin Myth*, Shurtleff broached this subject in considerable detail especially for New England and Virginia, and Professor Thomas J. Wertenbaker and others have restated many of the points he made. One may question why it is necessary to cover the same ground again, but I feel it important to do so for two reasons. First, a new generation of readers has difficulty obtaining Shurtleff's book, and my present objective is to bring all the pertinent log cabin data together in a single, up-to-date volume for the general reader. Secondly, Shurtleff's treatment of Maryland, New York, Delaware, New Jersey, and Pennsylvania was far from exhaustive, and my chapters are by no means a supererogation. In his anxiety to extirpate, "the myth," which he did with notable success, Shurtleff did not dwell on Pennsylvania's importance as an originating point of the cultural waves that carried the concept to other parts of the country. Nor did he treat New Sweden with the depth I will give it, and which it deserves as the colony where the Scandinavians built the first log cabins along the American seaboard.

NOTES—CHAPTER 3

1. "Fortescue Cuming's Sketches of a Tour to the Western Country," *Early Western Travels, 1748–1846*, ed. Reuben Gold Thwaites (Cleveland, 1904), IV, 107.

2. Allan Nevins, *American Social History* (New York, 1923), 43.

3. *Marquis de Chastellux's Travels in North America in the Years 1780, 1781, 1782*, trans. Howard C. Rice Jr. (Chapel Hill, 1965), I, 388.

4. Captain Basil Hall, *Travels in North America in the Years 1827 and 1828* (Philadelphia, 1829), II, 69–71.

5. John Woods, "Two Years Residence in the Settlements on the English Prairie in the Illinois Country," *Early Western Travels*, X, 277–278.

6. Zerah Hawley, *A Journal Tour Through Conn., Mass., N.Y. and the North Parts of Pa. and Ohio* (microfilm, Univ. of Delaware), 54.

7. Martin Wright, "The Antecedents of the Double-Pen House Type," *Annals* of the Assoc. of American Geographers, XLVIII, No. 2, June 1958, 109–117. C. G. Parsons, *Inside View of Slavery, etc.* (Boston, 1885), 108, reported in his southern tour of 1852–1853 that the two-unit dwellings of round pine logs were common.

8. Edna Scofield, "The Evolution and Development of Tennessee Houses," *Journal* of the Tennessee Academy of Sciences, XI, No. 4, Oct. 1936, 229–240.

9. *Early Western Travels, op. cit.*, 107.

10. Frederick Law Olmsted, *A Journey in the Back Country* (New York, 1860), 199.

11. *Ibid.*, 111.

12. John Davis, *Travels of Four and a Half Years in the United States of America, etc.* (New York, 1909), 372–373.

13. Personal letter, Nov. 12, 1952.

14. John Bradbury, "Travels in the Interior of America in the Years 1809, 1810, 1811," *Early Western Travels*, V, 283. Gustav Unonius vividly describes the raising of his log cabin at Pine Lake, Wisconsin, assisted by other cabin dwellers; see Chapter 13 of *A Pioneer in Northwest America, 1841–1858*, trans. Jonas Oscar Backlund, ed. by Nils William Olsson (Minneapolis, 1950), I.

15. Carl W. Drepperd, *Pioneer America, Its First Three Centuries* (New York, 1949), 14.

16. "Journal of André Michaux, 1793–1796," *Early Western Travels*, III, 34.

17. F. A. Michaux, *Travels to the West of the Allegheny Mountains, 1802*, 2nd edition (London, 1805), 100.

18. Joseph Smith's cabin is illustrated in Robert Bruce Flanders, *Nauvoo, Kingdom on the Mississippi* (Urbana, 1965), 20. I am indebted to Jay A. Johnson for bringing this reference to my attention.

19. Stuart Piggott, *Ancient Europe* (Chicago, 1965), 29: see also Grahame Clark, *The Stone Age Hunters* (New York, 1967), 31.

20. *Time* Magazine, May 16, 1960, p. 46, contains an article about the discovery and an illustration of the log dwellings; also see illustration of the same dwellings in Piggott, *op. cit.*

21. Richard Hakluyt, *The Principal Navigations Voyages Traffiques & Discoveries of the English Nation* (Glasgow, 1903), II, 269–270.

22. *Loc. cit.*

23. M. Tikhomirov, *The Towns of Ancient Rus* (Moscow, 1959), 150, 152.

24. Raphael Pumpelly, *Across America and Asia* (New York, 1870), 417.

25. Jeremiah Curtin, *A Journey in Southern Siberia* (Boston, 1909), see illustrations pp. 158, 236, 258.

26. Henry C. Mercer, "The Origin of Log Houses in the U.S.," reprint of a paper read at a meeting of the Bucks County, Penna., Historical Society, Jan. 19, 1924, reprinted from the Society's collections of papers, V, 568–583 (n.d.).

27. George R. Stewart, *American Ways of Life* (New York, 1954), 152, n. 3. In *The Complete Journal of Townsend Harris* (Garden City, N.Y., 1930), the first American Consul General and Minister to Japan, there is reference on p. 246 to the prison at Shimoda in 1856 which consisted of "cells of squared joists of timber placed some three inches apart."

28. Wilbur Zelinsky, "The Log House in Georgia," *Geographical Review*, April 1953, 184–185.

II

LOG CABINS IN THE ORIGINAL COLONIES

4 *Virginia Cavaliers, Carolinians, and Georgians*

President John Tyler helped perpetuate the persisting legend that Virginia's first colonists lived in log cabins in a speech he made in 1857 at the 250th anniversary of the settlement at Jamestown. Tyler described the hardships faced by the early English settlers, and using the present tense for emphasis, which I have italicized, he declaimed, *"The log cabin is built*, its covering of reeds, and the fortification made of logs and brush to guard against surprise from a savage foe is hastily constructed." [1]

Virginia's governor, Henry A. Wise, who followed Tyler to the rostrum, further dramatized the situation by telling his audience that, "Here the Old World first met the New. Here the White Man first met the Red for settlement and colonization. Here the White Man first wielded the axe to cut down the first tree for the first log cabin. *Here the first log cabin was built* for the first village, etc., etc." [2]

The facts are that no log cabins were built in Virginia until more than a century *after* the founding of Jamestown! And the log cabins in Georgia and the Carolinas came even later!

The colonists Sir Walter Raleigh sent to Roanoke Island in 1585 were the forerunners of the English settlement at Jamestown, and they indirectly paved the way for the later settlements in North Carolina. Unfortunately they spent too much time looking for gold, and too little in building houses and cultivating the soil, and the effort failed. The colonists abandoned their settlement and returned to England with Sir Francis Drake who found them destitute upon his arrival.

In 1587 Raleigh sent out his second colony, and although he intended them to make a settlement farther north, the colonists rebuilt the crude fort their predecessors had erected on Roanoke Island and threw up a few huts. As their supplies began to run low, John White, whom Raleigh had appointed governor, was persuaded against his wishes to return to England for provisions where he was detained because of the war then raging with Spain. When White returned to Roanoke Island, he wrote "we went to a place where they were left in *sundry houses*, but we found them all taken down, and the place strongly inclosed with a high Palizado, very Fortlike." The colonists had disappeared, according to White's familiar account, leaving only the letters C.R.O. carved on a tree and the word CROATAN in capital letters on one of the posts at the entrance to the fort. To the still unsolved mystery about their fate must be added the question about what kind of "sundry houses" they lived in on Roanoke Island before they departed. There is no reason to believe that these dwellings in the first English settlement in the New World bore the faintest resemblance to log cabins; they were probably similar to the huts erected shortly thereafter by the Jamestown settlers described below.

Jamestown came into existence about 20 years after Raleigh's ill-fated attempts at colonization, and thirteen years before the Pilgrims made their historic landing at Plymouth. Although much has been written about Jamestown, misunderstandings about its architecture still persist. What I have to say may not be new to most historians, but it will give the general reader a better understanding of why log cabins were missing in the Virginia colony.

The colony had its beginning on May 13, 1607, when three small vessels anchored at Jamestown Island—the *Susan Constant* of one hundred tons, commanded by Captain Christopher Newport, the *Godspeed* of forty tons, commanded by Captain Bartholomew Gosnold, and the *Discovery*, a pinnace of twenty tons, under Captain

John Ratcliffe. On May 14 the Englishmen landed and broke ground for the fort and town that ultimately won distinction as the first permanent English settlement in America and the capital of the Virginia colony for almost a century. It was only a precarious toe hold in the beginning, and the colony almost foundered during its early years due to living hardships.

The total complement of the three vessels was 160 men, of whom 104 remained as colonists, and the others returned with Captain Newport who was back in London in August of the same year. He left England for Virginia in October with 120 additional settlers, and his second arrival at Jamestown was greeted as "the first supply." All told, Newport made five round trips between England and Virginia, bringing new colonists and supplies on each voyage before his career ended.

The leaders of the Virginia colony were men steeped in generations of English culture. In addition to Newport, Gosnold, and Ratcliffe, there was Edward Maria Wingfield, heir of a landed family, and incidentally, one of few seventeenth century Englishmen bearing a middle name. There were also John Martine, who had commanded English vessels under Sir Francis Drake; George Kendall, a cousin of Sir Edwin Sandys, who was later to play a dominant role in the colony; George Percy, brother to the Earl of Northumberland; Gabriel Archer, an English lawyer; the Reverend Robert Hunt, an Anglican vicar; and Captain John Smith, an adventurer who had fought in bloody campaigns against the Turks in Transylvania and along the Hungarian border. The financial sponsor of the colony, the Virginia Company, represented not only the commercial interests of the port of London, but its membership included gentlemen and noblemen of consequence and influence in the kingdom. Virginia was, in short, a project of, by, and for Englishmen seeking profit for their chartered company coordinated with a vision of a more prosperous England. They were British to the core, shackled by the traditions and customs of their society, and by the strictures of a rigid class system.

To understand why these Englishmen transplanted to the New

World did not build log cabins, one must recognize that a nation's way of life, like an individual's, is also a product of heredity and environment. The environment of Virginia consisted of the land, the rivers, the bay that bordered the land, and the multiplicity of natural resources associated with these physical features. The heredity comprised the acquired habits the settlers brought with them from medieval England. By and large, these Englishmen adhered to their hereditary habits of housing which had a stronger influence on them than the Virginia environment.

During the Tudor and Stuart periods, when a strong central government put down lawlessness and private armies, ideas in England about house styles underwent significant changes. Previously, defense had been of primary consideration in houseplanning, and fear of armed attack led to the building of walled towns to enclose the family dwellings. In the houses themselves, small doors and windows were placed where they were least vulnerable to attackers; in larger houses, whenever possible, rooms were built to face inwards on a courtyard for the protection of the family. In mediaeval times the strength of the gatehouse, the moat, and outer walls was more important than the internal living facilities. Such details as adequate light, fresh air, sanitary facilities, and comfortable living and sleeping quarters were considered secondary to the security of the family. There was little privacy, and even in the manor houses of the wealthy, the great hall was a general living room by day and a dormitory by night where the members of the family and the guests slept.

During the seventeenth century, when England was starting to explore and settle the New World, concepts of the Renaissance, which emphasized the supremacy of civil authority and the prime importance of the natural man, strongly influenced domestic architecture. Englishmen embraced new notions of beauty and convenience, with the result that new houses were built and old ones remodeled to permit better family living. They sought beauty and comfort in their homes, then heated by large open fireplaces attached to great chimneys; in their gardens and in their halls, parlors and drawing rooms. They began to glaze their windows, hang their walls with elegant tapestries, or panel them with oak, cedar, and pine. They removed the narrow twisting stone stairs from which one could repulse an intruder, and replaced them with wide, hardwood staircases, having molded balusters and heavy handrails, which provided ready access to the upstairs rooms.

Even the mean homes of the poor cottagers in the rural counties of England underwent improvement for the comfort of the family, although the change was slower than in the villages and towns. Most farm families continued to live in their stuffy, little kitchens, as they had in the past, but small parlors began to appear for use on special occasion to entertain guests and relatives. The upper story of the cottage came to be divided into two or three small bedrooms, usually unceiled and open to the rafters. The English people, in towns and on farms, grew to live free from fear of organized attack on their homes, and the domestic architecture began to show less concern for protective features and more for the daily needs of the family.

The same emphasis on the domestication of the home was felt in other European countries, and the people who migrated to America were influenced by these architectural traditions of the Renaissance. This is not to say that all the men and women who came to the New World lived in well-built houses, because many of them were pathetically poor, their families crowded into small dwellings, where they faced privations and a low standard of living. It was, indeed, the inadequacy of food and housing that motivated some of them— but by no means all—to leave their native countries and seek a new home and a better life in a new land.

In considering the development of the United States [George R. Stewart wrote], we are constantly inclined to forget one important fact— the utter and abysmal ignorance of the first colonists as how to cope with the wilderness. Transferred immediately, without experience or schooling, from the highly civilized countries of England and Holland, they can only be described as complete greenhorns. They were much more innocent and helpless, in fact, than the average American of today would be if placed in similar circumstances.[3]

One of the first needs of the Jamestown colonists, which was even greater when they were joined by women, was for food and shelter. Foremost in their minds as desirable dwellings were the types of buildings they knew in England—fortified manors, battlemented castles, half-timber houses, thatched and wattled cottages, and other types of mediaeval architecture built according to Anglo-Saxon, Norman, and Gothic styles. What was available to them for house building at Jamestown was not stone or bricks or tiles and pantiles, and strictly speaking not even wood—only trees. The chief difficulty the colonists faced was in felling and shaping the trees to produce the kind of building lumber with which they were familiar, and, at the same time, to carry on the necessary pursuits of planting, fishing, and hunting in order to keep alive.

The idea of extravagantly using whole logs by notching them and setting them horizontally one on the other to form the walls of a house apparently never entered their heads. But even if it did, or had they specific directions for building log cabins, they probably would not have done so. Their one consuming desire was to build framed houses as quickly as possible, and they were content to occupy makeshift shelters in the meantime. Although the selection of wood for their new homes was determined by the availability of trees in the Virginia environment, the building styles they employed was a hereditary factor. Their difficulty adjusting to the new environment was in not being able readily to sever the ties that held them to their English cultural heritage. "Our drink was water," wrote Thomas Studly, "and our lodgings castles in the air."

They went hungry, and some even starved to death, where native but un-English foods abounded. They suffered during a miserable winter, and some even froze to death, when they should have been warm, because they persisted in wearing torn and patched English clothing when they might have adopted the fur and deerskin dress of the Indians. They laboriously split timbers to make familiar clapboards, sawed tree trunks into boards and planks, and gathered and bound thatch, instead of simply cutting down the trees and notching the round logs to build cabins. When Sir George

Somers was shipwrecked in Bermuda, en route to Virginia, his party made "their cabens of Palmeta leaves" even though they were amid great stands of virgin cedars and had at their disposal a full assortment of carpenter's tools salvaged from their vessel.

The first structure the Virginia cavaliers erected was a fort fronting on the James River which was "triangle wise, having three Bulwarkes [one] at every corner like a half Moone," protected with a palisade.[4] Within the three "Bulwarkes" they mounted pieces of artillery as protection against Indian attack. This fort covered about an acre and within the palisaded enclosure they built storehouses, living quarters, and a place of worship. The palisades, consisting of planks and posts set vertically in the earth, was a type of defensive structure well known in English military science, and familiar to every soldier.

Captain John Smith in the following quotation describes the first shelters erected within the palisades of the fort at Jamestown. I have supplied the italic:

> When I went first to Virginia, I well remember wee did hang an awning (which is an old saile) to three or foure trees to shadow us from the Sunne, our walles were *rales* of wood, our seats unhewed trees till we cut plankes, our Pulpit a bar of wood nailed to two neighbouring trees. In foule weather we shifted into an old rotten tent; for we had few better, and this came by way of adventure for new. This was our Church, till we built a homely thing like a barne set upon *Cratchets*, covered with *rafts*, sedge and earth; so was also the walls: the best of our houses [were] of the like curiosity; but the most part farre much worse workmanship, that could neither well defend [from] wind nor raine.[5]

To understand fully Smith's words the reader should recognize that in their seventeenth century English meanings, a *raft* (dialectic for *rafter*) was a pole or spar, thinner than a log, usually used as a supporting member of a roof; a *rale* was a horizontal bar of wood or small tree limb fixed on upright supports or posts as part of a fence. What Smith is saying is that the first church services at Jamestown were held outdoors under the shade of an old sail in an area fenced off with rails. The exposed pulpit was nailed to two trees, and when the weather was bad services were held in an old tent. The first church building was set on *cratchets*.

Cratchet, a variant of *crotchet, crotch, cruck*, or *crutch* was a forked post to support the ridgepole of a structure. The term *cruck* came to be used in England to describe an architectural form in which a pair of bent or curved tree trunks were placed together in the form of a Gothic pointed arch. The exterior of a cottage built on crucks was usually covered with thatch, but Smith explains that the first church on crucks at Jamestown was covered with tree limbs, sedge, and turf. He adds in the quoted passage that the best of the first Jamestown houses were also set upon cratchets, but the workmanship was so poor that the occupants were inadequately protected from wind and rain.

Forman, an authority on Virginia colonial architecture, stated:

No horizontal log walls were ever used in a building set on crucks or crotches. The arched roof of a house set on crucks is but an extension of the walls, whereas the walls and roof of a log house are two separate entities. In crotched houses the walls may be removed and the roof will stand up, but take away the walls of a log house and the roof will collapse.[6]

Another early house type of Virginia was constructed by the old method previously cited of setting timbers or posts upright in the ground and closely together. The space between these vertical members was then filled with "wattle and daub," a basketwork of branches, twigs, and roots, coated on boths sides with loam and lime mixed with straw. In England this filling was often called "post and pan," and the method of construction sometimes known as "puncheoning."

Gabriel Archer refers to the English colonists "cutting down a great oke for Clapboord," and that "we wrought upon Clapborde for England." The clapboards were also used for house construction in Jamestown, replacing the canvas tents, and they were also carried back by Captain Newport to be sold in England for the benefit of the company's stockholders. Clapboards were split from a section of log, not sawn, by the use of a riving tool called a frow, a coarse knife with a wedge-shaped blade having a handle set at right angles. The blade was pounded with a wooden mallet called a frow club to split the clapboards from the log. These clapboards were smaller than the long boards known today by that name, and an important commercial use was as barrel staves. The English gentlemen in the party, unused to hard work, undisciplined, and unadaptable, had to be taught how to rive clapboards, and on one occasion Smith took thirty of them five miles into the woods to teach them to make clapboards, with the result that the axe handles blistered their tender fingers.

Following Newport's departure, Captain Smith "who by his own example, good words and fair promises, set some to mow, others to binde thatch; some to build houses, others to thatch them." Smith himself refers to these houses by that misleading term "cabins," and wrote that the thatched roofs constituted a serious fire hazard. There was a series of fires in Jamestown, which spread rapidly because the flammable huts were built too close together. Here, too, the Englishmen were traditionally motivated by the character of the tightly-packed streets of mediaeval English towns, and in laying out the streets of Jamestown they transferred Old World conditions which were nonexistent in the new land.

After the fires, the houses were rebuilt along sturdier lines, and when Sir Thomas West, the third Lord Delaware, arrived as governor in 1610, he found, "The houses which are built are as warme and defensive against wind and weather as if they were tiled and slated, being covered above with strong boards and some matted round with Indian mats." [7] A board in the seventeenth century, as today, was a piece of timber sawn thin, having considerable extent of surface and greater length than breadth. Reference to boards and clapboards leaves no doubt that cut lumber, as opposed to unmodified logs, was the type of wood used in the Jamestown houses.

When he left Virginia because of ill health, Lord Delaware turned over his responsibilities to Sir Thomas Dale. During Dale's administration the towns of Henricopolis and Bermuda City were laid out further up the James River, and new buildings erected at Jamestown.

An observer noted in 1614 that Jamestown "hath two rows of houses of framed timber, and some of them two stories and a garrett higher, etc." The new town of Henrico had at each corner, "A high commanding watch-house," and there was built a church, storehouse, and "three streets of well-framed houses." Some of the latter houses had their first stories of bricks made by brickmakers brought from England by Sir Thomas Gates. By 1621 bricks were being made in such quantities in Virginia that they were exported to the Bermudas to be traded for fruit, fowls, and other commodities.[8]

The "well-framed houses" and the houses "of framed timber" were constructed along timber-framing styles which consisted of upright posts placed some distance apart, and tenoned into a bottom sill and a wall-plate at top. Brick or plaster was used to fill the space between the timbers, and the entire structure was then covered with plaster, or clapboards.[9] Less than ten years after the founding of Jamestown the colonists were living in timber-framed dwellings similar to those in England.

Henrico during this period contained "five faire Blockhouses or commaunders" and the records refer to "two Blockhouses" at Jamestown. All seven structures were garrisoned by persons who farmed and also acted as sentinels to warn the colonists against Indian attack. The primary purpose of the blockhouses was military, not residential, and years later in New England they were called "garrison houses."

Although garrison houses and blockhouses were frequently built of individual wooden members placed horizontally, the beams were not generally notched and held together at the corners by their notches, but butted into corner posts, and herein lies their essential difference from a log cabin. In blockhouse construction, the beams were set one on the other, flush at the corners, but not having open or luted joints between them. Thus the tiers were characteristically even in contrast to the uneven tiers of the walls of a notched log structure.

In the former, the beams forming the tiers of the four walls lie even one with another, and in the latter, the logs or beams lie as much as half or a full thickness above or below those of the corresponding tiers in the adjoining walls. Halved cornering, tongue and groove, and the butt joint were three of the several methods in which the beams were jointed at the corner in the even tier construction (see Figure 29). In the uneven tier construction, typical

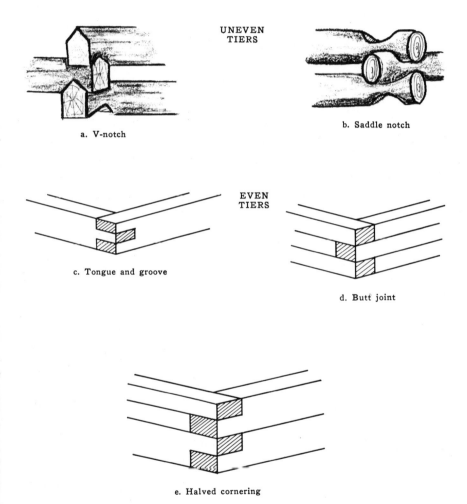

UNEVEN TIERS

a. V-notch

b. Saddle notch

EVEN TIERS

c. Tongue and groove

d. Butt joint

e. Halved cornering

Figure 29

of the log cabin, the interlocking corner joints were fixed into position without the need of supporting vertical posts. In the even tier construction of the blockhouse, support was given in several ways: vertical posts with continuous grooves were set at each corner of the house and the ends of the beams were tapered to fit; sometimes the posts were mortised to receive the tenoned ends of the horizontal beams, and there were other constructional variants. An English blockhouse, or garrison house, was definitely not a log cabin although it was an old form of military construction found in many Old World countries. The even tier construction of both round and hewn logs, butted or fastened to corner posts by wooden pegs, was a prevailing method of traditional wood construction in French Canada, including residences described as *pièce sur pièce*. So far as I am aware, this method of construction did not survive in residential architecture in Virginia.

"Yet," wrote Shurtleff, "log cabins were plentiful in eighteenth-century Virginia, both as pioneer dwellings in the Valley, and for slave quarters on the Tidewater. When did they come in? That is for others to find. . . ." There is no question about the widespread distribution of the log cabin in Virginia in the eighteenth century, particularly in the Piedmont, where many are still standing. To date there has not been published any detailed regional account of log housing in Virginia and the Carolinas, and the area merits careful individual study.

In trying to find a reasonable answer to Shurtleff's question, the authors of the WPA-sponsored Virginia guidebook stated:

> The log cabin was known in Virginia, as in England, at this date, and for many years afterwards. The roofed pen of logs was a contrivance of Scandinavian origin and did not establish itself on this continent until the Swedes brought it over to Delaware. Once it was introduced, diffusion of the type was inevitable, peculiarly adapted as it was to rough-and-ready shelter in a rude country of forests.[10]

I can only partially agree with this statement. To attribute the log cabins built in the eighteenth and nineteenth centuries in Virginia directly to the Swedes on the Delaware is a gross exaggeration, because there was no influx of Swedes into Virginia, and there was little or no direct Swedish influence on Virginia colonial culture. One must look elsewhere for the social and economic forces that brought log cabins to Virginia, and in a later chapter the reader will find that it was the Germans and Scotch-Irish who were responsible for introducing log dwellings to the Old Dominion.

Following Raleigh's failure to plant a colony, there was no further attempt to found a settlement in North Carolina until after Jamestown was colonized. Restless people from Jamestown started to migrate southward in search of better lands, following the streams in southeastern Virginia flowing into Albemarle Sound. This territory that later became North and South Carolina was originally called "Carolina" in honor of Charles I, and in 1664 an English settlement was made on the Charles (Cape Fear River) called Charles Town. The English continued to expand their settlements in what is now the tidewater area of North Carolina, building the typical framed dwellings characteristic of the Jamestown colony. Thomas Newe, writing in 1682, said that in Charles Town on the Ashley River (present Charleston, South Carolina, a different town from the above-mentioned Charles Town) there were one hundred houses wholly built of wood.[11] He probably meant frame houses, because there is no reason to believe that any of these dwellings were built of logs, but a letter written in 1690 leaves little doubt that there were a few structures built of logs in the upriver, wooded country of South Carolina. John Stewart writing that year from "Wadboo Barony" at the head of Cooper River on Biggin and Wadboo Creeks said in a letter to William Dunlop, ". . . Sr. Nath [Sir Nathaniel Johnson who settled there in August 1690] has built a silk howse 50 foot long with logs not a nail in it . . ."[12] This structure was apparently intended for the breeding of silkworms, and in other letters written the same year Stewart refers to residential "Log houses." Regrettably no detailed descriptions are given, and it is uncertain whether these dwellings were of horizontally-placed notched timbers or of logs set vertically in the earth. If of horizontal construction, they represent further examples of seventeenth century log techniques overlooked by Shurtleff.

Actually, there were no log houses in any significant numbers in the Carolinas until the next century when the Moravians, Swiss, and Germans from the Palatinate, as well as Scotch-Irish, infiltered the region, and this, too, will be brought into focus in a later chapter.

Georgia, the last of the thirteen colonies to be settled by Englishmen, was strongly under Spanish and French influence from Florida in the seventeenth century where the missions and presidios were made of wood, adobe, brick, and sometimes tabby, a cement concocted of oyster shells, lime, and sand. The English settlements in Georgia originated with James Edward Oglethorpe, who founded Savannah in 1733—almost 125 years after Jamestown was colonized. Although log dwellings at that late date were being built in Maryland, Virginia, and the Carolinas, the colonists in Oglethorpe's settlement had no opportunity to acquire log cabin skills from their American neighbors, occupying, as they did, a terminal position in British America. Like the first Virginians they built their dwelling houses according to English tradition.

Consequently, the log cabin was late in arriving in Georgia, making its appearance long after Oglethorpe's colony was established, and when Scotch-Irish and other English-speaking frontiersmen, who had learned the craft from Pennsylvania Germans, Swiss, and Swedes, moved down through the Carolinas, and finally entered the Georgia Piedmont. This is not to say that direct German influences in early Georgia were nonexistent, because two of the rare references to log buildings in the tidewater area of the state are specifically attributable to Germans. Henry Michel and Henry Myers, immigrants from Germany, each built a house of hewn logs on St. Simons Island, both of which were standing in 1738. The first dwellings of the Salzburger settlers at Ebenezer, some twenty-five miles up the Savannah River from the city of Savannah, were also made of logs. A professional geographer, Wilbur Zelinsky, conducted a comprehensive study of surviving log houses in Georgia, a project that sets a standard for other regional scholars to follow. Although I have visited Georgia and examined many of the log structures still standing, my comments below are based largely on Zelinsky's published account.[13]

With the exception of Georgia's tidewater area, log dwellings today can still be found throughout the state. The greatest number occur in the Blue Ridge, the inner edge of the Piedmont, and a small corner of the Cumberland Plateau; and next most frequently, in the intermontane basins of the extreme north-central parts of the state. Round log tradition dominates in the southern portion of the state and hewn log houses are more numerous in the north. The two-story log house is rare in Georgia and most log dwellings are built with a ground floor only. The general architectural pattern of houses, barns, sheds, schools, and churches was dominated by log construction almost until the eve of the Civil War when frame construction began to increase in importance, first for the well-to-do, and then for the poorer classes, as sawmills made cheap lumber available.

Zelinsky estimated that in 1951 there were between ten thousand and twelve thousand log houses still standing in Georgia, exclusive of barns and other utility structures of logs.[14] This was a decline from the fifteen thousand log dwellings estimated for the state in 1934, indicating that the forces of log cabin attrition were being felt in Georgia, as they were elsewhere. Log courthouses, jails, forts, and churches have now completely disappeared, although one school house of logs was still in existence in 1953.

Oak or pine was the most common building material, but the old-time practice noted by Olmsted (see pp. 249–50) of leaving the logs unchinked vanished during the Civil War. Most often the interstices between the logs on the existing structures are chinked with twigs, with added clay, lime, or some other variety of cement, and in recent times some of the cabins have been sealed by nailing short lengths of narrow boards across the gaps between the logs. The catted, stick-and-mud chimney attached to the gable ends of the earliest log cabins is now only a memory in the state, having long ago been supplanted with chimneys of brick or stone. The incidence of surviving log houses in Georgia, as in other areas of log housing is in inverse proportion to the rate of traffic in goods and modern ideas. City and town environment are nonpreservative factors, whereas economic backwardness and isolation have tended to perpetuate the log house in the rural sections of Georgia and elsewhere in the South.[15]

NOTES—CHAPTER 4

1. *Southern Literary Messenger*, XXIV, No. 6, June 1857, 437.

2. *Ibid.*, 462.

3. George R. Stewart, *American Ways of Life* (New York, 1954), 145.

4. *Travels and Works of Captain John Smith*, ed. Edward Arber, A. G. Bradley edition (Edinburgh, 1910), I, lxx.

5. *Ibid.*, II, 957. George C. Gregory in "Log Houses at Jamestown, 1607," *The Virginia Magazine of History & Biography*, XLIV, No. 4, Oct. 1936, 287–295, distorts this reference to mean that Smith was referring to log houses. Gregory omitted forty-four words from the quotation which I have given in full, and he also misinterpreted the seventeenth century meaning of "rales" and "rafts."

6. Henry Chandlee Forman, *Jamestown and St. Marys* (Baltimore, 1938), 31–32. See also by the same author, *The Architecture of the Old South* (Cambridge, 1948), 14–15, wherein he comments on the prevalence of houses on crucks in seventeenth century England, citing that in the middle of Queen Elizabeth's reign a survey was made of the village of Crackhorn which indicated that every house and barn stood on "crocks" and was covered with thatch. During the seventeenth century the cruck method of construction gave way to timber-framing.

7. *Smith's Works*, II, 502.

8. Philip A. Bruce, *Economic History of Virginia in the 17th Century* (New York–London, 1896), II, 137.

9. *Jamestown and St. Marys*, see p. 50 for illustration and discussion of timber-framing. Forman calls the period in Virginia between 1607 and 1620 "the Cottage Period"; *cf.* his *Virginia Architecture In The Seventeenth Century* (Williamsburg, 1957), 28.

10. *Virginia, A Guide to the Old Dominion*, American Guide Series (New York, 1940), 174.

11. "Letters of Thomas Newe, 1682," *Narratives of Early Carolina*, ed. Alexander S. Salley, Jr. (New York, 1911), 181.

12. "Letters from John Stewart to William Dunlop," *The South Caro-lina Historical and Genealogical Magazine*, Vol. XXXII (1931), 17, 85, 97. Note his reference on p. 19 to "Swedes."

13. Wilbur Zelinsky, "The Log House in Georgia," *Geographical Review*, April 1953, 173–193.

14. *Ibid.*, 182.

15. Eugene M. Wilson of the University of Alabama has made an intensive study of folk housing in Alabama, and Alabama log houses figure prominently in his dissertation, "Contributions to Southern Appalachian Folk Housing," submitted to the Louisiana State University in 1968 in partial fulfillment of the requirements for the doctoral degree.

5 Pilgrims, Puritans, and Dutchmen

Like the Virginia cavaliers, the Pilgrims also brought an English cultural heritage to America, although there was both a regional and religious difference in their backgrounds. Pilgrim history began about the middle of the sixteenth century when small groups of people called Separatists or Brownists (after one of their leaders, Robert Browne), who disagreed with the doctrines of the Church of England, began to assemble secretively for worship. The southeastern counties of England was the home of spiritual nonconformity, whereas the Virginia gentlemen, who settled Jamestown, adhered to the Church of England, came mostly from London, and were strongly under the influence of the Crown.

Although the Pilgrims were represented in all of the southeastern counties of England, of a New England population in 1640 estimated at 25,000, fully two thirds were from six counties: Essex, Cambridgeshire, Hertfordshire, Middlesex, Surrey, and Kent. In 1932, the British architect, Martin S. Briggs, made a thorough study of the residential architecture of the southeastern area of England for the purpose of ascertaining exactly what type of houses were built by the hard-working, thrifty, middle-class folk who became known in America as Pilgrims. He found that although brick and stone houses were not unknown, the majority of the Pilgrim fathers occupied dwellings of wood.[1] This was not unusual because the six counties had formerly been deeply wooded, and the forests cleared, and the trees sawed, hewn, and riven to make beams, planks, and clapboards for house construction, as well as lumber and masts for ships. Here New England architecture was cradled long before the *Mayflower* set sail for the New World.

Typical of the houses in the southeastern English counties were those timber-framed, the sides covered with weatherboarding, usually fixed horizontally across the vertical posts or studs of the framing, the steep-pitched roofs thatched with thick layers of straw or reeds. The roof covering, applied by craftsman called "thatchers," was both a fire hazard and a breeding ground for vermin, and since there were no gutters or rainspouts on this type of roof, it was not unusual for leaks to develop as the house aged. Some of the better cottages were roofed with plain tiles and pantiles, imported from the Netherlands before England developed its own tile manufacture.

Brick-making was practiced in southeast England, as in other parts of the country, and bricks were widely used in the walls of churches, great halls, and manor houses, although their use in the Pilgrims' wood cottages was confined to plinths and chimneys. Characteristic of the dwellings were small casement windows, with leaded glazing in diamond patterns, commonly called lattice windows, which swung open on hinges. The window sash that was raised and lowered was still unknown in the time of the Pilgrims.

The volume written by Briggs and listed in the chapter notes is recommended to the reader who would like to have further details about the features of the cottages built by the Pilgrims in their homeland. My only purpose in making these brief references is to emphasize that they did not live in cabins of horizontally placed logs, and had little knowledge about this type of residential architecture.

It is well known that the Pilgrims sought refuge in the Netherlands (having been preceded there by other Separatists), because if offered freedom of worship in contrast to the harassment they suffered in England. Before the decision was made to go to America, the Pilgrims, from 1609 to 1620, were exposed to Dutch residential and commercial architecture in Amsterdam and Leyden, with its warm multicolored bricks, bold and fanciful tiled gables, colorful shutters, cream and white wood trim, and pantile roofs. Holland was devoid of forests, and most of the lumber used for house building was imported. The scarcity of native wood was the principal reason Holland's builders found it necessary to develop extensive brick and tile industries, and also explains why the Pilgrims saw no log houses during their sojourn in the lowlands of the Netherlands. Had they sought asylum in one of the Scandinavian countries or in Germany, they might have assimilated ideas about log dwellings from their surroundings, but this was not the case.

In view of their cultural background, it would have been unnatural and illogical to expect the Pilgrim fathers to fell the trees and notch them for log cabins when they landed at Plymouth, yet it is difficult to dispossess William Bradford, Miles Standish, Elder Brewster, and their associates of their nonexistent houses of logs, which we have been erroneously told they erected. The error, as Shurtleff stated, has been perpetuated in a number of historical volumes, and among the earliest was the Reverend Alexander Young's *Chronicle of the Pilgrim Fathers* (1841), in which he mistakenly said of the Pilgrims, "Their houses were probably log-huts, thatched and the interstices filled with clay." This was sheer nonsense, having no basis in fact as the contemporary documents clearly show, and Young was probably influenced by Harrison's Log Cabin Campaign, which will be discussed in a later chapter.

As in Virginia, the first structure erected by the Pilgrims was a temporary fortification of sorts, intended as a protection against the Indians. Built on December 6, 1620, by a landing party from the *Mayflower*, which lay at anchor in Provincetown Harbor, it was described as "a barricado with logs and boughs." [2]

The next afternoon after exploring the shore line, the landing party under command of Miles Standish, carrying guns and wearing armor, erected a second crude fortification. This also served the men as a shelter, consisting of "logs, stakes, and thick pine boughs, the height of a man, leaving it open to leeward, partly to shelter them from the cold and wind (making their fire in the middle and lying round about it) and partly to defend them from any sudden assaults of the savages if they should surround them, etc." [3] The place where they had landed did not offer a satisfactory anchorage for large vessels, and after exploring the coast line Miles Standish returned to the *Mayflower* and the Pilgrims sailed to Plymouth Bay where they again landed and selected a site for their settlement.

On December 25, the Pilgrims began to erect their first dwelling and utility house, a structure "for common use to receive them and their goods." [4] It was twenty feet square and probably no better than a shanty, for on January 14 it caught fire, and the thatched roof was consumed, sending the shore party back to the *Mayflower* for shelter. During the ensuing winter most of the party continued to live aboard ship, but weakened by scurvy, chilled by the damp winter cold, men and women sickened, and before summer came, half of the *Mayflower's* 102 passengers were dead. Those who kept their health took care of the sick, and when weather permitted carried the dead ashore to bury them in unmarked graves lest the Indians learn of their weakness. Early in March, the first signs of spring appeared, and they went ashore and began to prepare their fields for planting and to build houses.

Like the Virginians, the Pilgrims brought carpenter's tools with them, including broad and pitching axes, chisels, augers, whipsaws, two-handed saws, and frows for the riving of pales, laths, and clapboards. They set about to fell the trees and saw the logs into boards, and they had a good supply of nails of several sorts for building purposes. Seven small dwelling houses were built before the *Mayflower* returned to England in April of 1621. In November of 1621, the *Fortune* arrived from England with thirty-six new settlers, and when she headed for home, she carried a cargo of clapboards, but only two hogsheads of beaver and otter skins, not a rich reward for Thomas Weston and the other English merchants who had invested in the voyage. [5] Somewhere in the North Atlantic a French warship captured the *Fortune*, and her cargo never reached England.

It is likely that the Pilgrims used the clapboards they rived to construct wood cottages having thatched roofs and wood chimneys probably lined with clay. Governor William Bradford called these flimsy dwellings "cabins",[6] which may also have misled the Reverend Mr. Young and others to conclude they were made of logs, and it wasn't long before fires consumed three or four of them. Like their countrymen in Virginia, the Pilgrims made the mistake of building their cottages too close together in the manner of crowded town life in England making them especially vulnerable to the spread of fire. The houses were woefully inadequate, and one of the reasons given by Bradford for the death of almost fifty persons before the summer of 1621 was that of "wanting house and other comforts." As the Plymouth colony grew, sturdier frame houses were built following mediaeval housing styles of the southeastern English counties, and the settlers were then able to live more comfortably.

Turning to the Puritan colony at Massachusetts Bay, settled in 1630, the first temporary shelters were tents, and huts, termed English wigwams, built of thatch, reed, saplings, and tree boughs. Although the word was borrowed from the Algonkian, the English wigwam differed somewhat from the Indian huts, and some of them were probably conical in shape, like the old Yorkshire charcoal burner's hut illustrated by Kimball.[7] Individual tastes dictated their size and shape, but they were crude, uncomfortable, and like tinder to a spark. John Winthrop wrote that one of the colonists named Finch "has had his wigwam burnt and all his goods," and the same fate befell another named Firmin who also "had his wigwam burnt." [8] Winthrop refers to six colonists from Boston driven ashore near Cape Cod who received assistance from an Indian who "fetched a hatchet and built them a wigwam and covered it." [9] Since the latter structure was native-made it was probably a true Indian wigwam.

Other settlers built "cabins" of thatch and wood with wood and clay chimneys, which also constituted a fire hazard. Winthrop wrote, "the chimney of Mr. Sharp's house in Boston took fire (the splinters not being clayed at the top) and taking the thatch burnt it down." [10] To make matters worse the wind spread the flames to Mr. Colburn's house and burnt it down. The house of John Page was also burnt, "a coal fell by the way and kindled in the leaves." [11] Mr. Oldham built a small house "made all of clapboards, burnt down (fall of 1632) by making a fire in it when it had no chimney." [12]

As time went on, it was written that "The Lord hath been pleased to turn all the wigwams, huts and hovels the English dwelt in at their first coming into orderly, fair, and well-built houses," but at the beginning the dwellings of the Pilgrims and Puritans were a far cry from the log cabins of the western frontier.

Rhode Island, an offshoot of Massachusetts, had its beginning when Roger Williams, expelled from the Bay Colony, fled to the upper Narragansett Bay region, and he was followed by others who migrated to lands farther south on the bay. Williams started the plantation that became Providence, and Anne Hutchinson, another of the banished zealots, founded Newport. There is a paucity of information about the kinds of houses standing in 1647 when representatives from Providence, Newport, and Warwick formed the first general assembly of Rhode Island, but there seems to be little question that the settlers followed the domestic architectural styles of Massachusetts. By 1700 the population of Rhode Island had substantially increased, and there were numerous well-built houses mostly framed cottages with stone chimneys on the ends—but cabins of round logs were missing.

Vermont had no true domestic architecture at this early date since it was still largely an unsettled passageway for French and Indian raiding parties seeking to harass the English settlements to the south and east. There were a number of fortified trading posts, such as the one Captain La Mothe built on an island in Lake Champlain, and an outpost erected several years later at Chimney Point in present Addison Township, but Vermont remained the New England frontier when the seacoast towns further south were settled and displaying various styles of residential architecture.

Maine and New Hampshire were closely related, and although the territory the Council for New England transferred to Sir Ferdinando Gorges and Captain John Mason in 1622 lying between the Merrimac and Kennebec Rivers was called the Province of Maine, it also included land encompassed by present New Hampshire. There were settlers at Monhegan in 1622, Saco in 1623, and York in 1624, but no specific descriptions of their houses was recorded.

When Mason and Gorges divided the province in 1629 with the Piscataqua River as the middle boundary, Mason called his portion New Hampshire. In the earliest settlements in Maine, and those at the mouth of the Piscataqua near present Portsmouth, the first dwellings were probably huts of branches, rushes, turf, and thatch, replaced as soon as building materials were accessible by typical English framed cottages. In time a number of garrison houses were built of squared timber, referred to in the previous chapter, and some were used secondarily as residences, but during the early period of settlement true log cabins were scarce in both Maine and New Hampshire. A single documentary reference to a "log house" in Maine (1662) was found by Shurtleff, but this may have been a garrison house (see Figure 30).

It is regrettable that so few of the old garrison houses have been preserved. In the vicinity of Dover, New Hampshire, along Oyster River and Great Bay there were originally twelve or fifteen of these structures, some built to protect the settlers during King Philip's War, which broke out in 1675, and others were built earlier. The New Hampshire garrison houses were almost invariably positioned on high knolls and were usually surrounded by palisades. If the Indians carried the palisades by assault, the defenders could retire to the garrison house, and when they did so the importance of the overhanging upper story becomes apparent. Tradition has it that the women, who retreated with the men to this upper story, poured down kettles of boiling water on the heads of the Indians, while the men discharged their guns at the attackers. The Indians used every artifice to drive out the defenders by setting fire to the citadel, even pushing carts of burning hay against the walls (see Figure 31).

As the years rolled by the garrison houses lost their utility and a few were clapboarded and some even bricked over for residential use, but there seems to have been a general indifference to their

Figure 30. Fort Halifax, Winslow, Maine, a garrison house built in 1791, as it appeared when photographed by the writer in 1957.

preservation. Some were used as hen houses and tool sheds, and in more than one instance when a later resident was building a new barn, he pulled down an old garrison house to salvage the timbers for use in his barn. Others were destroyed accidentally by fire. The William Damme Garrison House on the grounds of the Woodman Institute in Dover is the last of these buildings in the immediate area, the hewn logs halved at the corners and pinned to upright posts.[18]

There was also a scarcity of log cabins in seventeenth century Connecticut, which, like Rhode Island, was largely colonized by Massachusetts people. The Reverend Thomas Hooker and members of his congregation established an English community in Connecticut, and the three "river towns," Hartford, Windsor, and Wethersfield, had their cultural antecedents in Massachusetts, as did New

Figure 31. Wood engraving of an earlier day shows Indians trying to set fire to a New England log garrison house.

Haven settled as a separate colony by Puritans from Massachusetts Bay.

It is, however, incorrect to conclude that no buildings of horizontally laid logs were built in Connecticut, for a number of garrison houses of squared logs are on record. In 1937 the two walls remaining from a log structure, the Lieutenant James Bennett House, were pulled down in Easton, Connecticut, by order of the local water company on whose land they stood. This one-room log building, built *circa* 1671, which originally measured 17 x 10½ feet, was made of even-tiered, hewn oak logs which were halved at the corners, and some of the joints secured with oaken pins. The hewn logs were fitted so closely together that an observer said a knife blade could scarcely fit between them, although here and there the builder had caulked some of the seams with flax or hemp fibers.[14] There was apparently no overhanging story on this particular building, which leads one to assume it may have been primarily built as a residence; if so, it was definitely an exception.

The six New England states, like Virginia, were dominantly English, and the colonists could no more escape the architectural influences of seventeenth century England than they could divest themselves of English language and custom. As a matter of fact, no significant method of wood construction was developed in New England during the colonial period—the ideas were all European imports. To labor the issue further would be tiresome and repetitious, for the evidence is overwhelming and well recognized by informed historians—true log cabins were missing in the Plymouth and Massachusetts Bay colonies, nor were they part of the settlement housing in the neighboring colonies of Rhode Island, Vermont, Maine, New Hampshire, and Connecticut. It goes without saying that at a later date log cabins were built in New England, but this was only after non-English influences diffused into the area.

J. A. Graham, writing in 1797, described the "log huts" with bark roofs, the walls daubed with a mortar of clay and wild grass, which had recently appeared in Franklin County, Vermont. Graham said that three men could build one of these dwellings in six days.[15]

When New Englanders migrated westward in the early nineteenth century in what Stewart Holbrook called a *Yankee Exodus* (Macmillan, New York 1950) many of them built log cabins wherever they settled. By that time they had broken away from many of their hereditary ties with England, and the majority of them had no difficulty in conforming to their new environmental needs, especially since they were thrown into close contact with frontiersmen thoroughly experienced in log cabin techniques. There were some conservatives like Henry Trumbull's Dr. Jeremiah Simpleton who could not adjust to log cabin life. In the fall of 1814, Dr. Simpleton and his family headed for Ohio in a covered wagon containing "three feather beds, one table, three chairs, two spinning wheels, one reel, one brass kettle, two iron pots, a tea kettle and a frying pan, four axes, three hoes, two ox yokes, a plough and harrow, two saddles, and a bag of seed corn." [16]

Dr. Simpleton's wife, three daughters, and two young sons rode in the wagon, while he rode forward and drove the team, and another son rode the forward horse. His oldest son, "and my faithful dog Watch brought up the rear on foot."

The family's initiation to log cabin life was in a one-room log inn on the summit of Laurel Mountain in the Alleghenies built and operated by a Pennsylvania German. The Simpleton family "spent a wretched night" in the single room with the owner, his wife, the owner's six children, a dog, three cats, and a sow with nine pigs!

The cabin the Simpletons built when they arrived at their destination in Ohio was swept into the Ohio River during a heavy rain. This and other unpleasant experiences caused them to retrace their steps and return to their New England home.

Probably the first European observer in what is now upstate New York was Samuel de Champlain, who, in 1609, explored southward along the valley of the lake named for him in his efforts to establish a French North America. During the same year Henry Hudson, sailing under the flag of the Dutch East India Company, entered the river that still bears his name, but neither explorer built any houses during his travels. It was more than a decade later before a newly-formed Dutch West India Company attempted to lay down a commercial colony in America, although Dutch traders and navigators explored the coastal waters and certain parts of the inland areas drained by the Hudson, the Connecticut, the Delaware, and their tributaries. They returned to the Netherlands with cargoes of valuable beaver and otter pelts; increasing this profitable Indian trade was their principal interest—not colonization or house building.

Dutch commerce in the seventeenth century surpassed that of any other European country, and by the middle of the century, Holland was a center of intellectual, social, and commercial life in Europe. Hundreds of Dutch trading vessels, owned by the prominent West India and East India Companies, sailed back and forth to America and the Orient, but with prosperity and religious free-

dom at home there was no compelling reason for Dutch families
to leave the comfort of their homes to settle the American wilderness.

There is a record of one of the seventeenth century Dutch explorers in New York state building crude shelters, but this happened
only because of unusual circumstances. When Adriaen Block's ship
Tiger caught on fire in the waters off Manhattan Island and was
destroyed, he and the members of his crew, including Herman
Hillebrantsen, a shipbuilder, spent the winter of 1614 constructing
a yacht, given the Dutch name *Onrust*, usually translated as *Restless*,
although a modern Dutch scholar believes a more accurate translation is *Trouble*.[17] This interruption in their explorations and trade
with the Indians necessitated living on the land during a bitter cold
winter, and it was written of them that the Indians "assisted our
people with food and all kinds of necessaries." [18] The huts they occupied were probably the earliest white men's residences in New
York state—and certainly the earliest on Manhattan Island. The like-
lihood is that these shelters were bark wigwams made after the
fashion of the Algonkian-speaking Manhattan Indians who later sold
the island to the Dutch for merchandise worth sixty guilders.

Dutch explorers later built a trading post on Castle Island at present Albany, which they called Fort Nassau. It was surrounded by
a stockade of logs set vertically in the earth, as was the later Fort
Orange, but there isn't the slightest reason to believe that log cabins
were erected at either location.

The first successful effort toward permanent Dutch colonization
occurred in the spring of 1624 when the ship *New Netherland*,
under the command of Cornelis May arrived in the Hudson River
with a company of thirty Walloon families intent on wedging a
settlement on behalf of the West India Company between the English of Virginia and those in New England. One of the members
of this expedition, Catelyn Trico, later deposed as follows concern-
ing the nature of the residences built by these first settlers at Fort
Orange, now Albany. The italic is mine:

. . . there were about 18 families aboard who settled themselves att
Albany & made a small fort; and as soon as *they had built themselves some
hutts of Bark:* ye Mahikanders or River Indians, ye Maquase: Oneydes:
Onnondages Cayougas & Sinnekes, wth ye Mahawawa or Ottawawaes
Indians came & made Covenants of Friendship. . . .[19]

These bark huts were doubtless patterned after the wigwams of
the neighboring Mohawk, and since it was then the spring of the
year the Walloon families were not exposed to the severe weather
that Captain Block's men experienced at Manhattan. Catelyn Trico
also testified as to what happened to some of the other Walloon
families, prior to their arrival at Albany:

. . . as soon as they came to Mannatans now called N: York they sent
Two families & six men to harford River & Two families & 8 men to
Delaware River and 8 men they left att N: York to take Possession and
ye rest of ye Passengers went wth ye Ship as farr as Albany which they
then called fort Orangie.[20]

The party sent to "harford River" may have been responsible
for erecting Fort Good Hope, or perhaps it may not have been
built until a later date when the Dutch attempted to protect the
bounds of the New Netherland from incursion by the Pilgrims of
the Plymouth Bay colony. In any event, it was described in a contemporary Dutch account as a "blockhouse," a type of fortification
previously discussed. Unfortunately there is no description of the
houses built by these first Walloon settlers in Connecticut nor by
those sent to live on the Delaware. A trading post built on the Delaware in 1626, also called Fort Nassau, had a large dwelling house
within the stockaded area for use as living and sleeping quarters by
the garrison which occupied the fort intermittently. When this house
fell in decay, a master carpenter from Manhattan was sent, and he
"built the large house in Fort Nassau." [21]

The colony established by patroons of the West India Company
at Swanendael in Delaware Bay in 1631 was intended to develop
whale fishing and cultivate grain and tobacco. There were no wom-
en or children in the contingent of settlers consisting of twenty-
eight men under the command of Gillis Hossit. They erected a log

stockade with bastions at the corners, and within the stockaded area built a dwelling house and cookhouse of yellow bricks brought with them from Holland on *de Walvis*. The main brick structure was a sort of barracks occupied by the men, and it had a loft where merchandise was stored for use in the Indian trade. Despite the abundance of virgin pines, cedars, and other trees growing at the Swanendael site no log cabins were built in this ill-fated settlement. This colony was wiped out by the Indians, the fort burned, and the men massacred. The patroons lost their interest following this tragedy and Holland did nothing to advance her interests along the Delaware.

Since two of the permanent and most populous settlements in the New Netherland were at Albany and on Manhattan Island, it is in order to review briefly selected contemporary accounts for clues to the architectural styles of the residences built at both locations. The temporary bark huts at Fort Orange were shortly replaced by sturdier frame residences, and in 1644 there were twenty-five or thirty homes in the community known as Rensselaerswyck, described thus: "All their houses are merely of boards and thatched. As yet there is no mason work except the chimneys. The forests furnishing many large pines, they make boards by means of their mills which they have for the purpose." [22]

The sawmills, like the grist mills, were built on the banks of suitable streams and operated by water power. In the absence of pantiles, and since the Dutch were not experienced in riving shingles unknown in Holland, they covered their houses with thatch, which presented the usual fire hazards that had plagued the Pilgrims. The problem was worsened in the event of attack by unfriendly Indians, and in one of his letters the patroon Kiliaen van Rensselaer wrote to his cousin van Curler, "Use the tiles, which I sent over for the roof of your house to protect it against fire arrows." [23]

In 1656, Willem Juriaensz's thatched roof was condemned as being hazardous, and his Albany neighbors contributed boards, nails and timbers for a new roof.[24] In the numerous references to the frame houses in contemporary journals, letters, and court records one can readily infer that log cabins were absent.

Even as late as 1652, an inhabitant of Albany who wanted to erect a temporary residence was given permission by the court to erect "a small bark hut" on her lot.[25] The bark hut appears to be the Dutch substitute for the log cabin as a provisional dwelling at Albany. This was also true of Manhattan, where towering skyscrapers now stand, as indicated in a description of the residential architecture written in 1626, with italic supplied, "The counting house there is kept in a stone building thatched with reed; *the other houses are of the bark of trees*." [26]

In 1628, Michaelius, a Dutch pastor on Manhattan Island, made reference to another type of temporary dwelling as follows, "They are therefore beginning to build new houses in place of the hovels and *holes* in which heretofore they huddled rather than dwelt." [27]

Van Tienhoven, writing in 1650, gives a detailed description of these holes or pit houses,

Those in New Netherland and especially New England who have no means to build farm houses at first, according to their wishes, dig a square pit in the ground, cellar fashion six or seven feet deep, as long and broad as they think proper, case the earth inside with wood all round the wall, and line the wood with the bark of trees, or something else to prevent the caving in of the earth; floor this cellar with plank and wainscot it overhead for a ceiling, raise a roof of spars, clear up and cover the spars with bark or green sods, so that they can live dry and warm in these houses with their entire families for two, three and four years, it being understood that partitions are run through those cellars which are adapted to the size of the family.[28]

The bark huts, pit homes and frame cottages with thatched roofs were poor and unsatisfactory substitutes for the comfortable, step-gabled brick residences which the Dutch knew in their homeland. The ambition of every Dutch settler occupying what he must have considered a home of inferior quality on Manhattan Island, and elsewhere in New Netherland, was to rebuild at the earliest opportunity along the hereditary lines of the mother country.

It was natural that brick-making would be given impetus by this motivation, and as early as 1628 bricks of a low grade were baked on Manhattan Island, and a brick kiln was operating in Rensselaerswyck in 1634. Stones were also quarried, at first for use in churches, inns, and other public buildings, and there is record of a stone inn at Manhattan in 1642, and soon thereafter a stone church was built within the palisades of the fort, measuring fifty by seventy-two feet. In the absence of suitable roofing tiles, it was covered with "overlapping shingles cleft from oak" by an English carpenter.[29]

Before the seventeenth century ended, the architectural posture of the New Netherland began to resemble Leyden and Amsterdam as the crude bark and frame dwellings, particularly in the growing towns, were replaced by houses of brick and stone, roofed in the Dutch manner. Pictorial evidence in contemporary engravings indicates that the chief features of the dwellings were brick and tile construction, with stepped gables rising to the chimneys or to ornaments at the top of the roof.[30]

Dutch farmhouses beyond the limits of the protection afforded by the forts centered in the towns, were usually surrounded by palisades, consisting of vertical logs or board pales. These palisades kept Indian attackers at a distance from the house, making it more difficult for them to ignite the thatched roofs with their fire arrows. The residents could defend their properties by firing through the palisades. In addition to this protection given the individual houses, the Dutch also built a number of blockhouses, similar to the English "commanders" or "garrison houses," strategically placed for defense. Some of them were provided with light pieces of ordnance.

One of the blockhouses erected on Staten Island was described as "a small, slight wooden, Block house about 18 @ 20 feet square, [situated] in the center of their houses which were slightly constructed of straw and clapboards." [31] Similar blockhouses were built at Albany, on Long Island, and at New Utrecht, the latter described as having several portholes and housing a cannon.[32] Although even-tiered squared logs were used in building these blockhouses, the information herein presented can be summed up by saying that the cabin of uneven-tiered, horizontally-placed notched logs was a missing element in Dutch architectural patterns in New York state in the seventeenth century.

After the English seized control of the New Netherland, rechris-
tening the largest town New York, the colony developed very slowly, and the typical English frame house began to appear in increasing numbers, although brick buildings continued to be built. New
Englanders, with the support of the English authorities, moved down
to settle along the east bank of the Hudson; Highland Scots and
Scotch-Irish settled on the west bank in Cherry Valley and in the
northern parts of the state. About 2500 or three thousand Germans
from the Palatine, comprising the largest mass immigration up to
that time, came to the Hudson Valley to produce naval stores, under
a plan sponsored by Governor Robert Hunter who abandoned the
project in 1712. With the failure of that enterprise, many disil-
lusioned Germans scattered along the Hudson with the greater number moving to the Schoharie and Mohawk Valleys (see Figure 32).
In 1743, John Bartram noted in his journal that Oswego had seventy

Figure 32. Saddle-notched one room cabin at Schoharie, Schoharie County,
N.Y., typical of the eighteenth century round-log dwellings built in the area.
(Reproduced from the collections of the Library of Congress)

log houses, and here we begin to see German influence on the housing.

By 1760 the frontier settlements in the state extended to about forty miles north of Albany along the Hudson, and eighty miles west of Albany on the Mohawk. In these settlements the log cabin was well represented, but it was a latecomer in the settlement housing of New York state, and it persisted longer than the builders anticipated. As late as 1855, seventeen thousand families in the state were still living in log houses.[33]

NOTES—CHAPTER 5

1. Martin S. Briggs, *The Homes of the Pilgrim Fathers in England and America* (New York, 1932); see also George D. Langdon Jr., *Pilgrim Colony* (New Haven, 1966).

2. William Bradford, *Of Plymouth Plantation, 1620–1647* (new edition) (New York, 1952), 68.

3. *Ibid.*, 69.

4. *Ibid.*, 72.

5. *Ibid.*, 94.

6. *Ibid.*, 78, 92.

7. Fiske Kimball, *Domestic Architecture of the American Colonies and of the Early Republic* (New York, 1927), 4.

8. Winthrop's Journal, *History of New England, 1630–1649*, ed. J. K. Hosmer (New York, 1908), I, 53, 54.

9. *Ibid.*, 55–56.

10. *Ibid.*, 59.

11. *Ibid.*, 63.

12. *Ibid.*, 90.

13. Louis W. Flanders, M.D., "The Garrisons of Ancient Dover, New Hampshire," *Old Time New England*, XII, No. 2 (Oct. 1926), 51–62; see also Stuart Bartlett, "Garrison Houses Along the New England Frontier," the Monograph Series, *Records of Early American Architecture*, XIX, No. 3 (1933).

14. John Frederick Kelly, "A 17th Century Connecticut Log House," *Old Time New England*, XXXI, No. 2 (Oct. 1940), 29–40.

15. J. A. Graham, *A Descriptive Sketch of the Present State of Vermont* (London, 1797), 161.

16. *Western Emigration: A Journal of Doctor Jeremiah Simpleton's Tour to Ohio*, by H. Trumbull (Boston, 1819), 8.

17. Simon Hart, *The Prehistory of the New Netherland Company* (Amsterdam, 1959), 28.

18. From "a rare tract"; see fn. 48, John R. Brodhead, *History of the State of New York*, N.Y., 1853, vol. 1.

19. *The Documentary History of the State of New York*, ed. E. B. O'Callaghan (Albany, 1849–1851), III, 51.

20. *Ibid.*, 50.

21. *Documents Relative to the Colonial History of the State of New York*, ed. E. B. O'Callaghan (Albany, 1856–1887), XIV, 16.

22. *Documentary History of the State of New York*, IV, 23.

23. *Van Rensselaer Bowier Manuscripts*, trans. and ed. A. J. F. van Laer (Albany, 1908), 551.

24. *Minutes of the Court of Fort Orange and Beverwyck, 1652–1656*, trans. A. J. F. van Laer (Albany, 1920), 255.

25. *Ibid.*, 22.

26. *Narratives of New Netherland, 1609–1664*, ed. J. F. Jameson (New York, 1909), 83.

27. *Documents Relative to the Colonial History*, I, 422–423.

28. *Documentary History of the State of New York*, IV, 31–32. I have also made reference elsewhere to Dutch colonists living in holes dug in the banks of the creek at the Whorekill (present Lewes, Delaware) about 1670; see Appendix of my "Log Structures in New Sweden," *Delaware History*, V (1952), 79.

29. *Narratives of New Netherland*, 213.

30. Thomas Janvier, *The Dutch Founding of New York* (New York, 1910); see plate opposite p. 66 for a Dutch view of New York *circa* 1630 and opposite p. 64 for a view *circa* 1650.

31. *Documents Relative to the Colonial History*, XIV, 443.

32. *Minutes of the Court of Fort Orange*, 249; *Documents Relative to the Colonial History, op. cit.*, XIV, 261, 449, 494; II, 402.

33. Jared van Wagener, *The Golden Age of Homespun* (Ithaca, N.Y., 1953), 4.

6 The Maryland Planters

Cecilius Calvert, the second Lord Baltimore and the first Proprietary of Maryland, issued detailed instructions on November 13, 1633, to the commissioners he had selected to settle colonists in his American province named for the consort of Charles I. He emphasized that after finding a suitable site for the colony, they should first erect a fort, and within it, or near it, they were instructed to build a convenient house and a church, or chapel, as the seat of the government. Cecilius did not specify the kind of houses he wanted built in his colony, but he obviously meant ones constructed in the English style. The *Ark*, a vessel of three hundred tons burden, and the *Dove*, a pinnace of fifty tons, which transported the settlers, were well stocked with broadaxes felling axes, handsaws, augers, chisels, gimlets, hatchets, frows, pickaxes, as well as nails, locks, hinges, bolts, and glass and lead for windows.

The first company of Maryland colonists was composed of two classes, gentlemen adventurers who intended to take up lands and become planters and lords of manors, and indentured servants who were to serve the ruling class until their indebtedness was discharged, usually about four years. The planters were instructed to "build their houses in as decente and uniforme a manner as their abilities and the place will afford, and neere adjoyning one to an other, and for that purpose to cause streets to be marked out where they intend to place the towne, and to oblige every man to buyld one by another according to that rule . . ."[1] On the backs of the

135

house plots, gardens were to be laid out, and the planters were told to employ their servants to plant corn and other commodities.

Lord Baltimore conceived of the main town in his province as being a small part of mediaeval England transplanted to the New World, with houses, streets, gardens, and a society modeled after the English class system. He dreamed of English lords ruling in baronial splendor, but time proved that a feudal atmosphere was hard to create in the New World. Cecilius' instructions were uppermost in the mind of his brother Leonard Calvert, whom he appointed his deputy governor of the colony, when Captain Henry Fleete guided the two vessels into a convenient harbor in a tributary of the Potomac River on March 27, 1634. There they founded a town called St. Mary's.

When Leonard Calvert landed, the site on a high bluff overlooking the river, which had been partially cleared of trees, was a thriving village of peaceful, Algonkian-speaking Indians known as the Yoacomacoes. Recognizing that it would be far easier to make a beginning for his brother's colony on land already cleared, instead of laboriously reducing a forested area, Calvert negotiated with the hospitable sachem of the Yoacomacoes, and for an assortment of metal axes, hoes, hatchets, and cloth, brought approximately thirty miles of land along the river which included the entire Indian town. It was agreed that the Indian families would immediately vacate some of their wigwams which would then be occupied by the Englishmen. Temporarily the Indians would continue to occupy part of the town, but after their harvest (their corn had already been planted), they would move away leaving the entire village area to the English.[2]

This was more of a gesture of hospitality than a sacrifice on the part of the Yoacomacoes, who were accustomed to move from one location to another, and could readily construct new wigwams wherever they decided to settle. The sachem, in fact, lived in a second village on the other side of the river from the site Calvert had selected, and the Indian families who gave their wigwams to the English were welcome to join him there. One thing the Indians had in plenty was land—like the air it was everywhere, and their wigwams could be built on short notice. Furthermore, the Yoacomacoes had been subject to attack by an enemy nation, the Susquehannock, and had already resolved to move their towns in the fall to a less vulnerable position further upstream.

During the several months the English and Indians shared the facilities of the Indian town, the hospitality of the Yoacomacoes was shown in many ways. The Indian women taught the English how to grind corn into flour in stone mortars, and how to make pone and the various other Indian corn dishes. The Indian hunters showed the Englishmen how to track down deer and hunt wild turkeys in the surrounding woods, and taught them their manner of netting fish and gathering clams and oysters in the bay and rivers. In return the English gave the Yoacomacoes beads, bangles, and baubles that they had brought from Europe, and to which the Indians attached greater value than their monetary worth.

One of the wigwams in the Indian town became St. Mary's first Catholic church, according to Father Andrew White, a member of the expedition, and the first Superior of the Maryland Mission of the Society of Jesus. He wrote, "In one of these houses we now doe celebrate [the Mass] haveing it dressed a little better then by the Indians, till we get a better, which shall be shortly as may be." [3] Cecilius Calvert would probably have been as astonished to witness the sacred rituals of the Catholic Church exemplified in a primitive bark hut built by pagan Indians, as he would have been to see English gentlemen huddled on the earth floor of the wigwams brewing tea over an open fire whose smoke escaped through a hole in the roof. But it wasn't long before brickmakers were at work in the colony, and within three or four years a brick chapel, eighteen by thirty feet, was built, and there a few Indian converts were baptized and mass celebrated in less pagan surroundings.

Since there were insufficient wigwams in the Yoacomaco town to house the entire English company, some of the gentlemen continued to live on shipboard as the house-building program got under way on the shore. Trees were felled, and planks, beams, and clapboards produced to build a "court of guard" (guard house) as well as a storehouse for stocking supplies and provisions. Work was then started on the fort and private residences, and some of the indentured servants were assigned to plant Indian corn and the vegetable and fruit seeds that had been brought from England. The Maryland colonists had the good fortune to have the well-established Virginia colony close by, and hogs, poultry, and cows were obtained from the colonists at Jamestown, and a water mill was erected for grinding the corn into flour.

After reviewing the contemporary source material, a well-informed student of Maryland's architectural history concluded that Maryland's first fort at St. Mary's was built along the same design as the fort erected by the cavaliers at Jamestown. It consisted of a palisade one hundred twenty yards square with four flankers or bastions at the corners. He believed that what was probably used in the residential architecture was "timber-framed construction common at Jamestown in their period." He emphasized that he had not discovered a single, original historical reference to log houses at St. Mary's in the first half of the seventeenth century.[4] This absence of documentation has nevertheless not deterred a number of other writers from making positive, but erroneous statements, that log houses were built by Maryland's first English settlers.[5]

It goes without saying—in view of what has already been presented in this volume—that if the Maryland colonists had been disposed to log cabin construction they would not have lived for months in crude Indian huts, surrounded as they were by many kinds of trees and having tools at their disposal. They suffered this inconvenience only as a temporary measure until they could build the kind of houses they knew in the mother country, as instructed by Lord Baltimore. Fortunately, there exist two contemporary references to the type of dwellings built at St. Mary's after the Indian wigwams were vacated. The first is found in a letter written from St. Mary's on April 16, 1638 by Thomas Cornwallis, one of Lord Baltimore's commissioners and for many years the chief military officer in the colony. I have supplied the italic:

. . . I am building A house toe put my head in, of sawn Timber framed A story and a half high, with A seller and Chimnies of brick toe Encourage others toe follow my Examples for *hithertoe wee Live in Cottages.*[6]

A "cottage" to the English at this date meant a wigwam, a crude hut, or some other frail structure unrelated to a log cabin. When Colonel Norwood's party, marooned on the Eastern Shore of Maryland in 1650, were rescued by Indians, Norwood referred to the wigwam of an Indian fisherman as "this poor man's *cottage* which was made of nothing but mat and reeds and the bark of trees fix'd to poles." Thomas Cornwallis obviously meant the Indian wigwams in which the Maryland colonists were first sheltered when he used the word "Cottages."

The second reference, occurring a number of years later, is found in Lord Baltimore's report to the Lords of the Committee of Trade and Plantations on March 26, 1678. Therein he stated that Maryland's principal town was St. Mary's, and except for his own dwelling and public buildings, there were about thirty houses "very meane and Little and Generally after the manner of the meanest farme houses in England." [7] He used the word "meane" in the sense of humble, unimposing, or of low quality, which aptly described the timber-framed houses constructed by his colonists.

Shurtleff stated that he had found only one authentic contemporary reference to a log structure in seventeenth century Maryland. Dated 1663, he cited it as one of five documented references known to him of log buildings in the full sweep of the English colonies during the seventeenth century. It refers to a proposal to build a jail in what is now Cecil County, but what was then Baltimore County, and reads, in part, as follows: ". . . be it Enacted . . . that there be a Logg House Prison Twenty Foot Square Built at Augustine Harmans in Batlemore [sic] County."

This structure was probably of the type the English usually called a blockhouse, possibly built of squared logs along the lines of some of the garrison houses previously described.[8] In this connection, *Block House Cove* was an early name given to a creek or cove of Humphrey's (Sparrow's Creek), and the name *Block House Creek* was cited in a Maryland land survey of 1681.[9] One may speculate that the structures from which these places apparently derived their names may also have been of logs, although block houses were also built of other materials.

The Maryland log jail was by no means unique since many jails in the early American colonies were built of logs laid horizontally and usually, but not always, squared. In 1680 there was a log house jail in North Carolina; in 1682 a "Convenient Logg House" was built as a jail in Burlington, New Jersey; Philadelphia's first prison, as the reader will find in a later chapter, was of logs; in Georgia, for a time, the term "Logg-House" was almost synonymous with prison and used as one uses the word "hoosegow."[10] There was also a log jail in New Hampshire in 1699, where log cabins at the time were scarce or nonexistent, and other examples could probably be cited.

As the Maryland colony grew, settlers of non-English origin left New Sweden on the Delaware for various reasons and settled in Maryland's tidewater area. As early as 1655 the Swedish governor, Johan Rising, was complaining in reports to his superiors that Swedes had deserted the colony and fled to Maryland, and he specifically referred to two men who deserted their wives and children to go to the neighboring province. After the Dutch seized control of the Swedish colony, a number of Swedes and Finns recruited for military duty at Fort Casimir (present New Castle) deserted the garrison and ran away to Maryland. Abraham, the Finn, fled to Maryland taking his Dutch paramour with him, and others unable or unwilling to pay taxes demanded by the Dutch government left the Delaware to settle in Lord Baltimore's colony. Several Indian traders from the Delaware also moved to Maryland to live, including Jacob Young, who eloped with the young wife of the Lutheran pastor, Larentius Carolus Lokenius, in 1661, and Godfrey Harmer who settled in Gunpowder Neck, Baltimore County, now Harford County.[11] A number of Finnish families moved from the Delaware colony to set themselves up as farmers along the Sassafras River on Maryland's eastern shore.

Lord Baltimore encouraged this movement of aliens into his province through the issuance of a declaration July 2, 1649, authorizing his governor to grant lands to non-English and non-Irish immigrants, although the foreigners were not given the political rights of Englishmen. A number of years later several parties of non-English settlers, who had taken advantage of Lord Baltimore's offer, appeared before members of the Maryland Council asking that they be naturalized and given full citizenship rights inasmuch as they had long been property owners in the colony. In October of 1671, Hans Hansun "born in Delaware Bay of Swedish parents," asked to be naturalized.[12]

In June of 1674 a group of residents who petitioned the Council for naturalization included eleven men all born in Sweden, among whom were such familiar Scandinavian names as Axell Stille, Marcus Syserson, Mounts Anderson, Cornelius Peterson, etc. One Hans Peterson, born in Denmark, was also a petitioner at this time; on another occasion John Elexon and Andrew Toulson, both born in Sweden, also requested citizenship, pointing out they had lived in Maryland for some years.[13]

These newcomers—as well as those from other countries—introduced alien cultural influences in what had hitherto been, with a few exceptions, a strictly English society, and the Swedes and Finns brought with them the concept of log housing, the typical form of residential structures constructed by their countrymen in the nearby Delaware River colony. Thus, one would expect to find scattered references to log dwellings in Maryland once this cultural interaction was set into play, and there are a number which Shurtleff overlooked, and which are cited chronologically below. The contemporary documents leave not a scintilla of doubt that Swedes and Finns had early contact with the English of Maryland, and it naturally follows that their log work spread from New Sweden into the neighboring province. One is tantalized by these documentary references because they are of such brevity that they reveal little typological detail and even the sites of the structures cannot be precisely identified. The names of the builders in most cases is a mystery nor is there any way of knowing how long the houses survived.

For instance, an entry in the court records of Charles County, Maryland in 1662 refers appositively to the residence of a planter named John Neville as a "loged hows," and another named Richard Roe is also described as living in a "loged hows." [14] Although the litigation took place in 1662, the events in the case actually transpired in 1658, at which time both log structures were standing. One would like to be able to introduce convincing evidence that a "logged house" in this early period of Maryland's history had direct and specific reference to what we would now call a log cabin, but such proof has not been forthcoming. Yet in the adjective use of the noun "log," years before the term log cabin came into popularity, one has the impression that the respondents had coined a term with identical meaning.

An entry in the same court records for 1663 refers to "giles glovers loged house."[15] Giles Glover was a carpenter who lived at "Portobaco" in Charles County, and one might infer that the log house may have been his own handiwork. If so—and if he were an Englishman as his name suggests—perhaps he had tried to imitate a log dwelling built by one of his non-English neighbors.

In 1680, a blustering Irish kinsman of the Calverts, George Talbot, obtained a patent for a tract of land known as "Susquehanna Manor." To protect his property, as well as the unsettled boundary of Maryland then disputed by William Penn, Talbot, about 1684 or 1685, erected a number of small log redoubts along his property line. The description of one of these miniscule strongholds, situated at Christiana Bridge in an area occupied and previously claimed by Swedes, has been preserved in a manuscript reference. It was, according to a contemporary observer, "a little house built of Round logs about twelve foot square with a few Punchins or Split pieces of Wood before the Door . . . the house was often called Talborts fort." Another deponent said "it seemed to be Called so by way of a joke for it was a poor little thing not worth above forty shillings." [16]

The following two Maryland references are more specific, and it should be noted that both refer to log dwellings containing lofts:

On August 17, 1693, a contract was drawn up between Michael Judd and John Oglesby, both of Baltimore County, to supersede a previous contract whereby Oglesby agreed to build four houses for Judd. In the more recent document it was agreed between the two principals that a log house be completed according to the following specifications: ". . . the said logg house being twenty foot in length & fifteen foot in width in the inside and to cover and lay the loft & to make a door sufficient to the said house and sufficiently to cover the same." [17] The site of this log house was in Gunpowder Neck, lying between Bush River and Gunpowder River.

In 1694 a deposition was made by Katharine Lomax, a runaway servant, who found refuge at the log house of Thomas Heath in the fork of Gunpowder River between the mouths of the Great and Little Falls of that river. She deposed that Heath said to her, "Your master will not think you are here. Then he asked me if I would eate any vitell and he went into the log house and sent me out some vittles by his doughter and then I went to work along with them to digging in the pese." A day or two later one Robert Bright came to Heath's farm and inquired about the girl who was then in hiding "in the log house loft." [18]

Reference to an old log dwelling house standing in the eighteenth century, but obviously built in the previous century, occurs in an assessment made by Roger Matthews and Thomas Cord of the properties of Susannah Utie, daughter and heiress of the deceased George Utie and Mary Utie. One of the tracts called "Uties Addition" lay in that part of Harford County which was erected out of the northeastern part of Baltimore County, and specifically lay across the neck between Rumley or Romney Creek and Chesapeake Bay about eight and one-half miles in a direct line southwest from present Bear Point, the extreme southern end of Spesutia Island.

Although the assessment was made in 1703, the wording leaves no doubt that the log dwelling was erected some years before. It reads, in part, as follows, with italic added:

"We also find upon another tenament called Uties Addition whereon Mr. Mark Richardson lives at Rumley Creek one twenty-five foot logged dwelling house with a shedd on one side and one other dwelling house thirty foot long and 20 foot wide *both old and ready to fall*, etc." [19]

In summation, the references to John Nevill's logged house; Giles Glover's logged house; Richard Roe's logged house; Talbot's log fort; the log house to be built in Gunpowder Neck; the log house containing a loft in the fork of Gunpowder River; the aged Utie logged dwelling; and the log house prison leave no doubt that log housing was known in Maryland in the seventeenth century. These examples all occur in the latter half of the century long after the St. Mary's settlement was well established and during the period when the colony was beginning to feel the influences of the Swedes and Finns in the nearby settlements on the Delaware River.

Direct personal contact by Marylanders who travelled to the Delaware River settlements, like Colonel Nathaniel Utie and his party who came to New Amstel in 1659 to warn the settlers that they were seated on land claimed by Lord Baltimore; and contact by Swedes who visited Maryland, like the mission sent by Governor Printz in 1651 with letters of friendship for the Maryland government, contributed to this cultural interchange. The influence became even stronger when Swedish colonists, soldiers, and traders moved to Maryland to live. Yet, one should not magnify it, for the Swede-Finn influence was not a strong and persistent one, and it was felt only in the tidewater area of Maryland. Not until the eighteenth and nineteenth centuries were log dwellings and log farm buildings constructed in large numbers in the central and western parts of the state, particularly the mountain counties of Garrett, Alleghany, and Washington, as well as the Piedmont counties, especially Frederick and Carroll. Hagerstown, for example, in 1775 was a town of two hundred dwellings, some of stone and brick, "but the greater Part of the Houses are built with Logs neatly squared." [20] In 1811, Sir Augustus J. Foster made a trip on horseback from Washington, D.C., to Harpers Ferry; after leaving Montgomery Court House, present Rockville, on the road to Frederick, he noted, "The Cottages are universally made of Logs and small." [21]

Other contemporary diaries and journals contain references to the log housing that spread to Maryland, and a rich log cabin tradition has been preserved in the state.[22] A number of fine examples still remain which are deserving of detailed study since Maryland's log housing is still largely unchronicled and no systematic investigation has yet been made (see Figure 33). The log dwellings at Frostburg, Clearspring, Flintstone, Grantsville, Lukins, Hagerstown, on Polish Mountain; in Harford County, and elsewhere, many of which I have seen and photographed, were largely a product of the movement of German and Scotch-Irish families into Maryland, which will shortly be discussed.

Figure 33. Log barn, Harford County, Maryland, built circa 1832, which shows influence of the Pennsylvania Germans who settled in Maryland.

NOTES—CHAPTER 6

1. "Instructions to the Colonists by Lord Baltimore, 1663," *Narratives of Early Maryland,* ed. Clayton Hall (New York, 1910), 22.

2. "Father White's Briefe Relation," *ibid.,* 42.

3. *Ibid.,* 44.

4. Henry Chandlee Forman, *Jamestown and St. Mary's* (Baltimore, 1938), 198.

5. *Ibid.,* fn. 13, p. 197, lists erroneous statements about Maryland settlers living in log cabins made by Wilstach, Ives, Thomas, and Andrews. To these the present writer regretfully adds William Hand Browne, *Maryland, The History of a Palatinate* (Boston, 1895), 165; I. Marshall Page, *Old Buckingham by the Sea on the Eastern Shore of Maryland* (Philadelphia, 1936), 13; Edward Noble Vallandigham, *Delaware and the Eastern Shore* (Philadelphia, 1922), 85.

6. *Calvert Papers,* I, No. 28 (1889), 138, Maryland Historical Society Fund Publication. As early as 1634 bricks were being made at St. Mary's, see "A Relation of Maryland," *Narratives,* 81. In *Maryland Archives,* I, 538, there is a description of a house to be built in 1665 having a hip roof, tile or shingled, and a brick cellar.

7. *Maryland Archives,* VIII, 266.

8. *Maryland Archives,* II, 224; *cf.* Shurtleff (*The Log Cabin Myth*), 128; also Forman, *op. cit.,* 293.

9. Wm. B. Marye, "Place-Names of Baltimore and Harford Counties," *Maryland Historical Magazine,* XXV, No. 4 (Dec. 1930), 345–346.

10. Francis B. Johnston and Thomas T. Waterman, *The Early Architecture of North Carolina* (Chapel Hill, 1941), 5; Frederick D. Nichols and Francis B. Johnston, *The Early Architecture of Georgia* (Chapel Hill, 1957), 26.

11. Wm. B. Marye, "The Early History of The Site of Havre de Grace," *Maryland Historical Magazine,* XIII, No. 3, Sept. 1918, 197; see C. A. Weslager, *The English on the Delaware* (New Brunswick, N.J.), Chapter 11, fn. 9.

12. *Maryland Archives, Proceedings of the Assembly, 1666–1676,* 331. Baltimore's declaration occurs in *ibid., Proceedings of the Council, 1636–1667,* 231–233.

13. *Op. cit., Proceedings,* 1666–1676, 282, 400.

14. *Maryland Archives,* LIII, 232, 381–382.

15. *Ibid.,* 356, 357. I am indebted to Dr. George B. Scriven for bringing these references to my attention.

16. I am indebted to Professor A. R. Dunlap for calling to my attention these depositions made in 1735 and found in the Penn Manuscripts, Historical Society of Pennsylvania, liber 15, folio 165 ff. The log fort was in ruins when the depositions were taken.

17. Baltimore County Court Proceedings, June Court, 1694, folio 338, Hall of Records, Annapolis. Wm. B. Marye brought this reference to my attention as well as the following one.

18. *Ibid.*, September Court, 1694, folio 303.

19. Baltimore County Land Records, liber H.W., n2, folio 235; Susannah Utie, report, 1703. Wm. B. Marye kindly furnished this reference and identified the location of the property for me.

20. *Philip Vickers Fithian Journal*, 1775–1776, ed. Robert G. Albion and Leonidas Dodson (Princeton, 1934), 9–10.

21. "Sir Augustus J. Foster in Maryland," ed. Margaret Kinard Latimer, *Maryland Historical Magazine*, XLII, No. 4 (Dec. 1952), 295.

22. Wm. B. Marye in his exhaustive studies of the records of the Land Office of Maryland at Annapolis has brought to my attention several references to log houses which may have been built in the seventeenth century. In the valuation of lands in Baltimore County of the deceased Aquila Price, located on a tributary of Gunpowder River, there is reference to a framed dwelling with "one *old* Logg Kitchen 20 x 16 stone chimney [,] 1 *old* logg smokehouse 20 x 16, logg cornhouse 16 x 12, etc. [August 30, 1774.]"

There was an old log house on a tract called "Matthews Enlargement" on the north side of Romney (or Rumley) Creek in Bush River Neck, Harford County, which was pulled down in 1913.

Patented Certificate No. 394, Baltimore County, for a vast tract called "Arabia Petrea" lying on the north side of Deer Creek in present Harford County, for Charles Carroll, dated 1721, refers to "an *old* logg house."

Patented Certificate No. 5105, Baltimore County, for a tract called "Warrington" on the west side of the mouth of Bush River, for William Rumsey and James Baldwin, dated 1734, refers to "one new and *one old* log house." This was one of three tracts taken up in 1658 by the Indian trader from the Delaware, Godfrey Harmer, and the older dwelling may have been built by him.

"Dixons Neck," a 525-acre tract taken up by John Dixon between Middle River and Back River in Baltimore County contained "an *old* log house 15 foot long and 12 foot wide," referred to in a survey dated 1744.

7 Swedes and Finns on the Delaware

The nucleus of the first Swedish settlements in the Delaware Valley was at Fort Christina, built at a rock outcropping constituting a natural wharf on the western bank of the Christina River at present Wilmington, Delaware. Here Peter Minuit, an ex-governor of the New Netherland who sold his services to Sweden after his recall from his official post on Manhattan Island by the Dutch West India Company, brought the first Swedish expedition in 1638. The area was already claimed by both England and Holland, and the Dutch had made several unsuccessful attempts at colonization.

Minuit was one of several non-Swedes who persuaded Swedish merchants to form a commercial company under the aegis of the Crown and invest in stock in a project aimed at exploiting the resources of the New World, particularly the beaver trade with the Indians. He played a leading role in planning the expedition, selecting the crew, and outfitting two vessels, the *Kalmar Nyckel* and *Fogel Grip*, placed under his command for the first voyage to America.

After sailing up the Delaware River, and entering the mouth of the Christina, Minuit purchased land from the Indians, supervised the building of the fort which he named for Sweden's child queen, and left there as the beginning of a colony a commander and a handful of Swedish and Dutch soldiers. Within the log palisades set in the earth around the fort, Minuit's men built two small houses,

The heart of New Sweden in the Delaware River Valley where the log cabin made its American debut, with the approximate locations of places mentioned in this chapter.

one to serve as a magazine to store ammunition and merchandise for use in the beaver trade with the Susquehannock and Delaware Indians, and the second to be occupied as a communal dwelling place by members of the garrison. Both structures are believed to have been made of logs, with gabled ends, probably roofed with split limbs set close together according to Swedish custom. Five hundred bricks brought from Stockholm were used to construct a fireplace and oven in the dwelling house.

In the spring of 1640, three new log houses were built within the palisaded area of the little fort, one of which was used as a chapel for Lutheran services, and the others for residences as the garrison was reinforced by additional men sent from Sweden. From Fort Christina the Swedes expanded their territory northward to present Marcus Hook and Chester, and across the Delaware to the New Jersey side of the river where their influence was ultimately to be felt in the area from Salem to Trenton. Coincident with this expansion, women and children with their husbands arrived from Sweden in a series of expeditions to increase the population of an indefinitely bounded territory called New Sweden, which included Delaware, parts of New Jersey, and southeastern Pennsylvania.

Because the use of horizontally-laid notched logs, both round and hewn, as an accepted form of settlement housing, made its American debut in New Sweden the area is of utmost importance for a thorough understanding of the origins and diffusion of what came to be known as the American log cabin. Many careless and unsupportable statements have been written about the so-called "Delaware Swedes" or "the Swedish log cabin" by those who have not examined the historical documentation on which this chapter is largely based. Moreover, the typology of the cabins that have survived is consonant with the documentation if these structures are examined as a series in context and not as isolated examples.

At the outset it should be emphasized that of the so-called Swedish settlers in New Sweden approximately *one-half were actually Finns*, a significant fact in tracing the origin of their log housing. Although the country of Finland through Swedish conquest had become part of the Swedish kingdom in the seventeenth century, the language of its people differed both in vocabulary and grammar from the Swedish language, and the cultural background and traditions of the Finns were unlike those of the Swedes despite the acculturative forces that had been brought into play. Among the educated Finns the Swedish language had made some headway, but the peasant classes, who constituted the majority of the settlers, were conversant only in their own language. They considered themselves a breed of people different from the Swedes even though they shared a common government.

Starting about 1580 A.D. and continuing over a period of years some 12,000 to 13,000 Finns, at the instigation of Swedish authorities, moved to the central and western parts of Sweden to settle on lands still untouched by axe or plow. They lived apart from the Swedes, followed their own customs, and spoke their own language. As time went on the Swedes found many of these Finns objectionable for a number of reasons, and to get rid of them they sent many of them to America in what virtually amounted to conscription when the expeditions were organized. A number of the "Swedish" colonists were recruited from Finland itself, and these people had not been directly exposed to the folkways of Sweden.

In the early records of New Sweden one finds such references as Knut Mårtensson from Vasa, Johan Frannson from Viborg, Mats Hansson from Borgå, Karl Jansson from Kexholm, Mårtin Thomasson from Österbotten, Mons Pietersen Staeck from Åbo, etc.[1] Of 105 colonists who came from Sweden in 1655 on the vessel *Mercurius* it was recorded that ninety-two were Finns—a rare instance when the passengers in an expedition were classified.

Swedish became the official language of the church, the school, and the government in New Sweden, and the names of the colonists were always recorded in Swedish, irrespective of whether they were Finns or not. As a result, an individual's ethnic background cannot be determined from his name unless he is specifically identified by his place of origin or with such appellatives appearing in the records as Lars Anderson, the Finn; Mans Mansson, the Finn; Bertil Eskelsson, the Finn; Abraham, the Finn; Askell, the Finn; Karin, the Finnish woman; Jurgin, the Finn on the Crooked Kill; etc. Without these modifiers, there is no certain way of knowing whether an individual named in an early Swedish-American document was of Swedish or Finnish origin. Scribal custom tended to minimize the cultural differences that existed and to leave the impression that Finns and Swedes were culturally one and the same people which is incorrect and ethnically naïve.

Although the rural log housing in parts of Finland in the seventeenth century did not significantly differ from that found in some parts of Sweden, there were definite typological variations in the east Baltic. One would like to be able to point to certain log house traits and say, "This is Finnish, and that is Swedish," but such oversimplification can not be made of a complex subject; at least the writer is unable to do so with certainty. Nevertheless, it should be crystal clear to the reader that prototypes of many of the log dwellings built in New Sweden were actually part of the housing complex of Finland, and this is of utmost significance when one recognizes that the majority of log houses in New Sweden were built by Finns (see Figure 34).

The Finns had a close attunement with the forests, and forest industries in both Finland and Sweden were well developed and extremely important to their respective economies. In the domestic households of Finland, wood from native trees was used for plates, bowls, spoons, forks, ladles, beer jugs with hinged lids and wood spouts, carved molds in which cheese hardened, etc. Birch bark was used to make shoes and baskets; and sleighs, skis, boats, and wagons of wood, as in Sweden, were all part of the economy. Like the Swedes, the Finns were accomplished in building several forms of log housing, having different methods of corner timbering, and they utilized both round and hewn logs. Their log buildings had undergone an evolutionary process from the crude *pirtii* (which the Swedes called *pörts*), a small gabled-roof cabin of round logs with an opening in the roof to vent the smoke, to more sophisticated structures of squared logs with interlocking double-notch joints,

Figure 34. Eighteenth century farmhouse, round logs, double-notch corners, Savo Province, Finland, photographed 1937. Many Delaware Finns came from this province. (Courtesy National Museum of Finland, Helsinki)

the timbers extending beyond the corners.[2] Log *saunas* or bath-houses of this type are still used by families in rural Finland.[3]

In Finland in the seventeenth century, and more so in Sweden, there was also found the hewn log house with the timbers cut off, evened at the corners, and held together by full dovetailing. This corner-timbering method common in the east Baltic was also widely practiced in Russia, Germany, and elsewhere in Central Europe. Finns who later came to Minnesota in the nineteenth century—and who influenced the log housing patterns in Alaska; see page 324— brought this identical method of corner timbering. Therefore, when full dovetailing and flush corners appear on old log dwellings in New Sweden one need not seek its antecedents in Germany or elsewhere in Central Europe when it was clearly a material culture trait of the Scandinavians.

In September of 1655, in dire need of supplies and moral support from Sweden, which did not materialize due to political changes that occurred in the homeland, New Sweden succumbed to a Dutch attack. The Swedish and Finnish population who lived in small, scattered farming settlements on both sides of the Delaware River became subjects of the Dutch. After an English force dispatched by the Duke of York defeated the Dutch in 1664, English customs, language, political, and social concepts began to take root, and with the coming of William Penn in 1682, it wasn't long before English institutions dominated New Sweden.

By 1819, the Swedish Baron Klinkowström observed during a visit to the Delaware River towns where many Swedish and Finnish descendants still lived, "Now our language is forgotten; the English laws have forced out the Swedish [laws] and there is no other trace of the oldest settlers except a few names of towns and country places and here and there some evidences of our building methods." [4] Klinkowström had reference to the log house techniques of Swedes and Finns which outlasted their language and political system.

When the Dutch took over New Sweden—and later the English —both were impressed with the proficiency of Swedes and Finns in the use of an axe. Thomas Paschall, an Englishman who purchased land along the upper Delaware, was so stirred by the axe skills of his Scandinavian neighbors that he wrote in 1683, the Swedish cabin builder could "cut down a Tree and cut him off when down sooner than two [English] men can saw him." [5] A Swede, he said, could fell twelve of the biggest Pennsylvania oak trees in a single day, and like most Englishmen who didn't know the difference, he used the word "Swede" in a generic meaning to include Finns.

"As they are People proper and strong of Body," William Penn wrote of the Swedes and Finns settled on the tributaries of the Delaware, "so they have fine Children, and almost every house full; rare to find one of them without three or four Boys, and as many Girls; some six, seven, and eight Sons: And I must do them that right, I see few Young men more sober and laborious."

Other English, as well as Dutch settlers, could not help but be

impressed by the industry of the Scandinavians and the log complex
that characterized their housing patterns, for, in addition to dwelling houses and forts, the Swede-Finns used logs to build storehouses, stables, bathhouses, mills, schools, and churches.

An interesting and unusual documentary note about log construction appears in the 1650 edition of a pamphlet published in England
entitled, *A Description of the Province of New Albion*, extolling
the virtues of a tract of land in America patented to Sir Edmund
Plowden by Charles I in 1634. The seat of the colony Plowden intended to establish in New Albion was a place known to the Indians
as *Watcessit* at or near present Salem, New Jersey. This was on territory claimed by Sweden as part of New Sweden, and where, by
1650, Swedes and Finns had built log cabins. In the updated 1650
edition of the pamphlet there appears a page describing six types of
dwellings which prospective English colonists could readily build
in New Albion, and one of the suggested houses was: "A log house
of young trees 30 foot square notched in at the corners."

Since this reference to a log house did not appear in the 1641
or 1648 editions of the pamphlet, it is apparent that the author had
become aware of the existence of log dwellings on the Delaware
prior to publishing the new text. So far as I am aware this is the
only reference in a seventeenth century English colonization tract
to a log house, and there can be little doubt that it reflects the influence of the Scandinavians.[6] The question is purely academic because Sir Edmund Plowden's New Albion was never colonized, and
the Earl Palatine died without fulfilling his ambition to become the
proprietor of a New World province.

In contrast to the scarcity of log cabin references in the contemporary literature of Virginia, New York, and New England, there
are a number of specific references to log structures in the seventeenth century records of New Sweden. This documentation is invaluable to the historian because it is confirmation (even if no
buildings had survived in evidence) that the emigrants from Sweden
and Finland did, in fact, transfer to America the techniques of the
vernacular log construction of their fatherlands. Although the lack

of details regarding typology is admittedly disappointing, it is historically of significance that during the adminstration of Johan Printz, New Sweden's most prominent governor (1643–1653), and immediately following, there is record of the following structures of logs, none of which remain today: [7]

Fort New Gothenburg on Tinicum Island, "a strong fort made of [round?] hemlock logs laid upon the other," built by Governor Printz when he moved the seat of the government from Fort Christina to Tinicum Island. (It was later moved back to Fort Christina by his successor, Governor Johan Rising who also built a log dwelling as his residence.)

Printzhoff (Printz Hall) on Tinicum Island, constructed in 1644 by Printz as his gubernatorial mansion, built of hewn logs, two stories high, referred to by Campanius as "a handsome mansion." Twelve men constructed it in eight days. Nearby stood a log storehouse on the land side of the island.

Swedish Lutheran Church on Tinicum Island, erected in 1646 of notched logs, having a clapboard roof. Nearby were built a number of small log cabins occupied by the parishioners.

Bathhouse on Tinicum Island, made of logs, built in 1644 for the use of Governor Printz and his family. Within this Swedish-type bathhouse, or *bastu*, water was poured on hot stones, and there the family sat unclothed and sweated in the steam arising from the stones. After a period of exposure to the heat the bathers ran from the building and plunged into the cold creek water. This routine was followed periodically in the winter as well as summer.

Fort Nya Korsholm on the Schuylkill River, "a fine little fort of logs, having sand and stone filled in between the woodwork, and surrounded by the palisades," built in 1647–1648 to protect the path used by the Susquehannock Indians in the beaver trade with the Swedes.

Log Blockhouse at Upland (present Chester), built in 1643, Printz described it as a "strong wooden house," and it was probably built along the same lines as Fort Nya Korsholm. It was later used as a courthouse.

Fort Vasa at Kingsessing (near Philadelphia), "not properly a fort, but substantial log houses, built of good strong hard hickory, *two stories high.*"

Grist Mill on Cobbs Creek, built in 1646 of logs, and in the adjacent Swedish community called *Molndal* there were a number of small dwelling houses built of hickory logs. Other so-called "Swedish Mills" built of logs were constructed on other suitable mill streams in New Sweden. (John Staelcop, Lucas Pieterson, and Hans Block built a mill on the Turtle-Kil (Shellpot Creek) in 1662 probably according to old types, although the structure is not described.)

Crane Hook Church (near Wilmington), a little church of logs resting on large rocks at each corner serving as foundation stones. Built in 1667, it served the Swedish congregation until 1699 when Old Swedes (Holy Trinity) Church built of stone was consecrated.

Wicaco Blockhouse (in Philadelphia), built of logs in 1699 on the site of the present Gloria Dei Church. Originally it was "a log house of defense," later converted for religious use.

The above references could probably be augmented by others, but they are ones I have gleaned from seventeenth century documents in which specific or inferential reference to logs occurs. The Swedish scribes quite naturally did not feel it necessary to give lengthy descriptions of a mode of construction that was common in Sweden and Finland, whereas log housing was an oddity to persons of other national origins who gave more details. In 1679–1680, two Dutchmen, Jaspar Dankers and Peter Sluyter, were in America looking for a colony for a sectist group called Labadists. En route from New York to New Castle, Delaware, they stopped overnight in a log house in New Jersey near present Burlington. Excerpts from their description of this dwelling have often been cited, but I am giving the complete passage below:

> The house, although not much larger than where we were the last night, [they spent the previous night in an English clapboarded cottage which was cold and uncomfortable] was somewhat better and tighter, being made according to the Swedish mode, and as they usually build their houses here, which are block-houses, being nothing else than entire trees,

split through the middle, or squared out of the rough, and placed in the form of a square, upon each other, as high as they wish to have the house; the ends of these timbers are let into each other, about a foot from the ends, half of one into half of the other. The whole structure is thus made, without a nail or spike. The ceiling and roof do not exhibit much finer work, except among the most careful people, who have the ceiling planked and a glass window. The doors are wide enough, but very low, so that you have to stoop in entering. These houses are quite tight and warm; but the *chimney is placed in a corner*. My comrade and myself had some deer skins, spread upon the floor to lie on, and we were, therefore, quite well off, and could get some rest. It rained hard during the night and snowed and froze. . . .[8]

This description applies to one form of the Swedish log house in which the hewn logs extended beyond the corner of the dwelling, but the owner, Jacob Hendricks, in the words of the Dutchmen was "from Holstein," and the dwelling may have reflected craft culture other than Swedish or Finnish. The description should not be interpreted to mean that it was the *only* kind of log house built in New Sweden, nor that it was necessarily typical, because the evidence is incontrovertible that the Swedes and Finns living in the Delaware Valley also built houses of round logs as well as those of hewn logs squared at the corners.

The placement of the fireplace in a corner appears to have been a characteristic trait of the earliest Swedish log houses, as it was in the crude log *pörts*, and in some, but not all, of the more sophisticated hewn log dwellings built by Finns.

The botantist, Peter Kalm, who visited the Delaware Valley in 1749 adds further details about the log dwellings built by the first settlers, also calling attention to the corner placement of chimney and fireplace in the earliest log houses, which I have italicized below:

The houses which the Swedes built when they first settled here were very poor. The whole house consisted of one little room, the door of which was so low that one was obliged to stoop in order to get in. As they brought no glass with them they were obliged to be content with little holes before which a moveable board was fastened. They found no moss, or at least none which would have been serviceable in stopping up holes or cracks in the walls. They were therefore forced to close them using clay both inside and out. *The chimneys were masoned in a corner, either of gray stone (or in places where there were no stones) of mere clay, which they laid very thick in one corner of the house* [9] [see Figure 35].

Kalm was undoubtedly correct in saying that the Swedish log cabins lacked glass windows, but he was in error in stating that no glass was brought to New Sweden. Governor Printz transported glass window panes with him on the *Fama* in 1644 which were installed at Printzhoff, but it was a commodity that poor Swedish and Finnish farmers could not then afford. The above description from Dankers and Sluyter indicates that by 1679–1680 some of the better log cabins had glass windows.

There are a number of documentary references to specific log dwellings built along the Delaware in the seventeenth century either by Swedes and Finns, or other settlers under the direct influence:

In 1659, the Dutch vice-director, Jacob Alricks, who then had all the Swedish and Finnish population under his jurisdiction, reported that a house of squared timbers fifty by twenty-two feet had been built at New Amstel (present New Castle), as well as a burgher watchhouse of logs twenty feet square, roofed with tiles. The tiles represented a Dutch trait superimposed on Scandinavian log construction—no tiles were used on log house roofing in Sweden and Finland at this time.

A deed dated December 20, 1675, reciting the sale of land along St. Georges Creek in New Castle County, Delaware, refers to a log house; a deposition made in 1792 by an elderly Wilmington woman of Swedish descent refers to an old log house that formerly stood on property in Wilmington patented to Dr. Tyman Stedham, one of the early Swedish settlers; and a deed of sale in the town of New Castle dated 1687 indicates that the property was bounded on the southwest by an old log house.[10]

The court records of Chester County, Pennsylvania (originally part of New Sweden), contain a reference dated 1686 to "the logg house of Jeremy Collett," and a petition dated 1696 refers to a road in Oxford Township being "neer Jno Wells Log House." [11] A court entry in 1678 refers to the building of a log house near Salem, New Jersey.[12] The Swede, Lasse Cock, prior to 1685 built a log house on present Second Street in Philadelphia which was intended to be used by the Quaker authorities as a jail, but, in lieu of £60 owed him for the job, they gave him the structure since they found it insufficient for its intended purpose.[13]

Future documentary research may reveal other examples, but these will suffice to make the point that the log house was a familiar dwelling in New Sweden. Like the pioneer families who settled the western frontier many years later, the Swedes and Finns intended their one-room cabins as provisional homes, to be replaced at a later date with larger and more commodious houses. The Swedish pastor, Israel Acrelius, writing in 1750 in New Sweden said of the area that fifty years before, "Then respectable families lived in low log-houses, where the chimney was made of sticks and covered with clay; now they erect painted houses of stone and brick in the country." [14]

Acrelius's reference to stick-clay chimneys dismisses any notion one might have that the first cabin builders in the Delaware Valley were so exacting that they were satisfied only with brick or stone chimneys. It also indicates that the stick-clay chimney was part of the earliest log cabin complex in America, long before chimneys of such materials appeared on the so-called pioneer log cabins—just as the double-unit log house made its first American appearance along the Delaware. (See description of Morten Mortenson house below.)

It should not come as a surprise to the reader that bricks were very scarce during the early period of New Sweden; bricks had to be imported from Sweden and the supply was so limited the peasant farmer had no alternative except to use other building materials. When the Dutch took over control of New Sweden they imported both boards and bricks from Fort Orange on the Hudson until they were able to build the first brick kiln on the Delaware, which was in operation in 1659.

There are numerous references to log houses in eighteenth century Delaware and New Jersey newspapers, and although there is no way of knowing when these houses were built there can be little question that some of them date back to the previous century. Typical of the many newspaper notices is an advertisement in the *Delaware Gazette* on January 10, 1798, describing property for sale in Pencader Hundred, New Castle County, on which there were *seven* log dwellings on adjoining parcels. In the December 1, 1792, edition of the same newspaper a log and frame house, and a log barn, on George Read's lands a mile from Newport were advertised for sale; and in the July 3, 1799, edition an advertisement appeared seeking buyers for a 160-acre farm in New Castle Hundred containing a log dwelling and a log barn. A complete search of the *Delaware Gazette* and other contemporary newspapers in Delaware would produce a long list of log houses offered for sale.

Advertisements from New Jersey newspapers for the period from 1742 to 1782 have been reprinted in the second series of the published *New Jersey Archives*. Typical of the numerous advertisements making reference to log structures are these: On March 21, 1780 property for sale in Morris County, two miles north of Hibernia furnace contained "a good log-house 24 x 20 feet." On March 17, 1780, fifty-two acres offered for sale in Greenwich Township, Sussex County, at Chelsea Forge included "a number of log houses sufficient for accomodating the hands necessary for carrying on the works." On December 11, 1780, a mill and lands on Waiding River in Burlington County which contained "two Log Houses for tenants" was put up for sale, and property advertised at sheriff sale on May 12, 1776 in Upper Penn's Neck, Salem County consisted of ninety-two acres "with a log dwelling house." There are, of course, many others.

Professor Peter O. Wacker of Rutgers University plotted all the advertised log houses in New Jersey on a map, concluding that the greatest cluster was in the southwestern portion of the state, well within the sphere of Swedish and Finnish influence. There was also a "generally continuous distribution of log structures up the Delaware Valley and into the Highlands." [15]

Log schoolhouses remained part of the architectural pattern in Delaware, and in 1728, the Rev. William Beckett wrote of the inhabitants of Sussex County, Delaware that the general custom is

to hire a Person for a certain Term and Sum to teach their Children to read and write English. For whose accomodation they meet together at a place agreed upon, cut down a Number of Trees, and build a Log House in a few hours, as illustrious as that in which Pope Sixtus Quintus was born, whither they send their children every day during the Term. . . .[16]

In 1876, there were still three old log schools in use in Delaware according to the first annual report of the Superintendent of Free Schools. None exists today, nor do I know of any log schools extant either in New Jersey or southeastern Pennsylvania.

In 1804, the taxables in Mill Creek Hundred, New Castle County, Delaware lived in twenty-one brick houses, forty-eight stone houses, and ninety-nine log houses.[17] Frame houses were not mentioned in this particular tax list, but they were doubtless very scarce in this farming area. The predominance of log houses is significant, and one can be certain that some of these ninety-nine log dwellings were built in the seventeenth century by Swedes and Finns.

In the holdings of the Historical Society of Delaware is a manuscript tax list for Christiana Hundred, New Castle County, *circa* 1797–1798. This hundred which adjoined Mill Creek Hundred included part of the then Borough of Wilmington and among its population were many descendants of the Swedes and Finns of New Sweden. The tax list unfortunately is not complete, but I abstracted from it a count of ninety log houses, six log and stone houses, two stone and log taverns, fifty-nine stone houses, twenty-seven brick houses, six frame houses, one stone and brick house, and approximately fifteen houses not described. The tax list also enumerates fifty-two log barns and stables.

Of particular interest are the names of some of the owners of log houses in Christiana Hundred, *e.g.*, Jonas Stedham, David Stedham, Isaac Stedham, Cornelius Stedham, and John Stedham (descendants of the Swedish physician, Dr. Tymen Stedham). Peter Walraven and Walraven Walraven (descendants of Walraven Jansen de Vos) lived in log houses, as did Charles Springer (descendant of a prominent seventeenth century Swede of the same name). The latter also owned a stone and log tavern with a small log barn on the property. Peter Hendrickson, another Swedish descendant, also owned a public tavern made of stone and logs.

In the Christiana Hundred tax list, the word "old" appears alongside many of the entries of log houses and barns, which suggests they may have been built—and probably were—in the previous century. By combining the number of houses for both Mill Creek and Christiana Hundreds, as revealed by the two tax lists, which are incomplete to be sure, it would appear that at the turn of the eighteenth century perhaps 40 percent to 50 percent of the houses in this area of northern Delaware were of logs, many built in the previous century when log house traditions were first introduced by Swedes and Finns.

In the holdings of the Chester County Historical Society at West Chester, Pennslyvania, is a series of original manuscripts, and microfilmed copies of manuscripts deposited in the National Archives, listing direct tax assessment lists for Chester and Delaware Counties, Pennsylvania, in 1798. At that time a federal tax was levied on glass windows, and the assessment lists give the details of the existing houses and other structures, the numbers of windows and "lights" of glass, the names of the owners, and other pertinent data. Hundreds of the existing houses in the two counties are described as being built of logs, many identified as "old" and the nonresidential log buildings include barns, stables, carthouses, spring houses, coopers' shops, tanning house, sheds, etc. Since these two counties were originally part of New Sweden, there can be little question that many of the older log houses still standing in 1798 were built under Swedish and Finnish influences. At that time, incidentally, the assessor tried to distinguish a log cabin from a log house, as indicated in two entries for West Bradford Township. Richard Humpton Esq., was assessed for:

> *1 Log Cabben small*
> *1 old Log House 18 by 18 feet*

Robert Young was assessed for:

> *1 Log Cabben Small*

If one could be transported back in time to the beginning of New Sweden when the first colonists were building their log cabins he might perhaps be disappointed in the quality of these dwellings. It is unlikely that many of the first log cabins were comparable to the finer log homesteads in Sweden where the logs were carefully selected, expertly hewn and planed to leave a smooth exterior surface, interlocked at the corners with exactness, and roofed with precision. The stone and brick fireplaces and chimneys in old Sweden were

Figure 35. Seventeenth-century cabin with loft, near West Chester, Pennsylvania, illustrates one form of crude dwelling, with low doorway in gable end, built by the first Swedes and Finns. Glass windows and frame wing were added later. White oak logs, partially hewn, were V-notched on undersides. Cabin was destroyed to make room for highway by-pass.

skillfully constructed, because the log house builders, except for the displaced Finns, were not frontiersmen in an unsettled new land, and they had the benefit of sawmills and carpenter tools, to say nothing of specializing in a craft culture handed down through the years from one generation to another.

The earliest cabins along the Delaware were hastily built of round, undressed logs by peasant farmers having relatively few tools at their disposal. These cabins, a reversion to an older Scandinavian form, were usually, but not always, saddle notched, had ill-fitted low doors, uneven apertures for windows, and the irregular open spaces between the logs were plugged with red and white clay instead of moss, with a view to utility rather than esthetics. The roofs of the cabins, to which the makeshift clay-stick chimneys were attached, were at first covered with turf, tree limbs, or boards laboriously sawn by hand, and were erected without benefit of square or level.

In view of the apparent primitiveness of so many of the earliest cabins and *pörts*, it is not surprising that so few of the round log structures have survived three centuries in a climate inimical to wood. Over a period of many years, I have thoroughly explored the area of the former New Sweden by automobile, boat, and on foot, in search of seventeenth century log housing, and the cabins that have survived, with a few exceptions, are built of hewn logs. They probably represent structures better than the average to begin with, which is why they have lasted, and some were built by Swedes and Finns during the Dutch period when bricks for fireplaces and chimneys and shingles for roofing became available.

All log cabins, other than those preserved as historic memorials, are becoming rare in the lower Delaware Valley because of the urbanization that has destroyed so many of the colonial buildings. Nevertheless, there are a few interesting examples to be found, and I will confine my remarks to those which tradition or other evidence indicates were built in the seventeenth or early eighteenth centuries. This was the period where one would expect to see the influence of the Swedes and Finns before other cultural waves engulfed the territory of New Sweden.

One of the most notable cabins of the Swedish period, renovated and administered as a memorial by the Pennsylvania Historical and Museum Commission, is located at Prospect Park near Essington, a few miles south of Philadelphia. The earliest section, a dwelling of closely-fitted hewn oak logs, dovetailed and flush at the corners, is believed to have been built by Morten Mortenson in the middle of the seventeenth century. This progenitor of the Morton family in America (including John Morton, the signer of the Declaration of Independence) was not a Swede, as is generally believed. The notice of his death on May 31, 1706, in the records of the Wicaco Church state he was believed to have been almost one-hundred years old, and was *born in Finland*.

A second unit of hewn pine and chestnut logs, also dovetailed and flush at the corners, was built alongside the first at a later date (1698

Figure 36. Morten Mortenson house Essington, Penna., before its reconstruction and renovation. Note low doorway typical of early Swedish-Finnish log cabins and how breezeway between two cabins was walled with stone. (Courtesy Pennsylvania Historical and Museum Commission)

Figure 37. Morten Mortenson house after its renovation showing full dove-tailing flush at corners. Gables have been added as well as doors and windows not in original structures. (Courtesy Pennsylvania Historical and Museum Commission)

is usually given for this unit and 1654 for the earlier one, but I have been unable to substantiate either date), and the two cabins were connected by a passage. The older unit has the characteristic Swedish-Finnish corner fireplace and chimney (see Figures 36, 37).

On the west bank of Darby Creek near Clifton Station, Pennsylvania, there is another seventeenth century log cabin traditionally said to have been erected 1643–1653, but in contrast to the Prospect Park house it is built of round logs. The top ends of the logs are cut in pear shape to mesh with the V notch in the bottom of each log. This dwelling has two rooms, but in reality it was constructed as two cabins butting against each other, and each has the distinctive corner fireplace (see Figure 38). The presence of corner fireplaces in these early cabins appears indicative of their Scandinavian antecedents.

Nearby at Clifton Heights is a second round-log cabin also of Scandinavian origin said to have been erected about 1650. Although this date has not been authenticated, the dwelling is unquestionably a seventeenth century survival. Like the first, it, too, consists of two rooms, although the logs are saddle-notched with their ends extending well beyond the corners of the walls. It has been considerably modified by modern owners through the addition of a new roof, windows, and a front porch (see Figure 39).

Probably the oldest remaining log dwelling in New Jersey sur-

Figure 38. Double cabin of round logs, some partially hewn, meshed at corners with V-notching, with corner chimney, dating from early Swedish period; still standing at Clifton Heights, Delaware County, Pennsylvania, along Darby Creek.

Figure 39. Cabin of round logs, saddle-notched, with corner chimney, built in early Swedish period; still standing at Clifton Heights, Delaware County, Pennsylvania, known as "upper Clifton Heights cabin."

viving from the Swedish period is the Nothnagle House located 2.3 miles northeast of Repaupo on the Paulsboro Road in Gloucester County. Built of hewn oak logs, with full dovetailing and flush corners, it also has the characteristic corner chimney and fireplace. The cabin is now a wing of a later frame dwelling built in several stages, and a common porch has been added which tends to alter the lines of the original cabin (see Figure 40). The one-room log dwelling was built on part of a one-hundred-acre tract which Benjamin Braman purchased from Andrew Robinson in 1686, and it is believed that the original was built by a Swede or Finn around this time. Charles A. Nothnagle, Sr., purchased the property in 1907, and the cabin, still occupied, has been in the Nothnagle family ever since, although much modified.[18]

A small one-room log cabin on the Schorn Farm (also called the Vanleer property) on the north side of Raccoon Creek in Glouces-

Figure 40. Nothnagle Cabin, Paulsboro, Gloucester County, New Jersey, a survival of the Swedish period. Although much modified, corner chimney and fireplace are intact.

ter County, New Jersey, is also believed to be a seventeenth century vestige of the Swedish period. Like the Nothnagle House, the hewn logs are closely fitted, flush at the corners, and notched with full dovetailing. It has no chimney, but it is likely the original chimney was removed when the structure was converted into a farm shed. Tradition has it that this cabin was owned by an abolitionist during the Civil War and was a station for underground activities in bringing slaves to the free North.

The identical method of full dovetailing was the mode of notching used on the Reall Cabin in Alloway Township, Salem County, New Jersey, which was in ruins when I visited it in 1952, and is no longer standing. This dwelling had a shingled roof, a central chimney, an off-center low door, and one window on the front (see Figure 41). A small colony of German glass makers settled in this immediate area in the early eighteenth century, brought by Caspar Wistar, who purchased one hundred acres of land on Alloway Creek where he erected a glass factory and a log residence.[19] It is quite likely that the Reall Cabin may have been erected by one of these Germans, since the central chimney is a trait generally associated with German builders. Nevertheless, the dovetailing is identical with that found on old cabins having corner chimneys, and it is not impossible that German, and Swedish or Finnish traits may have been represented.

The Emmell Cabin, approximately two miles northeast of the town of Alloway in Salem County was in a bad state of disrepair when I last saw it in 1952. It was notched with full dovetailing flush at

Figure 41. Reall Cabin, Alloway Township, Salem County, New Jersey, as it appeared in the 1930's; it is no longer standing. Central chimney is a German trait, and off-center door is often present in such houses. (Courtesy Salem County Historical Society)

Figure 42. Emmell Cabin near Alloway, Salem County, New Jersey, as it appeared in 1936. (Reproduced from the collections of the Library of Congress)

the corners, and was connected first with a one-story frame addition and later with a two-story frame dwelling (see Figure 42). It derives its name from an early owner of the property, Peter Emmell, although like most other New Jersey cabins the date when it was built is uncertain.

Another old log house, also one and one-half stories high, stood fifty yards west of Thompson's Bridge in Alloway Township on the north side of the Alloway-Denton-Salem Road, also notched with full dovetailing and having flush corners. This house had an overhanging roof, an extension of the roof proper to shelter the front door as indicated in the profile sketch in Figure 43. Although the overhanging roof is often associated with German log housing, this mode of construction is also found in Sweden.[20]

Full dovetail notching is also present on a hewn log cabin which formerly stood south of Leesburg in Cumberland County, New Jersey, and was later moved to Johnson Park in Salem where a stone

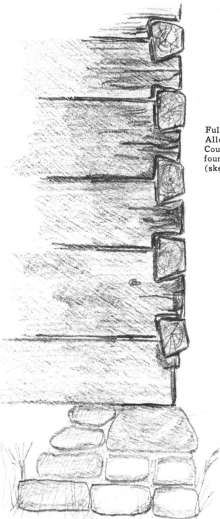

Full dovetailing, log house on n. side
Alloway, Denton, Salem Road, Salem
County, N.J., brick chimney, stone
foundation, overhanging shingled roof
(sketched by the author, 1952).

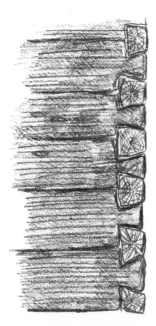

Full dovetailing, Emmell House,
Alloway Twp., Salem County,
N.J., shingled roof, brick chimney
(sketched by the author, 1952).

Figure 43

fireplace and chimney were reinstalled in one of the corners. It has recently been disassembled and removed to the property of the Smithville Inn near Absecon, New Jersey, for reconstruction. Another old cabin of hewn cedar logs having full dovetail corners was re-erected on the grounds of the Hancock House at Hancock's Bridge on Alloways Creek about five miles south of Salem. Currently used as a museum, this reconstructed dwelling formerly stood in the upper Salem County area, and like the Johnson Park log house it, too, is believed to date back to the Swedish occupation. Because both structures have been substantially modified I have not included illustrations of them which might confuse the reader.

In Figure 44 I have shown the Peter Bard Log House at Upper Mill, Burlington County, N.J. Although this house is known to have been built no earlier than 1720 the closely-fitted round logs, which extend beyond the corners of the structure are reminiscent of the

Figure 44. Built 1720 by Peter Bard, round-log cabin of white cedar at Upper Mill, Burlington County, N.J., originally had roof of white cedar slabs, later replaced with shingles. Typology reminiscent of early log dwellings in Sweden.

Figure 45. Main court of open air museum, Zorn Gammelgård, Mora, Sweden, with log houses dating from twelfth to eighteenth centuries. Low house with round entrance built c. 1100 A.D. (Courtesy Erik Forssman, Director)

walls on early Swedish log houses preserved at the Zorn Gammelgård in Mora, Sweden (see Figure 45). The reader can readily discern the differences in the roof construction.

These and other New Jersey houses require more thorough technical study before accurate comparisons and valid conclusions can be drawn. The dimensions, size of logs, nature of wood, and interior layout should all be taken into consideration, but from my observations I have been impressed with the scarcity of round log houses in contrast to the prevalence of hewn log dwellings with full dovetail notching on the surviving log houses in southwestern New Jersey. In this area of New Sweden, I see no reason for not associating this method of corner notching as a material culture trait of the Swedish and Finnish log housing, although I recognize that the Germans who founded Wistarburg probably used the same method. One thing is certain; the historical records of New Jersey make it crystal clear that Swedes and Finns built structures of hewn logs long before there was an influx into the state of German glass workers.

It is not certain when the first Swedes crossed the Delaware to settle permanently in New Jersey, but by the 1670's the entries in deed and early court records indicate that a number of Swedes and Finns were then in possession of land. "Finn's Point" in New Jersey is a place-name survival of the Finnish settlers. Although the Swedes and Finns living in Delaware complacently accepted the English authority established in 1664, some felt that by crossing the river to settle new territory they would be farther removed from possible government interference and that they would have greater freedom in preserving their own traditions and adhering to their own pattern of living. New Jersey's gentle rolling soil and rich meadows, drained by countless little creeks, and its expanse of woods were particularly attractive to a people who became primarily farmers, woodsmen, and fishermen.

Along the eastern bank of the Delaware and up into the land along such tributary creeks as Salem, Pensauken, Repaupo, Woodbury, Raccoon, Alloways, and others—including an immense tract between Big Timber and Oldmans Creek—Swedish and Finnish farm families carried their Old World traditions and customs. Although New Sweden had ceased to exist as a colony, the peaceful, conservative agricultural life in New Jersey permitted the continuance of Old World ways including old-time methods of log housing. Among the Swedish and Finnish settlers such names were recorded as Neilson, Rambo, Dalbo, Helm, Justafsen, Anderson, Swanson, Erixson, etc., including two still preserved in a number of New Jersey place names, Mullica and Steelman.

Held together not only by social custom and Old World ties, the Swedes and Finns were devout in their dedication to the Swedish Lutheran Church, and the church records and the letters of the pastors still preserved in the archives of Old Sweden are the main sources of information about the New Jersey settlements. Therein it is recorded that two separate centers, not to be considered as municipalities, but as communities scattered over an extensive geographical area, came into being, and each eventually had its own church—Swedesboro and Penns Neck. The latter congregation had the heavier concentration of Finnish families.

The early Swedes who settled in New Jersey attended services at the log churches at Crane Hook, where Finns dominated the congregation, and on Tinicum Island, which necessitated crossing the Delaware by canoe or rowboat. For those who lived back in the country it meant walking many miles to the canoe landing on the river, and even to those living along the river proper it was a time-consuming trip, and, at certain times of the year, hazardous. As the New Jersey population increased, the Swedish pastors were persuaded to cross the river to serve their parishioners, and the Reverend Andreas Rudman and Pastor Eric Bjork are known to have preached in New Jersey homes, performing other pastoral duties. Matts Mattson, the father-in-law of Pastor Rudman, was among the first Swedes to build a log house at Raccoon, as Swedesboro was first called, and no doubt early church services were held in his dwelling.

As time went on and the number of families in the Swedesboro area increased in numbers, the Swedes and Finns decided to build their own church and to contribute to the support of a resident pastor. In 1705, a log church was dedicated at Swedesboro by the Reverend Lars Tollstadius, an occasion of great rejoicing, and by 1714, the church members decided to improve the appearance of the building by covering the logs with boards. Unable to find suitable lumber, they simply whitewashed the edifice inside and out.[21] They also agreed among themselves to build a parsonage for a new preacher who had come to them, the Reverend Abraham Lidenius, provided their countrymen settled at Penns Neck "would cart the logs for it," and assume the responsibility for digging a cellar, laying the floors, and installing a fireplace.[22] Obviously this was to be a sizeable dwelling. A log schoolhouse was also built by the Swedesboro congregation in accordance with permission and instructions received from the Consistory in Sweden.

Regrettably there is no contemporary description of the first church built at Swedesboro, nor the parsonage or schoolhouse, except that they were all constructed of logs. It is not known whether they were of round or hewn timbers, but it would seem that the latter was the case. At this date, the settlers were well supplied with saws and other carpenter's tools, and there was a sufficient pool of manpower available to build worthy structures as indicated by the references to cellars, floors, and windows containing glass panes.

When construction began on a second church—this one to serve the congregation living at Penns Neck—the church records clearly state that it was to be made of *hewn* logs. "The logs were to be hewn 32 and 22 feet long, and were hewn and carted by the following:" (The records here list the names of the members of the congregation who donated logs.) [23] The edifice was completed in May of 1715 by four members of the congregation, Jan Minck, Lucas Peterson, John von Neeman, and Jacob Hindersson, the other church members helping to "heave up the logs."

By 1719 this second church building was covered with siding, and in 1720 logs were cut and hewn to build a parsonage.[24] Furthermore, the church records indicate that the Swedes had now become proficient in riving shingles, and during the winter of 1716 a group of workmen under the direction of Jacob von Devair made more than two thousand chestnut shingles.[25] In 1764 a new parsonage was built at Swedesboro "of Cedar logs 33 foot long and 23 feet broad two Storys high." The church records describe it as having three rooms on each floor and a commodious garret.[26]

In 1784, the old Swedesboro log church, then in a ruinous condition, was taken down and a new church erected on the same site— not of logs. At that time there were at least a dozen log dwellings still occupied in the community, also a log schoolhouse and a log parsonage, both of which were in use.[27] None of these log buildings remain today, nor have the old log church and parsonage survived at Penns Neck. This is regrettable because valuable data could have been obtained from a study of the log housing built by the two congregations, each of whom had received into their midst some German converts. No doubt the church and residential architecture at both locations was a synthesis of German, Finnish, and Swedish traits, although it should be clear to the reader that the first log structures were patently Swedish and Finnish products modified by New World resources, but not by strong German influences.

The settlement housing of southwestern New Jersey, particularly in Salem, Cumberland, and Gloucester Counties, was, at first, an extension of the basic log patterns found in the original Swedish and Finnish settlements in Delaware. The Swedes erected in New Jersey essentially the same kind of log buildings they had built in Delaware before sawmills and brick kilns made other material available for improved housing. There was one important difference: a German influence was manifest in southwestern New Jersey in the early eighteenth century, and this resulted in modifications attributable to Germans, although these cannot now be sharply defined, if ever. On the opposite side of the river in Delaware, strong Dutch and English influences were set in play at an early date, but there were no German settlements comparable to that at Wistarburg and vicinity, and no significant number of Germans, if any, infiltered the Swedish congregations. The early eighteenth century log housing in Delaware grew out of seventeenth century Swedish and Finnish forms. Thus from the log houses surviving in Delaware from this period one can expect to be able to gather a reliable impression about the methods of log construction in New Sweden, which, as I have suggested incorporated typological features different from those seen today in the log house exhibits in the outdoor museums in Skansen and Mora (see Figures 46, 47).

While engaged in field research in Delaware seeking log housing of the early period, I had the unusual experience of "finding" a long-lost log cabin along Love Creek, Indian River Hundred, Sussex

Figure 46. Seventeenth century Swedish log dwelling typical of farm houses in Dalarna; note brick chimney. (Courtesy Ingemar Liman, Skansen Djurgarden, Stockholm)

County, in 1957. What happened was that Edwin B. Perry, a resident of Baltimore, Maryland, purchased a farmhouse and parcel of land on which an old utility shed, ostensibly built of boards, stood in a field not far distant from the dwelling which Mr. Perry intended to convert into a summer home. While poking around at the shed, Mr. Perry discovered that an old log cabin, which had gone unrecognized for untold years, lay beneath the weatherboards. Mr. Perry brought the structure to our attention, and with his permission and assistance, we stripped away the boards which had been attached to vertical wood strips nailed against the logs with cut nails datable to the 1830's, and exposed a cabin of hewn white oak logs bearing the scars of a hand adze. There were no clues to enable us to date the structure with certainty, although we had the clear impression that it was originally equipped with a chimney and fireplace and used as a residence before it was converted into a farm shed.

After a newspaper article appeared reporting our discovery, we were fortunate in having a seventy-year old resident of Sussex County come to visit the project who told us that, as a boy, he had lived in the cabin and he showed us its original site in a pine woods some distance away before it had been moved to the farm property. Furthermore, he told us that his father, who was born in 1839, told him that the cabin was an old one when he was a boy. Additional information that our respondent gave us led us to conclude that the cabin dated back to the early eighteenth century and must have been built under Swedish-Finnish influences because there were then no German or other mid-European settlers in this immediate area. The full dovetailed notching and the flush corners were identical to those observed on the southwestern New Jersey cabins (see Figures 48, 49), and, incidentally, are similar to those found on an old squared-log storehouse reported from the Narke Province of Sweden.

Figure 47. Sixteenth and seventeenth century Swedish log houses at Zorn Gammelgård, Mora, Sweden. (Courtesy Erik Forssman, Director)

Figure 48. Dilapidated farm shed with tarpaper roof on Edwin B. Perry property, Indian River Hundred, Sussex County, Delaware, bore no resemblance to a log cabin until a board was torn off exposing the corner notching below.

Shortly after this experience, I was asked in 1958 to assist the members of the Board of Trustees of the Henry C. Conrad High School District in New Castle County, Delaware, by examining a shingled frame dwelling with a gambrel roof, locally known as the Eastburn House, which they were compelled to remove to make way for the building of the John Dickinson High School. Within this modern dwelling we found the four walls of a one-room cabin of white oak logs, measuring fifteen by nineteen feet. The house had been substantially altered, and siding was nailed to the log walls, and years later the siding was covered with composition shingles (see Figures 50, 51). When this exterior layer was stripped off, the log notching was found to be full dovetailed, and it was established that the original fireplace was in the center of one of the gable ends of the cabin. The school authorities later presented the log walls to the Smithsonian Institution for reconstruction and display in the Museum of History and Technology as an example of New Sweden's log housing. During the process of reconstructing the dwelling in Washington, D.C., I was invited to visit the museum and consult with the Smithsonian authorities about its features.

On the Taylors Bridge-Walker Schoolhouse Road in Blackbird Hundred, Kent County, Delaware, stands an unoccupied frame house which was originally a one-room cabin with a brick chimney and fireplace in one of the gable ends. A second floor and wing were later added and the entire structure covered with clapboards. Due to these modifications it is difficult to isolate the original features,

Figure 49. Assisted by Mr. Perry and others, the author removed the outside boards bringing to light a hewn white oak cabin with full dovetail notching similar to that found on numerous Swede-Finn cabins in Delaware.

Figure 50. Gambrel-roofed residence on John Dickinson High School property near Wilmington, Delaware, had a log cabin matrix which was salvaged when house was razed. Cabin walls were acquired by the Museum of History and Technology, Smithsonian Institution.

but the cabin is notched with full dovetailing, the log walls set on stones at each corner (see Figures 52, 53).

On the Hill Girt Farm, Route 100, near Chadds Ford, Pennsylvania, is a two-and-one-half hewn log dwelling which formerly stood in the Red Clay Creek Valley, near Wooddale, Delaware, east of the Lancaster Pike. In 1927, the structure was dismantled by H. G. Haskell, the logs carefully numbered, and reconstructed with faithful detail on the Hill Girt Farm. This dwelling is also notched with full dovetailing (see Figure 53).

In what is today the heavily-populated Richardson Park suburb of Wilmington there came into existence in the middle of the seventeenth century a scattered community of Swedish and Finnish farmers, the first settlers in an area described as on "ye north syde of

Christina Creeke." Here, as early as 1669, a tract of land was patented to Andries Andriessen, Broer Sinnex (both Finns), and Walraven Jansen. Andriessen and nineteen others also built and operated
a grist mill on a tributary of the Christina called the Little Falls
Creek. Although no specific descriptions of the houses built by
these Scandinavian farmers has been preserved there can be little
question that in this thickly wooded area, where no sawmills were
then in existence, that they all constructed log cabins. As the years
rolled by, the Richardsons, an English Quaker family, moved into
the area and purchased the old mill property, which they turned into
a thriving merchant mill. Before the end of the eighteenth century
the Richardsons had acquired considerable wealth, and they had also
purchased most of the farm properties on which the Swedes and
Finns had erected their log dwellings. They tore down these aged

Figure 51. Dovetailed oak logs on gambrel-roofed residence had been weather-
boarded over, and at a much later date, white composition shingles were nailed
on the weatherboards.

Figure 52. A frame addition was added to this log cabin on the Taylors Bridge-Walker Schoolhouse Road, Blackbird Hundred, Kent County, Delaware, and then the entire structure covered with clapboards concealing the underlying logs. (See Figure 53 for author's sketch of the dovetailed notching and brick fireplace.)

structures and replaced them with handsome brick and stone mansions, three of which, "Norwood," "Wayside," and "Ashley," are still standing, now hemmed in by streets and modern housing.

"Ashley," a brick mansion, and the most imposing of the three surviving Richardson houses, was built in 1804 by Ashley Richardson, who purchased the land from the descendants of Walraven Jansen. At the time of the purchase, and before the present mansion was erected, there stood on the property a small stone house with an older wing, a complete one-room log cabin. This cabin, one of the first structures built in the seventeenth century, was enlarged later by a Walraven descendant through the addition of the dwelling built of stone taken from a nearby quarry. He merely butted the

Two and one-half story log house, Hill Girt Farm, near Chadd's Ford, Pa., with notching detail at right.

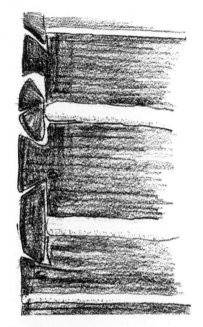

Notching on Taylors Bridge—Walker Schoolhouse Road Cabin, Delaware (left) and brick fireplace detail (above).

Figure 53

larger stone house against the old cabin. Ashton Richardson, a frugal Quaker, despite his wealth, elected not to destroy the dwelling but to use it as a house for one of his tenant farmers. Following Ashton's death in 1852, his spinster daughter, Hannah Richardson, continued to occupy "Ashley," allowing her hired man to live in the stone-log tenant house. After her death, the old structure fell into disuse and was ultimately removed, and no trace of it now remains. Fortunately, a photograph of it has been preserved (see Figure 54).

In this rare photograph the reader can see an example of the craftmanship of the Swedish-Finnish cabin builders who had learned to rive the shingles used on the roof, and had availed themselves of bricks from one of the early kilns to build a fireplace and chimney, which, incidentally, were centered in the gable end of the

Figure 54. Very rare photo of seventeenth century cabin in New Sweden, formerly located on Ashton Richardson estate, Richardson Park, Wilmington, Delaware. Stone wing was added long after cabin was built. Hewn, dovetailed logs, wood boards at window apertures, and loft (note ends of log joists across front) reveal traits of early Finnish builders.

dwelling. The logs were hewn and interlocked at the corners with full dovetailed notching, further evidence that this method of notching was commonly used on the hewn log structures in New Sweden. Evidently there was no glass in the original window apertures which were covered with boards. The ends of the log joists visible in the front of the cabin suggest that it had a loft or attic. This and other evidence negates the premise which has been recently advanced that the Swedes made little or no use of a loft or attic in their log cabins.[28]

The Public Archives Commission of the State of Delaware has preserved a hewn log cabin called "The Plank House" on the grounds of "The Lindens" at Smyrna, Kent County, Delaware. The house formerly stood on Smyrna's main street and was scheduled for destruction before it was moved and preserved by the Commission. Another hewn log house, which formerly stood near Cheswold, Delaware, has been re-erected by the Archives Commission on the grounds of the restored John Dickinson mansion south of Dover. Both of these houses are notched with full dovetailing—also a vestige of the oldtime methods.

It would be incorrect to convey the impression that all of the surviving log structures in the New Sweden area were built of hewn logs were full dovetailed corners, because this is not the case. Although this method of notching dominates the area, other corner-notching methods are present. For instance, in 1959 along Doe Run in nearby Chester County I stumbled on a ramshackle, unoccupied one-room cabin which has since been destroyed. It had a shingled roof, the diagnostic Swedish corner fireplace, and was constructed of undressed round logs which had been saddle notched. If not a surviving example of the Swedish period, it was unquestionably built under strong Swedish-Finnish influence. Two other examples are also worthy of description:

In 1957, when an old Delaware landmark, the so-called Price's Corner Log Cabin, which stood in a triangle of land southwest of Wilmington owned by Harvey C. Fenimore, was in danger of destruction due to highway and commercial expansion, the Delaware

Swedish Colonial Society undertook to investigate whether it was worthy of preservation. It was apparently built in the early eighteenth century, according to local tradition, and consisted of two full stories, and, unusual for log dwellings in this immediate area, it had a full cellar which was contemporary with the structure. There was a brick fireplace in the center of a gable end on the first floor and another fireplace immediately above it on the second floor, both venting into the same brick chimney. A deed search revealed that the house stood on land patented to Swedish owners in the seventeenth century.

At the request of the Delaware Swedish Colonial Society, a committee, of which I was a member, was appointed to examine the house, and in our report we recommended that every effort be made to preserve it. The house was thereafter removed by the State Archives Commission and re-assembled at Fort Christina Park in Wilmington where appropriate dedicatory services were held in 1963 in conjunction with the 325th anniversary of the landing of the Swedes at this very site. The original oak logs in the walls of this dwelling had been mostly left in the round, although crudely hewn on front and back surfaces, and both V and saddle notchings were used, not dovetailing. The boards in the two gable ends of this dwelling above the logs were nailed in a vertical position, but, as I have indicated earlier, this trait is found on houses having both German and non-German associations.

A cruder log cabin, which formerly stood on the Old State Road south of Wilmington, was removed and reconstructed as an exhibit in the State Museum in Dover by the Public Archives Commission. This dwelling provided an excellent opportunity for archeological study prior to its removal, which was prompted by a request that I, then the president of the Archeological Society of Delaware, received from the State Archivist, Dr. Leon de Valinger, Jr.

Dr. de Valinger noticed the ramshackle building as he drove between Wilmington and Dover. It stood in a field and appeared to be an abandoned farm shed covered with clapboards, but de Valinger learned that it was a log cabin when several of the clapboards rotted away. Under the clapboards lay a one-room dwelling eighteen by fourteen feet, with a front door slightly off center, having one front window, and a second window in the rear wall. The walls were of white oak logs, the interstices caulked with clay, and the base logs rested on a stone foundation, with a crawl space between the flooring and the earth. The logs were mostly round, although hewn on the front and rear surfaces, and the notching was the V method. The sawn board floor was laid on hewn log joists, and the ridge roof was covered with weathered cedar shingles, having under it a shelf-like loft apparently reached by a portable ladder since there were no pegs in the walls. The chimney in the center of one of the gable ends was of brick and there was a brick fireplace set on a stone foundation. A frame shed had been built against the chimney end of the house, having been recently used as a kitchen.

We began our archeological work on October 9, 1951, and continued intermittently, as time and weather permitted, until January 1952, following which the cabin was dismantled, the logs numbered and transported to Dover and reconstructed at the State Museum.[29] Since I have been unable to find any prior reports of log cabin excavations in American archeological literature, this may have been the first residential log cabin in the United States to be subjected to thorough archeological examination, and the reader may be interested in our findings.

Our initial excavations were conducted by digging a four-foot-wide trench completely around the building, after first clearing away modern trash—whiskey and soft drink bottles, tin cans, and the like. The humus in front of the cabin produced a number of clay marbles, a broken slate pencil, the fragments of a toy china doll, and a large stepping stone below the front door sill covered with six inches of earth. Near this stone stoop we uncovered an iron axe head and a hand whetstone. We also unearthed a variety of artifacts ranging from modern dishware fragments, broken glass from the windows of the cabin, forks, spoons, kitchen knives, a child's toy pistol, and other nondescript objects that had been lost or discarded by the cabin's most recent residents and subsequently covered with earth through natural forces.

After completing our work outside the cabin, we removed the floor boards from the six roughly-hewn white oak joists to which they were nailed and dug in the earth below. The black soil, varying in depth from ten to twenty-four inches, had been enriched with decayed organic matter and was heavy and loose, and animals had burrowed into it. All of this soil was completely removed by trowel and then sieved (see Figures 55, 56).

The quantity of artifactual material was almost unbelievable, illustrating an elementary lesson in archeology; namely, that wherever man lives, either ancient or modern, he leaves behind in the soil evidences of his occupation. How all of this material accumulated in the earth under the floor is a subject for speculation—some of it

Figure 55. Josh's Cabin, near Wilmington, Delaware, the clapboards partially removed, revealing charred logs of a fire which destroyed the logs under window to left.

probably dropped between the cracks in the floor boards; some may have been carried by children crawling in their play into the area about a foot high between the flooring and the earth; other material may have been deliberately discarded by successive residents of the cabin through the simple expedient of throwing it under the dwelling where the earth eventually covered it.

A variety of metal objects was found including rusted nails, spikes, horseshoes, two pairs of pliers, a garden trowel, a brass comb, four screw drivers, two axes, one hoe, an old-fashioned clothes iron, eleven knives, eight spoons, six forks, two buttonhooks, two thimbles, a conductor's ticket punch, and a small section of an iron rail which may have been from the New Castle-Frenchtown R.R., which once crossed near the cabin. The metal objects weighed seventy-four pounds, and there were also seventeen pounds of animal bones, among which were pig and cow (doubtless food remains), a boar

Figure 56. Aspiring young archeologists, including the writer's sons, assisted in sieving the dirt from under the flooring of Josh's Cabin.

tusk, fowl bones, a snapping turtle shell, groundhog skull, horse teeth, muskrat and small dog bones, and seven rat skulls.

A number of unbroken bottles were recovered dating from the nineteenth and twentieth centuries, including a small medicine vial bearing a pointille mark on the bottom. Only one of the bottles could be traced to its manufacturer. It bore the maker's initials "W.T.&Co.," referring to Witall, Tatum & Co. of Millville, N.J. who were in business between 1822 and 1880.

In addition to the bottles there were 217 fragmentary and complete glass objects including four bottle stoppers, fragments of four different lamp chimneys, one watch crystal, two lenses from eyeglasses, two Christmas tree ornaments, a mirror fragment, a vase fragment, a salt shaker, two toy dishes, and several portions of Mason jars.

Our archeological "loot" also included 114 complete or fragmentary ceramic objects, such as thirty-two pieces of jugs, a porcelain door knob, thirty-nine pieces of ornamented dinnerware, one cream pitcher, one shaving mug, two sugar bowl fragments, twenty-five fragments of glazed red pottery, and parts of baby doll heads, legs, and arms.

We also uncovered an interesting assortment of coins which included two Buffalo nickels, nine Lincoln head pennies, twelve Indian head pennies dated from 1902 to 1864, and five Liberty head pennies dated from 1840 to 1819. We found a one-half silver dime and one three-cent silver coin, and although neither was dated, we later established their coinage to the period between 1851 and 1872.

The earliest coin sieved from the soil was an English penny bearing the likeness of George III, worn so smooth the date was obliterated, but we determined that it was coined in the period from 1760 to 1820. Two other coins were worn so smooth that even the country of their origin could not be established, although the general contour of one of them resembled the George III penny. These coins had all apparently been lost over a long period of years because they were found at various places and at various depths in the earth.

Although not as exact in their datability as coins, buttons are a very useful chronological aid, and our excavation beneath the floor of the cabin produced 244 buttons of the "every day" type made of pearl, bone, horn, wood, glass, and hard rubber. The majority represented ordinary buttons used on wearing apparel during the last fifty to one hundred years, although there were also examples of the older "calico" buttons (1840–1870); the "ringer" (1840–1880); the "pie crust" (1840–1880); and there were seven older buttons, made of bone or horn, each perforated with five holes.

There were seventy-five metal buttons, some embossed with such designs as a butterfly, flowers, moon, and grapes. One pewter button had a faint intaglio design of a twelve-pointed star on the face, and ten of the metal buttons had back-marks, among which were those inscribed *Double Gilt, Warranted Fine Gold Surface, Gilt, Gold Color, Stanley London, ET.M.—Extra Rich,* and *R and W Robinson Extra Rich.*

The metal buttons also included a trainman's uniform button embossed PWB (Philadelphia, Wilmington, Baltimore R.R., predecessor the Pennsylvania R.R.), and a brass button from the uniform of a militiaman, which bore the Delaware state coat of arms.

This extraordinary series of buttons created much interest among button fanciers, and when I learned that there was an organization of Delaware button collectors, I sought the aid of several of the members to make identifications. Buttons, like clothing, change with the styles, and the "expert" can readily distinguish those of the colonial era from those of later periods.

Approximately fifty fragments of clay smoking pipes, including broken stems and portions of bowls, were uncovered beneath the cabin floor. Practically all of the bowls were charred on their interiors indicating they had been used by the cabins' occupants for smoking tobacco. All were of nineteenth or twentieth century manufacture, except four specimens which appeared to be older than the others. Experts in this specialized area examined the collections and were able to assist us in assigning dates which could then be cross checked with the buttons and coins. From four of the older stems, the thickness of the clay, the evidence of scraping to remove the marks of the mold in which they were made, and the off-center holes suggested they were made in England between 1750 and 1800. Two of the bowls carried the marks of their makers: the first bore a manufacturer's imprint, and the second the initials "ID" on the outside of the bowl facing the smoker. Both were identified as being of early eighteenth century manufacture.

Miscellaneous objects included a gold engagement ring with the stone missing, sixteen glass beads, an ornament from a horse bridle, a rusted key, a small conch shell ornament, a puzzle of two nails twisted together, a fragment of an ivory comb, a tiny clay doll marked "Made in Germany," a child's gold ring, ten glass "shooters," and an Indian arrowhead of argillite.

The typology of these artifacts clearly reflected the time sequence when the cabin was occupied, starting with objects used by the most recent occupants and continuing with earlier forms representative of their predecessors. Another clue to the age of the cabin was revealed through microscopic examination of the mortar used between the stones forming the foundation. It was made of sand and lime from pulverized shell, but contained no cement. Moreover, the mud chinking between the logs when examined microscopically was found to be tempered with rice or oat hulls, indicative of early practice.

Sections of the plaster which covered the interior log walls were also studied under the microscope and found to be composed of fifty-five different applications, some still tinted with the paint that had been applied. Assuming that a fresh coat had been laid on every three or four years, the time span represented by the laminations would range from one hundred fifty to two hundred years after the walls were first plastered. There was no certain way of ascertaining whether the plaster was applied immediately after the cabin was built or whether the first occupants were satisfied to live in a room with bare walls, which was probably the case. The age of the logs themselves was readily established by counting the rings, but this had no relation to the age of the cabin. The fact that trees seventy-five to one hundred years old at the time they were felled were used to construct the cabin did not reveal to us how long they had been in the walls.

All things considered—and in the complete absence of any reference to a log structure in the search made of the chain of deeds covering the property—we inclined to date the cabin as having been built about 1750, or perhaps shortly before. Although New Sweden had come to an end long before that date, we were nevertheless of the opinion that the builder had been influenced by older Swedish and Finnish cabins then still in existence along the nearby Christina River.

Inquiry among old residents revealed that the cabin had last been occupied twenty-five or thirty years before by an aged Negro, a countryside character and handyman whose shack was known simply as "Josh's Cabin." Josh, whose surname is unknown, came to New Castle County, Delaware, from unknown parts, taking possession of the old, unoccupied cabin, and he lived in it until he died, after which it stood vacant and began to rot away. If Josh were living today he would probably be surprised to see his humble log abode, with an assortment of the artifacts used by his predecessors, now fully restored and on display in Delaware's state capital (see Figure 57).

From a study of the contemporary documents and an examination of the surviving log buildings in Delaware, New Jersey, and southeastern Pennsylvania, it is clearly evident that the Swedes and Finns built a variety of structures of both round and hewn logs. These included one-room cabins, with or without lofts;[30] double-pen types; one and one-half, and two-story houses; churches, parsonages, schools, bathhouses, mills, and miscellaneous out housing. These structures were built not only while New Sweden existed as a Swedish-controlled colony—which was a relatively short time span—but continued to be built by Swedes and Finns during the successive periods of Dutch and English control of the lower Delaware Valley. Although the corner fireplace and chimney were characteristic of ancient Swedish craft culture, this does not mean that all

Figure 57. Restored in Delaware State Museum, Josh's Cabin has same shingle roof, loft, chimney, and logs in their proper positions. Several new logs were added to replace those destroyed by fire. (Courtesy Delaware State Archives)

the builders adhered to this trait, because some of the log residences in New Sweden were built with chimneys in the gable ends, and the stick-and-mud chimney was also built when necessity demanded it. Full dovetailing, with flush corners, was a common method of corner notching on houses built of hewn logs, although V notching was also represented. Saddle notching was the characteristic method of corner timbering on cabins made of round logs, and there is documentary reference by Dankers and Sluyter to a house having hewn logs extended beyond the corners.

Although these various forms of log structures had their origins in old Sweden and Finland during a long period of housing development and evolution, the American structures varied in typology from their Old World prototypes. As I have pointed out, the Swedes and Finns were quick to adopt wood shingles to roof their log houses, thus utilizing the natural resources of their Delaware Valley environment to manufacture roofs unlike those they knew in Sweden or Finland (see Figures 46, 47). Although living cypress and white cedar were both a source of wood for shingles, the fallen logs immersed in Delaware's Cedar Swamp and in New Jersey's Great Cedar Swamp made the best and most durable "mud" shingles.

Prior to the arrival of colonists in William Penn's Province of Pennsylvania, Swedes and Finns from the lower Delaware pressed north as early as 1664 to occupy the banks of the Schuylkill and upper Delaware and cultivate the lands where Philadelphia was later to be laid out. Of the nine members of William Markham's council, who initiated the Penn government, two were Swedes who had long resided on the Delaware.[31] The six justices of the first court at Upland in 1676, which had jurisdiction over the territory on the west bank of the Delaware from Wilmington as far as Trenton, were all Swedes or Finns. The court sat in a log house fifteen by fifteen feet built on lands owned by Neales Laersen.[32]

Peter Rambo, Peter Dalbo, Peter Cock, and the Swansen brothers, Andries, Swen, and Oele, acquired large tracts of land within the environs of present Philadelphia long before the arrival of the first English settlers to Penn's province. The log house the Swansens built on their tract at *Wicaco* facing the Delaware River was described as one and one-half stories high, with a piazza running all around it. It was standing at the time of Peter Kalm's visit in 1748, a forlorn, unoccupied antique, which was demolished by the British during the Revolution and used as fuel.[33] Not far distant was the log house built in 1669, first used for defense against the Indians, and in 1677 adapted as the Wicaco Church.

In 1677, John Mattson, Swen Lom, and Lacey Dalbo took up three hundred acres at a place called *Wiessahitkonk* (*Wissahiccon*) on the west side of the Schuylkill.[34] Lawrence Cock, Erick Cock, Michael Nielsen, Otto Ernest Cock, and Peter Nielsen—sons of the

first settlers—owned a 1800-acre tract along the Delaware at Philadelphia, previously known to the Lenni Lenape as *Shackamaxon*,
where land had been patented to old Peter Cock as early as 1664.

Peter Peterson was part owner of land at *Pennypack*, and Erick
Mullock, Olie Nielson, and Christian Thomason owned land at
Tawacawomink where the home lots formed a farming community
of log houses that the Scandinavians called *Tacony*, their rendition
of the Indian word. *Quessinawomink*, a mill tract on present Frank-
ford Creek, was owned by Swedes, and between it and the falls of
the Delaware below Trenton, some twenty-six separate properties
had been laid out starting in 1677. Hans Monson was a property
owner at *Oronemink* (some scribes spelled this Algonkian place-
name *Arunamink*) on the west side of the Schuylkill, and between
Passayunk (formerly the site of a major Lenni Lenape settlement),
and the falls of the Schuylkill, there were eleven plantations of various
sizes mostly taken up by Swedes and Finns.[35]

These tracts cited above by no means constitute a complete listing of Swedish and Finnish land holdings in and around Philadelphia
in the pre-Penn period, but they are adequate to illustrate the point
that William Penn's colonists did not seat themselves on wilderness
lands occupied only by the Delaware Indians and wild animals, as
some writers have intimated. The fact is that Penn had difficulty
locating suitable unclaimed and unoccupied lands for the "great
Town or City" he visualized as the commercial center of his province. His first choice was land along the Delaware at present
Chester, but when he found the Swedish and Finnish farmers in
possession of all the choice lands, leaving only the marshes available,
he turned his attention farther north to land lying between the
Schuylkill and the Delaware. Before he could proceed with his plans
to lay out a town at the new site he had to acquire land from old
Swedish residents such as the Swansens and Cocks who were already
seated on river front tracts along both the Delaware and Schuylkill.

There were numerous log houses in existence long before Penn
arrived in 1682, not only in Delaware and New Jersey, as the reader
has seen, but also at present Chester and within the limits of Phila-

delphia. These dwellings, which housed large families of blue-eyed, tow-headed children who chattered in a strange tongue, were there waiting to be imitated by the English Quakers, Irish, Welsh—later the Scotch-Irish—and any other newcomer who was willing to break away from Old World cultural heritage and build and occupy rude cabins of logs taken from trees in the Pennsylvania forests. The cultural landscape in Penn's Province was different from that in Virginia and New England when the first English settlers arrived, and the fact that log houses and other log structures were already in existence in Pennsylvania was a significant difference.

When, for example, a Swede or Finn conveyed property to an Anglo-American, as many did, the sale often included a log dwelling. Jonas Juriansen Kien in 1677 sold a parcel of land at present Chester to John Test, a London merchant, who, in turn, conveyed the property to Marmaduke Randall, another English merchant. The conveyance stated that there was included "a certayne new Blocq-house by him the sd. Jonas built on the above mentioned Lott." [36] William Markham later occupied this identical log house when he came to Chester, a new experience for William Penn's cousin, and Pennsylvania's first deputy governor.

In 1690, Israel Helm, a Swede, sold his house at Chester to James Sanderlins, a Scot, who had married a Swedish woman.[37] There is adequate documentation to show that there were close relations between the Swedes and Quakers, which negates a statement made in an otherwise excellent article on log housing that "the Swedes had little contact with their English neighbors." [38]

The reader has already seen how restless Swedes and Finns left the Delaware River settlements and settled among the English in Maryland, which I have suggested led to the introduction of log housing in the tidewater counties of that province during the latter part of the seventeenth century. A pro-Swedish author was technically correct when he wrote, "From New Sweden the log cabin spread wherever American colonists moved into virgin country," [39] but it would be gilding the lily to credit the Swedes for being *solely* responsible for the widespread diffusion of log housing to

America's western and southern frontiers. It is correct to say that a relatively small number of Swedes and Finns first introduced the log cabin in an extensive settlement area on both sides of the Delaware River, not excluding Philadelphia itself. It is also true that two other migratory waves from Europe to America were of paramount importance in the development and dispersion of log housing, and this is the subject of the chapter which follows.

NOTES—CHAPTER 7

1. A. R. Dunlap and E. J. Moyne, "The Finnish Language on the Delaware," *American Speech*, XXVII (May, 1952), No. 2, 81–90; see also John H. Wuorinen, *The Finns on the Delaware* (New York, 1938). In 1809 Russia seized Finland, and not until 1917 did Finland declare her freedom as an independent state.

2. *Introduction to Finland*, ed. Urho Toivola (Helsinki, 1960), 149, for illustration of an old log barn with an overhanging second story, interlocked with double-notch joints.

3. Wendy Hall, *Green, Gold, and Granite, a Background to Finland*, 2nd ed. (London, 1957), illus. p. 48.

4. *Baron Klinkowström's America*, trans. and ed. Franklin D. Scott (Evanston, Ill., 1952), 52.

5. *Narratives of Early Pennsylvania, West New Jersey and Delaware*, ed. Albert Cook Myers (New York, 1912), 250.

6. Charles H. Browning, *Welsh Settlement of Pennsylvania* (Philadelphia, 1912), 38, quotes from a pamphlet printed in England *c.* 1682, and then states that these were directions that William Penn gave his colonists about building log cabins before they left England. The palpability of the error is apparent if one refers to the text of the pamphlet reprinted in the *Penna. Mag. of Hist. and Biog.*, IV, 1880, 331–342, wherein it is evident that the directions apply to building a house of clapboards. Browning also implies that all the Welsh Quakers built log cabins in Pennsylvania, making specific reference to the "comfortable log house" built by Dr. Edward Jones who arrived in Pennsylvania in 1682, *ibid.*, 65. Although there were, indeed, log cabins in the Welsh-occupied townships of Pennsylvania in the eighteenth century, contemporary documentation to log cabins having been built by Welsh settlers in the seventeenth century is meager. Susan Nancarro, who died at the age of eighty, said that her Welsh grandfather, Hugh Evans, remembered William Penn and his daughter Letitia (in 1699 or 1700) coming on horseback to visit his father, Thomas Evans, and,

"Their house then was superior in that it was of barked logs, a refinement surpassing the common rank," *Watson's Annals of Philadelphia* (Philadelphia, 1898), II, 79; see also Howard M. Jenkins, *Historical Collections Relating to Gwynedd*, 2nd ed. (Philadelphia, 1897), 62. In their homeland, the Welsh built cottages of stone and mud, with roofs thatched with turf, fern, heather, rushes, reeds, and straws, but they did not build log cabins; Iorwerth C. Peate, *The Welsh House* (Liverpool, 1944).

The Welsh settlers on the 30,000-acre Welsh Tract, which comprised Pencader Hundred, Delaware, and parts of Cecil County, Maryland, erected a log Baptist meeting house called "the Baptist Meeting House at the Iron hill," *circa* 1703. The later brick church built in 1746 is said to contain some of the timbers used in the first; see *Records of the Welsh Tract Baptist Meeting 1701–1828* (Historical Society of Delaware, 1904).

At Radnor, Delaware County, Pennsylvania, a Welsh Episcopal Church was built of logs, replaced in 1717 by a stone edifice; Sherman Day, *Historical Collections of Pennsylvania* (Philadelphia, 1843), 306.

7. The documentation pertaining to all the structures listed is cited in C. A. Weslager, "Log Structures in New Sweden During the Seventeenth Century," *Delaware History*, Sept. 1952, 77–95.

8. "Journal of a Voyage to New York, 1679–1680," Jaspar Dankers and Peter Sluyter, *Memoirs of the Long Island Historical Society* (Brooklyn, 1867), 175.

9. *Peter Kalm's Travels in North America*, trans. Adolph B. Benson (New York, 1937), I, 272.

10. Weslager, 89.

11. C. A. Weslager, "Log Houses in Pennsylvania During the Seventeenth Century," *Pennsylvania History* (July 1955), 263–264.

12. *Records of the Court of New Castle, 1676–1681* (Lancaster, Pa., 1904), 388.

13. John F. Watson, *Annals of Philadelphia and Pennsylvania* (Philadelphia, 1898), I, 300, 357; see also pp. 150–151 describing a boarded log cabin moved to Christian Street in Philadelphia from Chester County. There was also an old Swedish log house on Swanson Street near Becks Alley, see Ward Townsend, "South Second Street and its Associations," *Penna. Mag. of Hist. and Biog.*, IV, No. 1 (1880), 46. This cabin is also referred to by Sherman Day, see fn. 31 below.

14. Israel Acrelius, *A History of New Sweden*, trans. Wm. M. Reynolds (Philadelphia, 1874), 310.

15. Peter O. Wacker, unpublished paper. "The Log House in New Jersey."

16. "History of the Parish of Sussex County in 1728 by the Reverend William Beckett," in "Description and Travel Accounts of Delaware, 1700–1740," ed. Harold B. Hancock, *Delaware History*, Oct. 1962, 140.

17. J. Thomas Scharf, *History of Delaware* (Philadelphia, 1888), II, 914. For references to other log structures in New Castle County see 889, 919, 921, 940, 996, 1025. A Swedes' mill on Red Clay Creek built of logs was acquired by Robert Philips, p. 924.

18. The Nothnagle Cabin is also illustrated in *The Swedes and Finns in New Jersey*, 1938, p. 84. For a complete deed search of the property see a pamphlet by Elmer G. Van Name of the Salem County Historical Society, "The Benjamin Braman Log Cabin," and note the cabin was not on Anthony Nielson's property, as erroneously stated in *Swedes and Finns*, 142–143.

19. R. M. Acton, "A Short History of the Glass Manufacture in Salem County, N.J.," *Penna. Mag. of Hist. and Biog.*, IX, No. 3 (1885), 343–346. The author describes the Wistar log house which was still standing in 1885. I am aware of the log house classifications in New Jersey cited by Seymour Williams, *et al.*, *New Jersey Historic American Buildings Survey: Outline of the Development of Early American Architecture*, compiled by the Historic American Buildings Survey, 1939, N.J. Hist. Soc., Newark, N.J., but I do not agree that the three log house types cited in the survey are sufficiently inclusive. As indicated in the text, my remarks are confined to cabins in New Sweden, which excludes that part of New Jersey north of Trenton. There is no question that German log construction techniques from Pennsylvania strongly influenced structures in northern New Jersey.

20. See illustration of overhang on a Swedish farm building, *Sweden: Photos by Otto Siegner* (Ludwig Simon, Munich-Pullach, n.d.), 117; cf. Gerda Boëthius, *Den Nordiska Timmerbyggnadskonsten*, etc. (Stockholm, 1927), Figs. 58, 75, 76, 215.

21. *The Records of the Swedish Lutheran Churches at Raccoon and Penns Neck, 1713–1786*, American Guide Series (Elizabeth, N.J., 1938).

22. *Ibid.*, 7.

23. *Ibid.*, 2.

24. *Ibid.*, 20.

25. *Ibid.*, 8.

26. *Ibid.*, 134.

27. John Barber and Henry Howe, *Historical Collections of the State of New Jersey* (New York, 1844), 223.

28. Peter O. Wacker, *The Musconetcong Valley of New Jersey* (New Brunswick, N.J., 1968), 78.

29. A full account of this excavation appears in C. A. Weslager, "The Excavation of a Colonial Log Cabin near Wilmington, Delaware," *Bulletin, Archeological Society of Delaware*, XVI, No. 1, April 1954.

30. Lofts were, of course, present in log houses in Scandinavia; see Halvor Vreim, "The Ancient Settlements in Finmark, Norway," *Folkliv*, I, 1937, 175.

31. Hannah Benner Roach, "The Planting of Philadelphia: A Seventeenth Century Real Estate Development," *Penna. Mag. of Hist. and Biog.*, Jan. 1968, pp. 3–47; April 1968, pp. 143–194.

32. *The Record of the Court at Upland*, 1676–1681, Memoirs Hist. Soc. of Penna., VII, Phila., 1860, p. 137.

33. Sherman Day, *Historical Collections of the State of Pennsylvania* (Philadelphia, 1843), 558.

34. *Upland Court Record*, 62.

35. *Walter Wharton's Land Survey Register*, ed. Albert Cook Myers, Hist. Soc. of Del. (1955), 40, 41, 43, 45, 47, 69; see also Roach, for drawing of original surveys at Philadelphia of Swedes' lands, p. 15.

36. *Upland Court Record*, 90.

37. *Ibid.*, 160.

38. Fred Kniffen and Henry Glassie, "Building in Wood in the Eastern United States," *The Geographical Review*, LVI, No. 1 (1966), 58. If these two fine authors had not specifically issued an invitation to their readers to correct their observations, I would not presume to criticize a minor point in what I deem the most significant paper on log housing that has yet been written. In view of the data introduced in the present volume, the authors may want to reexamine their statement made in fn. 34 that "so-called" seventeenth century Swedish log houses reflect German log-construction techniques rather than Swedish. The statement on p. 58 that the first mention of log houses outside of New Sweden is in 1669 for Maryland is no longer correct; also the log churches I have described in New Jersey, Delaware, and Pennsylvania indicate that early Swedish religious architecture was not English-American.

39. *Swedes In America*, ed. Adolph B. Benson and Naboth Hedin (New Haven, 1938), 1.

8 Pennsylvania Germans and the Scotch-Irish

After receiving his royal charter from Charles II for a domain in America nearly as large as England itself, William Penn wrote a prospectus entitled, *Some Account of the Province of Pennsylvania*, published in London in April of 1681. Although the democratic colony Penn intended to establish in the New World was essentially Quaker in character, he hoped that his prospectus would attract other desirable Europeans seeking religious freedom and economic opportunity.

The prospectus, which described Pennsylvania in extremely favorable terms, was almost immediately issued on the continent in both German and Dutch translations, and its wide circulation included the persecuted Frankfurt Pietists that Penn had visited in 1677. The prospectus was an important factor in arousing interest in emigrating to America not only among the Pietists, but among other sectists living in the duchies of Baden, Würtemberg, and the Palatinate in the Rhineland, and the news about Penn's proposed colony spread to other sectist groups. Some were eager for the opportunity to leave Germany because of religious intolerance, and others, because of their pacifist beliefs, to escape the military regimes.

Strictly speaking, there was no Germany in the modern political sense during the period of American colonization, and the name has been loosely applied to a group of principalities, duchies, and kingdoms, which included parts of present Switzerland and Czechoslo-

Arrows show how the concept of the log cabin diffused from primary American source area in northern Delaware and southeastern Pennsylvania. Map shows approximate locations of certain places prominently mentioned in text.

vakia, Alsace, Lorraine, as well as Bavaria, Prussia, and Saxony. Due to annexations and partitions in the aftermath of two World Wars, the geography of central Europe has undergone such radical changes that it is difficult to relate ancient kingdoms to present political boundaries. Bohemia, Moravia, and Silesia, which became provinces of Czechoslovakia, have lost their separate political identities in new administrative units, and parts of the former Silesia are now included in Poland. Bavaria is now a state of West Germany, and its south-western portion was formerly eastern Swabia. Peoples from all of these places made up the early "German" population of Pennsylvania, and all were included in the catchall term "Pennsylvania Dutch," although their cultural backgrounds may have differed.

The start of the emigration was slow. On August 20, 1683, Francis Daniel Pastorius representing the German Society of Frankfurt arrived in Philadelphia with a few followers on the vessel *America*. On October 6, a group of Dutch Quakers from Krefeld landed at Philadelphia, and they moved on October 25 to a tract adjacent to Philadelphia, first called Germanopolis, which later became known as Germantown, incorporated as a borough in 1689. There were 13 adult males in the Dutch contingent who settled Germantown, and 21 women and children, and they built the first houses in the community. Pastorius was not the founder of Germantown as some historians have erroneously reported—actually he and his German followers did not move there until after May 30, 1685. However, as more Germans arrived, including members of the Mennonite sect, Germantown became truly German, and some of the Mennonites moved to the upper half of what was then Philadelphia County (now Montgomery County) and later into present Bucks, Lancaster, and York Counties where their descendants may still be found.

In 1719, a group of Brethren, also called Dunkards, arrived from Germany and they settled at Germantown forming a congregation separate from the Mennonites. In 1734, a contingent of a sectist group called Schwenkfelders arrived from Saxony and moved into what is now Montgomery County where they established their church. I will shortly comment on the housing of all of these people.

Penn's *Letter to the Committee of the Free Society of Traders*, published in London in 1683, was, in 1684, printed in Dutch, German, and French, and was also circulated on the continent. Like his previous tract, it, too, had the effect of arousing interest and stimulating new waves of sectist migrations. In this letter Penn pointed out that in less than a year his Quaker colonists in Philadelphia had built a town which contained "about four Score Houses and Cottages, such as they are, where Merchants and Handicrafts are following their Vocations as fast as they can." He included a plan of the growing town prepared for him by his surveyor-general, Thomas Holme, on which parallel streets were laid out in the area between the Schuylkill and the Delaware Rivers with numbered lots for the houses. In his *A Further Account of Pennsylvania*, Penn pointed out that Philadelphia had grown to 357 houses "divers of them large, well built, with good Cellars, three stories, and some with Balconies." By 1685 there were 600 houses, according to another account, and the town continued to grow. Although the residences were built of wood and brick, the wood houses prior to 1700 greatly outnumbered those of brick, and most of them were framed. Nails, wrought iron, glass, brick, and roofing tiles were imported from England.

It is a matter of official record that some of the settlers lived at first in caves they dug into the river-front banks of the Schuylkill as temporary shelters for their families. These subterranean hovels were not only unsightly, but caused the new streets to begin to cave in, and the Proprietor was forced to issue orders that the caves must be vacated and filled in with earth.

In an entry dated the 17th, 9th month, 1685, in the *Minutes of the Provincial Council*, the occupants of the caves were given final notice to remove within a month, although a number of families had not vacated the caves as late as 1687. In a land where trees were plentiful, these English and Welsh cave dwellers might have built log cabins, which were more comfortable than damp holes in the earth, but like their conservative countrymen who settled Virginia and New England, they elected not to do so.

Unlike the Virginia and New England colonists, who were the

first permanent white occupants in their respective area, Penn's colonists, as I have indicated, were preceded in the Philadelphia environs by families of Swedes and Finns who lived in log dwellings. Yet the English hereditary housing habit exerted such a strong influence, as it did in Virginia and New England, that the majority of the Philadelphia Anglo-American settlers initially showed no inclination to imitate Scandinavian log housing techniques. There were, as one might expect, several exceptions, and these are only briefly noted in contemporary documents. The manuscript records of the Philadelphia County Court for 1685–1686 indicate that one Patrick Robinson was the owner of a log house on Second Street which, in 1685, he agreed to rent to the county authorities for use as a jail.

This passage, now appearing for the first time in print, as transcribed for me by Professor A. R. Dunlap, reads as follows:

agreed also by the Court with Consent aforesaid with Patrick Robinson to give him 12 lb per annum for his Logghouse in Second street out of this yeares Levie Provided hee bring it under the sherrifs hand that the said Patrick hath made the same a sufficient goale [jail] and yt with ye sd sherrifs [shewing?] therein hee accompts it sufficient and will make no excuse hereafter for want of a goale and the said rent to Commence from the date of ye sherrifs acceptance yrof [thereof] and for what handbolts[,] fetters or other Irons the said Patrick Robinson furnishes the said sherrif withall[,] the Court engages to take the same and pay ye said Patrick Robinson w[hat] they cost him[.] [1]

Another exception has been brought to light in Hannah B. Roach's studies of seventeenth century Philadelphia deeds. By 1686, George Bartholomew had erected a "log house" on his front lot next to the lot to which the Blue Anchor Tavern was moved.[2] Like the Patrick Robinson log house, this is another example of a log house in the English colonies in the seventeenth century that Shurtleff overlooked. By and large, however, the English in Philadelphia built frame and half-timbered houses, after which brick dwellings were erected.

In 1740, another German sectist group called the Moravians, some of whom who had previously settled in Georgia, came to Pennsylvania seeking the religious and political freedom of Penn's colony. They settled at the forks of the Delaware and Lehigh Rivers at a place called the "Barony of Nazareth." Later they bought land where the Monocacy flows into the Lehigh and there established their most important American town which grew to become the present city of Bethlehem. The Moravians, who originated in Bohemia, called their order the *Unitas Fratrum*, or United Brethren. They started to be called Moravians when some of the German-speaking members, banished from their homes in neighboring Moravia, found refuge in heavily-forested Saxony on an estate of Count Nicolaus Ludwig von Zinzendorf. The Count forsook some of the comforts of wealth to pursue evangelical work and spread Moravian teachings both in Europe and America where the American church in 1847 officially adopted the name Moravian Brethren. Like most of the other sectists, the Moravians were separatists from the Church of Rome, and like the Schwenkfelders, who went from Silesia to Saxony, and thence to America; the Mennonites; and the Amish (a separate group of Mennonites who established their first American community in northwest Bucks County), they had a passion against war, and espoused the plain life giving them a moral kinship with the Pennsylvania Quakers.

Most of the German and Swiss farmers, weavers, and artisans composing the Protestant denominations and sects were familiar with log house construction in the Black Forest, the Swiss Alps, and in the wooded areas of Silesia, Moravia, Bohemia, and Saxony. Like their Swede and Finn predecessors in the Delaware River Valley many of them erected their first American homes and churches of logs. Like the variations in typology on the log structures in New Sweden, German log housing also varied in different parts of Germany itself, and these differences were seen in America. For example, the log cabin built by Christopher Yeakel in 1743 on Chestnut Hill in Philadelphia, but no longer standing, was said to be typical of the Schwenkfelders,[3] although precisely how their log structures differed from the other sectists is not, to the best of my knowledge, recorded in contemporary sources. Likewise, the specific nature of the typological differences in Germany itself in the seventeenth century has not been fully delineated. For example, it is known that on one form of the log house then common in Saxony and northern Bohemia, the upper story rested, not on horizontal logs of the lower story, but upon wooden columns, often rounded and decorated with hand carvings. On some Swiss log houses the logs were carried several feet beyond the walls to support the overhanging eaves of a roof, a balcony, or pent eaves. These typological differences, which still remain to be precisely characterized, are of especial interest to technicians intent upon isolating the various methodologies of settlement housing and relating them to the movement of peoples to America and their internal migrations during the transition from frontier life to settled communities. The problem lies not only in identifying the forms of log housing in the native European hearths, but the German sectists, like the Swedes and Finns, improvised when they erected their American log houses. Although their log housing was similar to certain Old World forms with which they had a familiarity, it was by no means identical. It is simply unrealistic to assume that *all* peoples of German origin who came to Pennsylvania in the seventeenth and eighteenth centuries built the same kind of log house which can be neatly and indisputably cataloged as the "German type."

In contrast to the relatively small Swedish and Finnish population, peoples from the principalities, duchies, and kingdoms, who were called Germans, poured into Pennsylvania by the thousands. Gottlieb Mittelberger wrote in a contemporary journal that between 1749 and 1754 more than 30,000 German immigrants settled in Pennsylvania.[4] Prior to 1717, these Germans came principally for political or religious reasons, but those who came later, with some exceptions, left Europe to improve their economic and social life in the New World.

They came—as I have already indicated—from different areas, bringing their individual group cultural backgrounds. These immigrants from Alsace, Swabia, Silesia, Saxony, Bohemia, the Alpine valleys, and other sections of Germanic Europe added new and different cultural ingredients (including their housing concepts) to a crucible already boiling with a potpourri of the folkways of Swedes, Finns, Holland Dutch, English, Welsh, Irish Quakers, Delaware Indians, and others. The much-discussed American "melting pot" dates much further back in time than is generally realized. It had its origin in the Delaware Valley in the buffer zone between the 38th and 41st parallels that James I established in 1606 between the Virginia Company and the Plymouth Company where peoples of differing nationalities were brought together.

In 1766, in a well-known quotation, Benjamin Franklin told Parliament that about one-third of Pennsylvania's population was of German origin, and at the outbreak of the Revolution, of a total Pennsylvania population of about 225,000, it has been reliably estimated that some 110,000 were Germans.[5] The sheer number of Germans, in contrast to the much lesser Swedish-Finnish population, and the continuing influx of Germans, leaves no reason to question which exerted the stronger influence in young America. When Shurtleff wrote that, "Delaware Bay was the principal center from which log-dwelling construction spread," he was not inaccurate, but he inclined to overrate the Swedes and to underestimate the influence of the Germans. As I have shown, the Swedes and Finns were responsible for the first wave of log housing and their influence must not be discounted, but it was by no means the most persistent nor the strongest.

Many years later, long after America was in an advanced stage of economic development, there was a strong Scandinavian influence in Minnesota because of the thousands of Swedes, Norwegians, Finns, and Danes attracted to the fertile farmlands and later to the iron mines. Scandinavian peoples set the pattern for the political, cultural, industrial, and professional life in the state. Log houses were widely constructed in Minnesota in the latter part of the nineteenth century with one of the earliest built in 1850 on Hay Lake in Washington County by three young Scandinavians from the province of Vastergotland.[6] The situation in Minnesota was entirely different from that in colonial Pennsylvania where German log house traditions were heavily superimposed on an earlier Swedish-Finnish log complex at a time when the population was almost entirely confined to the seaboard colonies.

In addition to the influx of German sectists to Pennsylvania, members of the Reformed and Lutheran Churches, some of whom came in 1723 from the Scoharie Valley in New York (survivors of the community of Palatines established earlier on the Hudson by Governor Hunter) founded congregations in Pennsylvania, and many of them also constructed log houses. John Weiser, father of Conrad Weiser, Pennsylvania's great Indian ambassador, was a leader among the Palatines settled in the Scoharie Valley, and the village there which bore his name, *Weiserdorf*, consisted of some forty log houses built by German settlers. When Conrad Weiser brought his family from Weiserdorf in 1729 and settled at a place in Pennsylvania's Lebanon Valley known to the Indians as *Tulpehocken*, the first thing he did was to build a temporary cabin of logs. Later his hospitable neighbors helped him erect a small stone house: square, solid, and simple, with a cool cellar, and one main room and fireplace with raftered sleeping quarters under the eaves.

Between 1735 and 1736, Pennsylvania's Quaker government issued fifty-two licenses to settle along the west bank of the Susquehanna River, and the settlers who went there were mostly Germans as some of the names indicate—Tobias Frey, Michael Tanner, Caspar Spangler, Frederick Ebert, Henry Hendricks, Valentine Heyer, Martin Schultz—to name a few who built log houses on Kreutz Creek.[7] Here in a land disputed between the Penns and Calverts, the Pennsylvania Germans were thrown into contact with the English from Maryland, setting off new cultural interactions.

It is a familiar story: the pious, hard-working German farmers and artisans went west and south from the fertile valleys of the Lehigh, the Schuylkill, the Perkiomen, and the Susquehanna. They plodded through the South Mountains at Crampton's Gap and followed the Monocacy into the Potomac Valley where they founded such towns as Monocacy and Frederick. Others crossed the Potomac at Old Packhorse Ford, where Indian warriors and hunters had long passed, and founded the town of Mecklenburg, later rechristened Shepherdstown. Pennsylvania Germans moved to the Great Falls at the junction of the Shenandoah and Potomac at Harpers Ferry, and then swept through the Valley of the Shenandoah.

Jost Hite, and others of his countrymen living in the Colebrook Valley in eastern Pennsylvania, requested protection from the government at Philadelphia against attacks from the Indians, but the peace-loving Quakers withheld assistance because they were not only reluctant to oppose force with force, but wanted to retain the support of the Indians who were later to be a balance of power between French and English. As a result, Hite purchased land in the Shenandoah Valley and left Pennsylvania in 1732 with the families of his three sons-in-law, and twelve other German families— a vanguard carrying new cultural patterns to the southern frontier, including German vernacular housing.

Aware of Germans passing through Maryland en route to Virginia, Charles Calvert, the fifth Lord Baltimore, issued a proclamation in 1732 inviting settlement in his province, offering two hundred acres in fee, subject to a nominal rent, to any head of a family who settled between the Patapsco and the Susquehanna within three years. This was a factor that encouraged the movement of additional German settlers to Frederick and Washington Counties of Maryland, which was, in effect, an extension of the migrations from Germany to Pennsylvania.

Many German immigrants, particularly those who came after 1727, arrived in America under discouraging circumstances. Either they had disposed of all their property, and most of their personal possessions, in order to raise passage money before they left Europe, or unable to pay their way, they came as indentured servants. This usually meant that a ship's captain brought them across the Atlantic without charge, and with their consent, sold them into limited servitude in return for the payment of their passage by the individual for whom they were bound to work to discharge the debt. Even many of those who could pay their passage and were able to retain their freedom and independence upon arriving in America, were in poor financial circumstances. Fortunately land was cheap and plentiful, and to the German peasant farmer its possession was of utmost importance. Limestone soil and black walnut trees meant richly fertile land, the most precious asset that any German could own. Some rented land and paid for it in annual installments; others became squatters, especially on disputed border lands, without making immediate payment. They had little money to buy building materials or to hire carpenters, and it was not by chance or choice, but through necessity that they built log cabins, not with the infinite care given the construction of a village house in Germany, but in a manner adequate to meet their immediate needs. If by chance the immigrant came from a city or a part of Germany where log housing was not in wide use, there was always one of his countrymen, familiar with log building techniques, willing to give the newcomer a hand in raising a cabin.

When the German farmers cleared the land they did not girdle the trees and allow them to stand and die an unsightly death, or burn down the forests as the Finns did in rural Sweden, but they felled the trees and laboriously plowed and cut out the stumps. In doing so they quickly converted the land into arable acreage, making farm fields adjacent to their houses and barns. The independent farm, in contrast to the agricultural village in Germany, became the basic ecnomic unit where Germans settled. As with the earlier Swedes and Finns, and the later pioneers who opened the western frontier, the Germans built their log cabins in the hope that they would be replaced later with larger dwellings of hewn logs, or preferably houses of native stone. Often this did not materialize until the next or succeeding generations, and some of the original log residences were so sturdily built that many are still standing. German-built dwellings of logs were not all confined to small cabins on individual farms; New Market, Winchester, and Frederick, all founded by Germans, were described by an early visitor as "log-house towns."

In contrast to the Scandinavian corner chimney, or the chimney on a gable end, some of the painstaking German craftsmen built their log dwellings with a central chimney, a type of house found both in Switzerland and the Rhineland. This kind of dwelling, also built of material other than logs, usually had three rooms on the ground floor, with a central chimney arising in the middle of the roof, and a deep fireplace measuring from four to sixteen feet long built in the center of the house, and opening into the kitchen. The front door was characteristically off center in a house with a central chimney and usually opened into the kitchen (see Figure 25). Some houses of this type consisted of only one story, whereas others had an upstairs.[8]

As time went on it appeared to some Anglo-American observers that German farmers were more intent on erecting spacious barns for their cows and horses than in enlarging the dwelling houses for their families. Barns were built of squared logs or stone, or of both, thatched with straw until shingles became available, with the livestock stabled on the ground floor, and an ample winter supply of hay and grain stored on the floor above. The earliest record of the number of barns in Pennsylvania is found in a direct tax list of farm buildings in 1798. It reveals there were then 15,885 barns, of which 6813, or 43 percent, were built of logs.[9] Today in the Pennsylvania Dutch country the big barn still overshadows some of the farmhouses, although both are now typically built of stone, and the residences are much larger than they formerly were.

Pastorius, who said of Pennsylvania, *"Es ist alles nur Wald"* ("All is forest"), wrote that initially there were no bricks available at Germantown for house construction and consequently the twelve earliest dwellings built by the Dutchmen who preceded him were made either of stone or wood. Since most of the Dutch were linen workers, and there evidently were no carpenters in the first contingent, the possibility exists that some of the first houses were of logs. Admittedly, the Krefelders who lived near the Holland border where bricks were the favored material for house building did not have as much experience in log house construction as Pastorius's followers and some of the other German sectists who later settled

Germantown and who came from forested areas. Five years after its founding there were fifty houses in Germantown, but regrettably they were not described.[10] Any wood houses in the original settlement were, in a large measure, displaced by stone dwellings as the community grew. However, the records are clear that a log meetinghouse was built about 1708, which survived until 1770 before it was replaced with a stone edifice.[11] The Heydrick-Yeakle log house, a landmark which stood at Mermaid Lane and Germantown Avenue, survived until 1909 when it was demolished.

Bethlehem, Pennsylvania, was the nerve center of the Moravian settlements in North America, and it was a carefully planned community designed as a major industrial complex where raw materials could be converted into finished products or exchanged for manufactured goods. The plans for the community made by the church leaders in Europe, which were fully realized as the settlement grew, included accommodations for tanners, dyers, hatmakers, wagoners, blacksmiths, coopers, brewers, locksmiths, millwrights, clothmakers, weavers, potters, silversmiths, and many other artisan callings. The Moravians, predominantly from Bohemia-Moravia and Saxony—although people of other national origins joined them at Bethlehem— were of a higher socioeconomic origin than many of the other German sectists. Belonging mostly to the craftsman class, they were brought together in towns with the objective of carrying out group endeavors—not as isolated farm families.

The first building erected in 1740 by the Moravian vanguard at Nazareth, about nine miles north of Bethlehem, was a small cabin of round logs, a temporary dwelling, which is no longer standing. Later a more substantial cabin of hewn oak logs, "the humble, quaint and historic gray cottage," as a Moravian bishop later described it, was built by the Brethren. This structure has been preserved at Nazareth at its original site on the grounds of the Whitfield House, a stone building owned by the Moravian Historical Society. Known as the "Gray Cottage" its hewn logs are dovetailed and flush at the corners, and when I visited it in 1968 it was occupied by a retired Moravian missionary.[12]

The first house built by the Moravians at Bethlehem, 1740–1741, was also constructed of hewn logs, one story high with an attic. It was divided into two sections, one part of the structure used to house people, and the other part animals. The Moravians celebrated their first Christmas in Bethlehem in this log cabin, the worshippers separated by a partition from the cows and horses. The resemblance to the stable of Christ's nativity is said to have been the reason the community was given its biblical name. This cabin was torn down in 1823, and it is supposed to have measured twenty by forty feet, although no accurate description exists, since it was intended only as a provisional structure until the master carpenters built the *Gemeinhaus*. This "community house" was two full stories high with two attics, one above the other, built of hewn white oak logs dovetailed and flush at the corners. The building was constructed in several stages, which makes it difficult to ascertain the original dimensions, given by one authority as thirty by forty-five feet and by another as thirty-two by sixty-three or sixty-four. Regardless of which dimension is the correct one, it was one of America's largest log buildings (see Figure 58). The *Gemeinhaus* had a steeply pitched roof, probably of red tile, from which two parallel rows of dormer windows protruded which ventilated the two attics. The Moravian Church built of stone at Neuwied-Am-Rhein had similar rows of dormer windows in the sloping roof, and the Moravian-American builders transferred this identical trait to their log *Gemeinhaus* in Bethlehem.[13]

The Crown Inn, the first hostlery at Bethlehem built by the Moravians, and completed in 1745, was also made of hewn white oak logs, two stories high, measuring a sizeable forty by twenty-eight feet, and having a steep red tile roof. Like the *Gemeinhaus* it was floored with white oak planks fastened with nails made by Moravian blacksmiths, and like the *Gemeinhaus* it was intended as a permanent building, and it lasted until 1858 when it was removed to make way for the railroad.

Separate living units were erected around a central open square, *Der Platz*, for the Moravian "choirs," the segregated groups, which

Figure 58. Artist's conception of the log *Gemeinhaus* in Bethlehem, Pennsylvania, built by Moravians in 1742. Still standing, the hewn logs are completely covered with clapboards. (Courtesy Moravian Historical Society)

included the Married People, the Single Brethren, the Single Sisters, the Widows, the Widowers, etc. The Married Brothers Building, a smaller structure built along the lines of the *Gemeinhaus*, was also of hewn logs, as were some of the other choir houses. There were also schools for the children, and buildings to accommodate Indian visitors, at least one of which, the Indian Chapel, is known to have been built of hewn logs dovetailed at the corners, according to a photograph in the Annie S. Kemmerer Museum at Bethlehem, taken when the building was moved.

By 1758, the Moravian community at Bethlehem was thriving, and in addition to the *Gemeinhaus*, the Crown Inn, and the numerous log or stone structures for housing the "choirs," there was a variety of special-use buildings such as the blacksmith shop, locksmith's house, potter's house, cabinetmaker and turner's shop, water works, oil mill, grist mill, flax house, sawmill, house for boiling soap, community laundry, at least three buildings having to do with tanning leather, charcoal shed, and a nailsmith's house. There were also a number of stables, barns, and miscellaneous log sheds in the agricultural *Hof*.

In Bethlehem, according to Murtagh, "the church leaders and master builders of the community erected perhaps the largest and purest concentration of vernacular German architecture in the United States." In this concentration of industrial, residential, and ecclesiastical structures, notched-log techniques were widely employed, although one will probably never know precisely how many of the buildings were of logs. Bethlehem continues today as the headquarters of the Moravians of the United States, but the removal of the old log buildings, and the covering of others with clapboards, like the *Gemeinhaus*, which is still standing although clapboarded in 1868, has destroyed much of the character of the original community.

This church-oriented and church-governed communal society of Moravian Brethren spread from the Bethlehem-Nazareth hub, and exerted a more widespread influence on American log architecture than is generally realized. For example, at Lititz, Pennsylvania, Moravians from Bethlehem built a log church when they started a religious community there; at Emmaus in 1742 they also built a log church, and in 1747 a log schoolhouse. They also built log structures at Gnadenthal, Christiansbrunn, and Oley. Moravians spread to Hope, New Jersey, where in 1769, one of the brethren, Peter Worbass, built a log dwelling house, and Moravians led by David Zeisberger, the Indian missionary, carried log housing concepts to Salem, Gnadenhuetten, New Schoenbrunn, and Goshen in Ohio. Also, as the reader will presently note, they established settlements in North Carolina where their first dwellings were built of logs.

Moravian log houses in the Bethlehem-Nazareth area apparently had distinctive features differing somewhat from the log housing of the other German sectist groups. These typological characteristics may never be fully identified because so much of the evidence has disappeared. The previously described Gray Cottage is the only extant Moravian-built log dwelling surviving in the Bethlehem-Naz-areth area in which portions of the original logs are still exposed to view; and it, too has been subject to alteration since it was built.

Despite the fact that Pennsylvania German log houses seem to have been as diverse in construction as the regions from which the immigrants came, the necessity of sacrificing traditions as an ex-pedient for cost and simplicity tended to erase many of the differ-ences as log housing spread southerly and westerly. When the Ger-man Seventh-day Baptists settled at Ephrata in Lancaster County, originally called Dunkerstown or Beisselstown, they, too, built log cabins as their first residences although none of these cabins remain. Later the Brethren erected the heavy frame structures known today as the Ephrata Cloisters where Johann Conrad Beisel's followers lived, worked, and worshipped in accordance with his rigid dis-ciplines.

Although Mittelberger could note in his journal in 1750 that in Philadelphia, "All the houses are built up to the fourth floor of stone or brick and are roofed with cedarwood shingle," the German log house by then was the most common family dwelling in the area north to the Lehigh and west to the Susquehanna. In Womelsdorf and Meyerstown practically all the residences were of logs, and in Schaeferstown in Lebanon County, German Jews built a log syn-agogue.[14]

German Lutherans who moved into Maryland from Pennsylvania built a log church on the Monocacy in 1743, and another log church in Frederick in 1746, as well as many log residences and outbuild-ings.[15] Germans who migrated into Virginia also built log churches, and the account has been recorded of a Lutheran pastor at New Market who helped fell the trees to build his church while his wife cooked food in wash kettles in an open field for the hardy parish-ioners who gathered to assist in the "hewing and log raising."[16] If one had gone inside one of the log churches he would have heard sermons delivered in a German patois and hymns sung in German (see Figure 59). If he visited a log school he would have listened to a teacher talking anglicized German. The Germans carried with them

Figure 59. Evangelical and Reformed Church at Schellsburg, Pennsylvania, typical of the hewn log churches, neatly interlocked at the corners, built by Pennsylvania Germans.

to Maryland and Virginia a culture which was not entirely of the old country, but of a polyglot German Pennsylvania society, a composite of the folkways and dialects of people from different sections of Germany brought together in America. Sir Augustus J. Foster said of the Germans settled in Maryland that "the language they speak is a jargon of English and German," and although he was conversant in the German language he said he could hardly understand a single sentence!

Another wave of immigration from Europe followed the German movement to America—the evacuation of the Scotch-Irish from the Province of Ulster in northern Ireland, which also had an important bearing on the evolution and diffusion of the American log cabin.

The term Scotch-Irish is peculiarly American and rarely used by

British historians. It does not designate, as some assume, a people of mixed Scotch and Irish ancestry, but is derived from a group of Protestants from the Scottish lowlands who settled with their families in the northern counties of Ireland starting about 1600. The most prominent and more prosperous Scots became tenants of the English Crown, receiving land grants for the underlying purpose of anglicizing Ireland, and the poorer Scots then became subtenants of their countrymen. As time went on, civil and religious oppression developed in Ireland, and the Scotch-Irish sought relief and a better life in America. By then these lowland Scots, who had lived in Ireland for three or four generations, considered Ireland as their homeland, not Scotland of which there was only folk memory, but they recognized themselves as a breed different from the Catholic Irish with whom they had little in common.

There was a certain synonymity between the Scotch-Irish and Presbyterianism, and the influx of the Scottish lowlanders to Ireland, based on an assessment made in 1717, created 140 Presbyterian congregations, eleven presbyteries, and nearly 200,000 members of the Synod of Ulster.[17] The exodus of these Scotch-Irish Presbyterians from Ulster is a striking feature of Irish history, and one that had a marked impression on American colonial life. Families left Ireland in droves, draining Ulster of an energetic and enterprising segment of her population. Between 1717 and the outbreak of the American Revolution it is estimated that 250,000 Ulstermen came to America in five major migratory waves.[18]

Scotch-Irish settlements were made in New England, Pennsylvania, Virginia, New Jersey, the Carolinas, and in Maryland where the Reverend Francis Makemie, pioneer Presbyterian pastor in the New World, lived and labored for many years, founding six Presbyterian congregations. Although the Scotch-Irish landed at a number of American ports, the majority made their entrance via the Delaware River ports at New Castle, Chester, and Philadelphia with the result that Pennsylvania and her then "three lower counties" (now the state of Delaware) became a hearth of Scotch-Irish Presbyterian communities. In 1729, James Logan, the provincial secretary of Pennsylvania, himself of Scotch-Irish extraction, wrote, "It looks as if Ireland is to send all its inhabitants hither, for last week not less then six ships arrived and every day two or three arrive also." [19]

Although New Castle was much smaller than Philadelphia and of lesser commercial importance, it was, nevertheless, the seat of the courts and the General Assembly of the three lower counties, and ocean-going vessels conducted a brisk trade with the town's merchants. The Reverend John Wilson preached to a small English Presbyterian congregation that met at first in New Castle's courthouse before a church was erected in 1707. Farther south at Lewes another Presbyterian congregation had been formed, with its own minister, and doubtless the existence of these two Presbyterian churches encouraged many of the Scotch-Irish families to debark at New Castle and settle in northern Delaware, even though they were not warmly welcomed by the other denominations.

In 1723, George Gillespie wrote from the Head of Christiana, a town at the head of tidewater on the stream at whose mouth Minuit settled the first Swedes, "There are a great many congregations erected, and now erecting; for within the space of five years by gone, near to *two hundred Families* have come into our parts from Ireland, and more are following: They are generally Presbyterians." [20]

The same year an Anglican missionary at New Castle wrote,

The Church at New Castle is environed with greater numbers of Dissenters than ever, by reason of these fresh recruits sent us of late from the North of Ireland. They call themselves Scotch Irish ignavum pecus, and the bitterest railers against the Church that ever trod upon American ground. I wish I had better neighbours or keener weapons to stop their carreer . . .[21]

It was recorded that 4500 Scotch-Irish arrived at New Castle in the year 1728,[22] a substantial increment to the population, which in the three counties combined, was less than 35,000 at the outbreak of the Revolution. Having no affection for the newcomers, the Anglicans and Quakers encouraged them to move on, which some did, but many remained to settle permanently on small farms, as well as in the towns, and to form new Presbyterian congregations. Wherever they went in New Castle County they were exposed to Swedish-Finnish log housing, and in Christiana and Mill Creek Hundreds, as indicated in the previous chapter, perhaps 40 percent of the rural residences were of logs. So far as the Scotch-Irish settlers in Delaware are concerned there was little or no direct German influence on their housing, and in the log houses that they built they revived, to some extent, Scandinavian craft cultures.

This was not true of the Scotch-Irish who landed at Philadelphia and settled in Pennsylvania where German influences dominated the log housing. Like the poor German redemptioners, unable for the most part to buy land, they sought isolated areas where they squatted beyond ready reach of the authorities and there imitated the German vernacular housing. Their life in Ireland had given them self-reliance which, added to their physical endurance, resulted in a defiant, aggressive, and somewhat contentious nature. When challenged for land titles or for payment of rents, their response was that Pennsylvania had invited colonists to settle the province, and here they were and intended to stay! Because they had long been oppressed they had a deep consciousness of freedom and social and political equality. They were later to become ardent supporters of independence, and during the American Revolution many of them fought valiantly in the colonial armies against the British Crown.

The story of their movements is also a familiar one: from New Castle County in Delaware, and from Dauphin, Lancaster, Lebanon Counties, and elsewhere in Pennsylvania, where Scotch-Irish place names are still found, they moved in a succession of waves south and west. They spread toward the Susquehanna, and then pressed south across the Potomac at Harpers Ferry and into the Great Valley of Virginia, and through the gaps of the Blue Ridge into the Carolinas and Georgia. Augusta and Rockbridge Counties in Virginia were said to have developed the largest concentration of Scotch-Irish per square mile than any other place in the country.

In their original homes in the Scottish lowlands, before they

crossed the twenty-mile channel to Ireland, these Scots occupied a
land practically devoid of trees because of the destruction of the
forests. They lived in squalor, occupying one-room shanties of
stone, banked with turf, without mortar, the crevices stuffed with
straw, heather or moss to keep out the winds and rain. The roofs
were covered with thatch or turf, and a hole in the roof served as a
chimney for the fire that burned in the center of the earthen floor.
Cattle were tethered at night, especially during the winter, at one
end of the room. These hovels were filthy and full of vermin, and
there was a folk belief that an accumulation of dirt kept the house
warm and the residents healthy—"the mair the dirt, the less hurt."
The lowlanders knew famine, plague, exhausted soil, insecurity of
life and property, and they learned to fight back blow by blow to
protect themselves.

When they settled in Ireland, these lowlanders found themselves
in a heavily wooded land, but there were no dwellings of round or
hewn logs in Ulster, and they did not bring this concept with them
as part of their culture. Nor did they bring traditions of horticulture,
orchards, and vineyards, nor skilled craftsmanship, whether for
house-building, furniture or farm implements. They built crude,
rush-thatched huts of mud or stone near the castles of their landlords, and they placed their sheep within his bawn, a walled enclosure of stone or clay, strengthened by stakes or hedges for protection against wolves, or theft by the native Irish who had no
affection for the lowland intruders. In a 1611 report describing the
holdings of the Scotch landlords in Ulster there are such references
as "an Irish house of coples," "large timber houses," "houses of fair
coples," "a good house of timber," "houses of oak timber,"
"houses of timber frames," "stone houses," etc. The landlords, it
would appear, lived in comfortable dwellings.[23]

A survey of the tenants in Ulster made in 1619 enumerated "a
poor thatched house," "a house of brick and stone," "a poor cabin"
(the latter in County Tyrone was doubtless a mud hut), "houses
covered with clods," "an Irish house with a chimney at the end
made of wattles," "a fair cagework house," etc.[24] In contrast to

these mud and stone huts, the survey went on to say, and I have added the italic:

It appears by the particulars that there are now built within the Counties of Ardmagh, Tyrone, Donagall, Fermanagh, Cavan, and London-Derry, 107 Castles with Bawnes, 19 Castles without Bawnes, 42 Bawnes without Castles or Houses, and *1897 Dwelling Houses of Stone and Timber after the English manner in Townreeds,* besides very many such Houses in several parts which I saw not. . . .[25]

The timber used in the dwelling houses was obtained from oak and other trees growing in Ulster, and squared beams were used for house construction, but neither the native Irish nor the Scotch immigrants built log cabins. After their arrival in the New World the Scotch-Irish lost no time in imitating this method of house construction used by their Swedish and Finnish neighbors in Delaware and their German neighbors in Pennsylvania, exhibiting an adaptability singularly lacking among the earlier Anglo-Americans. After examining their cultural and environmental background, and recognizing the character of the Scotch-Irish themselves, this rapid adjustment to the American environment through cultural borrowal should come as no surprise.

Adaptability, in fact, was the price of survival; the Scotch-Irish families had little money, and no government or commercial sponsorship of their settlements. Economic necessity forced the individual settlers to build their houses of the most accessible and least expensive building materials. The most natural thing in the world was to copy log cabin architecture to the best of their craft abilities, and that's exactly what they did just as they had adapted to a hostile Ulster environment. Indeed, the log cabin was not unlike the single-storied cottages of mud and field stones, some with lofts under the thatched roof, that they knew in Ireland. The open fireplace, as in the log cabin, was the heart of the house, and some of the Irish huts had a central chimney erected over a fireplace in the middle of the house, and others had chimneys in the gable ends (see Figure 60).

Robert Parke, an Irish Quaker, wrote from Delaware County,

Figure 60. One of the larger farmhouses in Ulster occupied by Scotch-Irish in the seventeenth century, with chimneys on boths ends and attached shed. (Courtesy Professor Estyn Evans, Queens University of Belfast)

Pennsylvania, in 1725 that his father (more prosperous than other of his countrymen) purchased five hundred acres after his arrival and soon thereafter built a small log house.[26] Others, like Robert Wither-spoon's family who came from Ireland direct to North Carolina in 1734, built "a mean dirt house" in which the family lived at first and later built a cabin.[27]

William Tennent (also spelled Tenant), a Scotch-Irish minister from Ulster and a graduate of Edinburgh University, established the "Log College" at Neshaminy, Pennsylvania in 1727, "a little log house about 20 feet long and nearly as many broad," adjacent to his manse. It was the first school higher than a common school associated with the Presbyterian Church in America.

In 1775, during his tour of the Scotch-Irish families in Pennsylvania's frontier settlements, Philip Fithian noted in his journal that the town of Sunbury then contained a hundred houses, all of logs, except one stone dwelling.[28]

In 1772, the Reverend David McClure, another Presbyterian minister, preached sermons at Ligonier in the Pennsylvania mountains, where the Scotch-Irish congregation then lived in "twenty or thirty log houses," and at Fort Pitt where there were "40 dwellings of hewed logs." [29] At this late date some Scotch-Irish families had already moved several times, leaving their crude log cabins in eastern Pennsylvania and Delaware to go farther west or south where they built better homes of hewn logs at their new locations. No doubt the quality of the first cabins erected by the Scotch-Irish was inferior to the homes built by Germans or Swedes and Finns long practiced in log house techniques. In 1784, Pittsburgh was described as "inhabited almost entirely by Scots and Irish, who live in paltry-log houses, and are as dirty as in the north of Ireland, or even Scotland." [30]

During the summer of 1775, the Reverend John McMillan made a preaching tour of the Presbyterian settlements west of the Alleghenies, and one evening he lost his way in the mountains. He sought shelter at a farm owned by one of his countrymen, but the owner was away and the door of the scrubby cabin locked and barred. It was a rainy night, and the minister climbed the side of the cabin "and went into a hole in the roof which served instead of a chimney." [31] It was the duty of a sanctified Presbyterian pastor to visit the homes of the members of the church and examine them on their knowledge and understanding of the faith, but this method of entrance was highly unorthodox!

Fitting a chimney into an end gable wall or in the center of the log house, as many Germans did, or into one of the corners, as some Swedes and Finns did, required experience and skill (see Figure 25a, b, c, d). Lacking in the traditions of skilled craftsmanship, some Scotch-Irish builders like Dominie McMillan's absent host merely left a hole in the roof to serve as a chimney, as their ancestors had done in their lowland hovels. Others attached a crude chimney to a gable end of the dwelling as they had learned to append a clay, stone, or wattled chimney to one end of their huts in Ireland ("an Irish house with a chimney at the end made of wattles"). Although some of the log dwellings in Germany were built with chimneys attached to the exterior it was not common practice either in Germany or Scandinavia. Thus, the popularization of the exterior, protuberant chimney on the American log cabin may be due, in part, to Scotch-Irish influences.

Whereas the skilled German or Swedish cabin builder was capable of hewing logs with two or four flat surfaces, and interlocking them with carefully executed notches to produce tight, square, even corners, Scotch-Irish builders, at least at first, did not possess this sophistication, and both their round and hewn log cabins were crudely notched, having wide gaps between the logs to be chinked with mud, moss, wood, and stones, just as they had caulked the stone

Figure 61. Hidden in the Allegheny Mountains, Fayette County, Pennsylvania, this log house built by a Scotch-Irish settler provided a comfortable family shelter. Note that the squared logs are not flush at the corners, but extend beyond. The rear lean-to is a later addition.

Figure 62. Built in the log cabin traditions of the early town settlers, the two and one-half Hearth Stone House at McConnellsburg, Pennsylvania, is caulked with large pebbles set in mortar between the hewn logs.

walls of their lowland shanties. The younger Michaux was principally referring to cabins built by Scotch-Irish when he observed, "The space between these trunks of trees is filled with clay, but so carelessly that the light may be seen through in every part; in consequence of which these huts are exceedingly cold in winter, notwithstanding the quantity of wood that is burnt." [32]

As the Scotch-Irish became more experienced their craftsmanship improved, and at the time of Michaux's visit there were hundreds of well-built cabins (see Figure 61). His generalization was based on limited observation, and must be evaluated in the context of a Frenchman's aversion toward log cabins in the first place. Other contemporary accounts describe log dwellings occupied by Scotch-Irish in the towns and rural sections of Pennsylvania in more favorable terms. When Henry Bradshaw crossed the Alleghenies in 1817 he noted in his journal "log Houses are the only habitations for miles." [33] He noted there were "17 log and 20 frame or brick houses at Loudon" (present Fort Loudon, a town founded in 1795); and "40 houses, chiefly of logs" at present McConnellsburg, which was laid out in 1786 (see Figure 62). Fithian writing in 1775 said of Abbottstown that, "All the Houses are built with Square Logs."

Thaddeus Harris described the town of Strasburg in 1803 as having "80 houses principally built of hewn logs," and he called attention in his journal to the predominance of log houses in other western Pennsylvania towns.[34] At this late date many of the log dwellings were of two stories, containing a number of rooms, and were built to last (see Figure 63).

Log house with full cellar room, near Old Bedford Springs Hotel, Bedford, Penna., with detail of full dovetailing at right, sketched by the author, June 1952.

Figure 63

In 1816, David Thomas, en route from Auburn, N.Y. to the Ohio frontier, commented on the 150 dwelling houses in the town David Mead, formerly of Sunbury, Pennsylvania, founded in 1788 in the northwestern corner of the state called Meadville. Most of these houses were of hewn logs.[35] If Thomas had gone farther south to Harmony below Pittsburgh he would have entered a thriving German community housed in fifty or more fine hewn log dwellings, many two stories high, built by the devout and industrious members of the Harmonist Society who settled there in 1804 (see Figure 64).

Objectivity has been conspicuously lacking in evaluating the influences on American culture of the Germans *vis-à-vis* the Scotch-Irish, particularly during the postpioneer period. One can read that the impetuous Scotch-Irish were the valorous frontiersmen who boldly pushed south and west from Pennsylvania opening up migration routes on the old Indian trails that the conservative German farmers later followed. The single farm characteristic of the

Figure 64. Two and one-half story hewn log dwelling near Harmony, Pennsylvania, built by Harmonists who settled in the area in 1804.

early American frontier was, according to some authorities, a product of the Scotch-Irish who built their individual cabins on the wooded hillsides, and in imitation of the native Indians, planted corn, beans, tobacco, pumpkins, gourds, and squash in place of the potatoes and oats they raised in northern Ireland.

In other sources one reads that it was the resourceful Germans who were responsible for the individual farms, planting orchards of fruit trees and well-fenced gardens, taking pride in caring for their lands, their crops and livestock. The impression has been left that the Germans created everything from covered bridges and long rifles to barns and Conestoga wagons; that they formed the spearhead that pierced the mountain valleys to open new frontiers. According to the pro-German observers, the enterprising Germans were followed by uncouth, illiterate, lawless Scotch-Irish, indifferent to comfort, beauty, and good manners.

"The Old West," wrote a European scholar, "also borrowed its outbuildings from German Pennsylvania," a far too inclusive statement, as anyone knows who has traveled west of the Rockies where the nondescript sheds, corrals, and water tanks clustered around a sprawling ranch house bear no relationship to the spacious barns of Lancaster and York Counties in Pennsylvania. Conversely, it was none other than Theodore Roosevelt who assured his readers in one sweeping, unwarranted generalization that the Scotch-Irish "with axe and rifle won their way from the Alleghanies to the Rio Grande and the Pacific."

Since both the Scotch-Irish and Germans constituted prime influences in the diffusion of log housing in postpioneer America it is desirable to arrive at an objective appraisal of their relative priorities if significant differences did, in fact, exist. That the German sectists were settled in Pennsylvania and were building log houses before the first wave of 1717 swept the Scotch-Irish vanguard to American shores has been adequately documented. By 1690 Pennsylvania Germans were manufacturing paper in a water-powered mill on the Wissahickon, were laying out farms in Germantown, and a mature German migration to America was getting under way in Europe.

Palatines in 1709 settled at a point of land on the south side of the Trent River in North Carolina called New Bern well before any Scotch-Irish influences were infiltering the South. In 1714, twelve German and Swiss families, who had been living in North Carolina, moved to the Rappahannock River where they were augmented by twenty families who came direct from Germany.[36] The reader has already seen that the Palatines settled on the Hudson and moved to upper New York state before the first major Scotch-Irish migration began.

Not until the third wave of immigrants from Ulster, 1740–1741, was there a movement of Scotch-Irish in any numbers away from Pennsylvania.[37] Germans by then had already moved into western Maryland to build their log houses, where they were later followed by the Irish, English, and Scotch-Irish. On the other hand, it is true that many conservative Germans who settled in Pennsylvania felt no urge to move, and there were areas where the Scotch-Irish settled first and dominated both in numbers and influence, such as the upper portion of the Cumberland Valley nearest Harris's Ferry. Whereas Germans settled in eastern Chester County, the Scotch-Irish went to the western part of the county; the Germans settled in the northern parts of Lancaster County and Scotch-Irish in the south. I can fully agree with the statement that from the Delaware River ports where most of the Germans landed that they "accompanied, slightly preceded, or slightly followed that of the Ulsterman; thus every chapter on Scotch-Irish settlement must have its German paragraphs." [38] Both ethnic groups, in fact, were so closely associated with the diffusion of the log cabin that it is strictly an academic exercise to try to assign weights of relative importance to each, except on a regional basis, and this is only a small part of the complex whole.

Differing in religion, cultural attitudes, social heritage, and separated by a language barrier, Germans and Scotch-Irish met their housing needs in the New World in the same way by utilizing the native trees. Moreover, the peoples of each group tended to influence others as log housing spread southerly and westerly.

Emphasis upon their Scotch-Irish, German, Welsh, Dutch—or

other national origins—was usually not characteristic of the pioneer families who crossed the Alleghenies and settled on the western frontier. After the mountain barrier was surmounted, a new phase began, for here peoples of many national backgrounds met and merged. There was intermingling and intermarriage at a very early date that became characteristic of the American people, a social process that continues down to the present day. The examples of ethnic groups who continued in endogamous communities have been in the minority in the growing population.

Not until the end of the nineteenth century did Americans begin to develop a consciousness of their genealogical histories, and to compare the contributions of individuals from one national group with those of another, which led to exaggerated and prejudicial claims for particular ancestral stocks. As a consequence, objectivity has often been lost in comparing Germans with Scotch-Irish and explains why unacceptable evidence in favor of one or the other has been introduced into American history.

Actually, the memory of Ulster or of the Palatinate meant nothing to the children or grandchildren of the original Scotch-Irish and German immigrants. The ancestral ties faded as a new generation assumed the role of Americans!

The late Professor Thomas J. Wertenbaker, with whom I spent a delightful and stimulating afternoon in the Woodrow Wilson Room of the Princeton University Library in 1952 discussing log housing, was of the opinion that the gable ends of log houses erected in America by German builders differed from those built by Scotch-Irish and Swedes in that he believed the Germans preferred to place planking in a vertical position under the gable above the log walls. I made the point that although vertical planking under the gable ends was, indeed, a common trait on log dwellings in the Pennsylvania Dutch country, I had also seen examples of planking placed *horizontally* on the eave ends of German-built log houses in Pennsylvania, not excluding some houses with central fireplaces. In a further effort to isolate building traits diagnostic of the nationality of the builder (which will be discussed further in Chapter 11), Professor

Wertenbaker said he had formed an opinion that there was a distinctive and unique method of corner notching found on German-built log houses, in contrast to those built by other people, called *schwalb en schwanz*, which gave added strength to the walls, reduced the space between the logs, and shed the water outward to retard rotting. He illustrated this trait in one of his books.[39] I replied that this mode of notching was practically identical with the full dovetailing so common on existing log cabins in Delaware where German influence appeared to be minimal or nonexistent. Not having examined a series of surviving log houses in Delaware, as I had done, he seemed surprised at this disclosure. I also argued that this method of notching was common in southwestern New Jersey where Germans had commingled with the Swedish and Finnish population; and there was every indication that all three peoples used this same method.

One thing we both readily agreed on was that the *schindeldach* (shingle roof) was known in Germany as far back as the first century A.D., and was often present on log houses in Germany, whereas shingles were rare in Sweden, Finland, Holland, and Ireland, and were never used on residential structures in these countries. Yet, in America, even before the German immigrations, shingles came to be used on all kinds of buildings, including log cabins, by peoples of differing nationalities in an architectural pattern that another writer has termed "appallingly eclectic." As the Scotch-Irish, for example, were quick to adopt the log housing of the Germans, Swedes, and Finns, the Scandinavians in the Delaware Valley, as the reader has seen, learned to make and attach shingles to the roofs of their log dwellings. Typological differences began to lose whatever national or ethnic diversity they once may have had, and personal tastes and individual genius played an important part in the design of a log cabin consonant with the environment and available materials.

In this acculturation an American log cabin finally emerged, incorporating basic Scandinavian and German traits, with modifications by the Scotch-Irish and others, and a point in time was eventually reached when it became utterly impossible to identify a log cabin during the postpioneer period in nationalistic terms. The log cabin became a syncretistic American product, even though its ancestry, like many other American institutions, lay in Europe.

In the middle of the nineteenth century, a visitor to the Virginia Piedmont, or to the back country of North Carolina—especially the counties of Orange, Granville, Rowan, Anson, and Bobbs—where both Germans and Scotch-Irish settled in large numbers, may have been astonished at the hundreds of log cabins, but it is unlikely that he could have identified the ethnic backgrounds of the occupants from the mode of corner notching, the placement of fireplace and chimney, or whether or not the planking was nailed vertically or horizontally in the gable ends. A statement was once made by a European visitor that when he saw a chimney at either end of a house he was sure it was the home of an Englishman, whereas the chimney in the center was a certain sign of German ownership. The facts simply do not support this contention.

Postpioneer Ohio, where log cabins were built by mobile peoples of many differing backgrounds, is an excellent example of how the diversity in log housing developed west of the Alleghenies. Following the Revolution strips of land in Ohio were claimed by Connecticut, New York, Massachusetts, and Virginia, and tracts known as the Western Reserve, the Virginia Military Lands, the Ohio Company's Purchase, the Symmes Purchase, etc., were settled by colonists who came from the East. One writer has said that Ohio was "settled at an extraordinary fast pace, and the people came from the most diverse and individual regions . . . all kinds of people from everywhere came in so quickly in search of Eldorado that the state was from its inception cosmopolitan and decentralized." [40]

Elsewhere in the present volume I have discussed the log dwellings in the first settlements at Marietta and Schoenbrunn, the heart and soul of the Ohio Company's Purchase, and how log housing also characterized the architectural patterns in the other tracts. The earliest settlement in the Symmes Purchase illustrates how a number of differing influences were brought to bear on the housing. Three men, one from New Jersey, another from Pennsylvania, and the third from Kentucky in December of 1788 founded the colony on a high bank of the basin opposite the mouth of the Licking River. Following the Latin vogue of the time they named it *L* for Licking, *os* for mouth, *anti* for opposite, and *ville* for town—*Losantville*. Later the town was called Cincinnati, but the first settlers all lived in log cabins, the members of the new community, originating in different states, joined together to fell the trees, notch the logs, and raise the dwellings.

Donald Hutslar, associate curator of the Ohio State Historical Society, suggested in personal correspondence I had with him that log cabins were built initially in Ohio's earliest settlements because no other durable family shelter could be easily or readily constructed, a fact that is undeniable. At a later date, and while timber was still plentiful, Mr. Hutslar pointed out that log dwellings continued to be built because they represented cheap housing for farm tenants even though other building materials were available. Finally, in the mid to late nineteenth century, log dwellings were erected by both agricultural and industrial laboring classes who could not afford to build frame and brick houses.

Although log cabins were built throughout Ohio, the southeast and southwest parts of the state were the most important in the early introduction of log housing because of the access routes from the South and East. At a later date, people from Pennsylvania, Virginia, Maryland, and Kentucky came for mining purposes, and there was an influx of Negroes after the Civil War, some of whom built log cabins. Log housing in Ohio included dwellings, barns, schools, churches, and other structures ranging from those with one room (see Figure 65), to double-pen houses as well as one and one-half to two-story dwellings and larger. Not only was a variety of corner notchings and chimney complexes employed, but the log housing was a synthesis of different roof pitches, improvised shed attachments, door fixtures of both wood and metal, sash-type windows without weights, round log and sawn log rafters, and several kinds of porches. Thomas Worthington, governor and senator, built a double-pen log house on his estate in Chillicothe in 1801–1802,

Figure 65. Relic of the past, rare photo of cabin that stood near Gallia Furnace, Gallia County, Ohio, with shake roof, front porch, appended stone chimney, and snake rail fence (see left above roof). An example of Ohio's earliest log cabins. (Courtesy of Donald Hutslar)

calling it "Belleview," later to be known as "Adena," a name which came to have significance to American archeologists because of the remains of a certain prehistoric mound culture found on Worthington's property. In due course the owner framed the breezeway of the dwelling and built additional rooms until the house grew to be more than eighty feet long!

It is generally recognized by cultural historians that homogeneous groups of people incline to adhere to their own cultural traditions, of which housing is one, unless forced to deviate from them by their environmental milieu or other influences. Deviations were a natural by-product of the great American melting pot which tended to destroy homogeneity in its ferment. For example, many of the cabin builders in Ohio were New Englanders, who had no true log house traditions passed down to them from their European ancestry, but who built log structures in imitation of their neighbors.

Others having log house traditions were forced to change their housing styles in adapting to the natural resources of a new environment. Ohioans, like other Americans, borrowed this and rejected that, consonant with their capabilities and the natural conditions to which they were exposed. Individual differences and preferences found differing expressions in their housing; all Scotch-Irish, for instance did not use the same method of corner notching, nor attach a protuberant chimney to the exterior gable end of their dwellings; nor did all German descendants build their houses with a central chimney, or with planks placed vertically in the gable ends under the roof.

The following quotation from a log cabin resident in Indiana enumerates different genre from which a contemporary builder could make his selection:

> . . . the order of the cabin architecture are various like those of the Greek; for instance, *the Scotched Order*. In this, logs are hacked longitudinally and a slice taken from one side, the primitive bark being left on the other side. The scotching, however, is usually done for pastime by the boys and young women, while the men are cutting or hauling other timbers. *The Hewed Order*, in which logs like the stones for Solomon's Temple, are dressed on purpose. *The Stick-out-Corner Order*, the logs left to project at the corners, and the reverse of this, *the Cut-off Corner Order*. I might name, too, *the Doubtful or Double Order*. In this, two cabins are built together, but until the addition of chimneys, it is *doubtful* whether the structure is for men or brutes, and also *the Composite Order—i.e.*, loggeries with stone or brick chimney.[41]

When different ethnic or social groups are thrown into contact with each other, the unities that held each individual group together tend to dissolve and new patterns of common expression begin to arise. For example, in 1790 there were 12,955 white families settled in five western Pennsylvania counties, mobile peoples who had left their homes in the South and in the East. Thirty-seven percent of these families were of English origin, 19 percent Irish (including Scotch-Irish), 17 percent Scotch, 12 percent German, 7 percent Welsh, and 8 percent unidentified.[42] What cultural interactions must have been set in play as these groups intermingled and intermarried, and the acculturative forces affected them in many ways, including their methods of housing, which the reader has seen was predominately of log.

Perhaps no better example of a deviation from traditional housing patterns can be found than in the architecture of the French settlement at Azilum (Asylum) in Bradford County, Pennsylvania. Following the French Revolution emigrés from France and those from Santo Domingo after the slave uprising, founded the settlement in 1793 under the leadership of Viscount Louis de Noailles, brother-in-law to Lafayette, and a general in the French army, and Antoine Omer Talon, a prominent French attorney. These French aristocrats, accustomed to the luxuries of Parisian life, found themselves in a forested land with the nearest source of lumber and building materials at Wilkes-Barre, which had to be boated up the Susquehanna, a four or five day trip. Under the strong influence of German, Scotch-Irish, and other log cabin dwellers, "M. Talon caused the first log houses to be erected there, and the land to be prepared for the reception of the new inhabitants," according to La Rochefoucault who visited the settlement in 1795.[43]

La Rouchefoucault noted the thirty houses, all built of logs, "inhabited by families from St. Domingo, and from France, by French artizans, and even by Americans. Some inns and shops have been established the business of which is considerable." These log houses, were of hewn logs, notched, and laid horizontally to form the walls, typical of the American log cabin, but the French added some additional frills, as the following description written in 1797 indicates:

On [lot] No. 416 stands a log house 30 X 18 covered with nailed shingles, the house is divided into 2 lower rooms and 2 in the upper story, the lower ones are papered, on both sides of the house stand two small buildings of the same kind, one is used for a kitchen, the other being papered is called the dining room, both of these buildings have good fireplaces and a half story. The rooms in the biggest house have fireplaces, the two side buildings and the other are joined together by a piazza, there is a good cellar under the dining room. . . . On No. 417 stands a good log house 20 X 18 covered with nailed shingles, which is used as a barn, but might be inhabited as there are two good grooved floors and a winding staircase. . . .[44]

The most pretentious house known as *La Grande Maison* or the Queen's House, Talon had erected for his own use, but it is believed he intended it as the retreat for Queen Marie Antoinette and her children whom Noailles, Talon, and others were plotting to rescue from prison and bring to America. The Queen was executed before the project was completed. *La Grande Maison*, which survived until 1846 when it was torn down, was the largest log house ever built in America. Its hewn log walls measured eighty-four by sixty feet; it was two and one-half stories high, having a shingled roof, eight fireplaces on each floor, and glass windows covered with wood shutters. The walls were papered and the floors polished, and the entire structure had been erected by American workmen, laborers, and mechanics engaged by the French owners, who were advised by John Keating, an Irish-American entrepreneur.

La Grande Maison provided a sharp contrast to the log houses described by William Byrd in 1728 which housed peoples of differing cultural backgrounds living in the area where Byrd and the other commissioners were then establishing the border between Virginia and North Carolina. Byrd wrote as follows:

> Most of the Houses in this Part of the Country are Log houses, covered with Pine or Cypress Shingles, 3 feet long and one broad. They are hung upon Laths with Peggs, and their doors to turn upon Wooden Hinges, and have Wooden locks to secure them, so that the building is finisht without nails or other Ironwork.[45]

The Anglo-Americans living in the border swamps and forests of the deep south had learned the techniques from the peoples moving south from Pennsylvania in increasing numbers.

In 1765, residents of Hillsboro, North Carolina, counted a thousand wagons going through their town bringing new settlers—all potential log cabin builders. When the first contingent of Moravians, under the leadership of Bishop August Spangenburg came on horseback from Pennsylvania in the fall of 1752 in search of a suitable site for a new settlement, they traversed North Carolina from east to west as far as the summit of the Blue Ridge. With their broad-brimmed, flat-crowned hats, severe dark coats without lapels, and knee-buckled breeches, they set tongues wagging wherever they stopped to inspect the land.

These Moravians eventually selected a tract in present Forsyth County, North Carolina, containing upwards of 100,000 acres which they named Wachovia in honor of Count Zinzendorf's ancestral estate. Here they founded a community called Bethabara, then another about three miles away called Bethania, and finally, in the central part of the tract, the town of Salem, later consolidated with Winston. The Moravians brought the concept of the log cabin with them, as did other Germans and Scotch-Irish who preceded them, and once the technique became known in the South it was widely imitated by settlers to fit their individual housing needs irrespective of their national origins and differing cultural backgrounds.

The English minister, Bishop Francis Asbury, who wielded an influence second to none in the establishment and development of the Methodist Episcopal Church in America, found himself preaching in crude log churches built by his parishioners during his forty-five years as an itinerant minister. Neither he nor John Wesley had ever seen a log church in England, but descendants in America of English Methodists borrowed this method of construction from their neighbors and probably added individual touches of their own just as English Quakers learned to build log meeting houses (see Figure 66).

Thus the evolution of the American residential log cabin, as well as other forms of log housing, was a matter of ingenuity, adaptability, and resourcefulness of peoples of differing cultural legacies. Even the enslaved African Negroes became builders of log cabins, a phenomenon that uniquely illustrates the point. As early as 1793, the young Unitarian minister, Harry Toulmin, wrote of the farm of a Virginia slaveholder, "Adjoining the [frame] house of the master was a hut for his blacks, formed of small pine trees, laid one upon another and fastened at the end by a notch; but they were not plaistered, either on the inside or the outside." [46]

Figure 66. Quaker Meeting House, Catawissa, Pennsylvania, started in 1774, finished in 1776. Measuring 20 x 25 feet it is built on one floor with a loft.

As time passed, there came into existence in the agricultural south a class of planter aristocracy whose white-columned mansions gave America some of its outstanding Georgian architecture, although low-quality cabins hacked from pine logs, many without windows, became typical of the dwellings occupied by the colored slaves who worked in the fields of the plantation and served as household domestics in "the big house." Clusters of cabins, squalid and unpainted, sordid little villages of their own, stood a respectful distance from the owner's mansion house, usually well-hidden by intervening trees, flower gardens, and box hedges. Here the Negro families lived and bred, sang their spirituals, their standard of life depressed to a pitiful level compared to that of their affluent owners. Stephen Foster's young folks who "rolled on the little cabin floor, all merry, all happy, and bright" were, in most instances, living in log dwellings having damp, earthen floor, leaking roofs, and in a far less healthful environment than their masters' carpeted halls and drawing rooms.

Gunston Hall at Lorton, Virginia, home of George Mason, is a splendid example of the architectural beauty of the finer southern plantations. Its Palladian drawing room, impressive center hall, library, and the hand-carved woodwork of its interiors are among America's best examples of Georgian architecture. Some distance from its entrance portals and the boxwood *allée* there originally stood an assemblage of squalid cabins occupied by the colored slaves which bore a name given it by a long-forgotten satirist—Log Town. Slave cabins like those at Gunston Hall, which have long since been removed, were an integral part of the operation of a southern plantation, but are rarely accurately depicted in restorations. When replicas are constructed, as at the Andrew Jackson estate "The Hermitage" a few miles out of Nashville, the visitor usually sees tidy, well-built log structures, bearing little resemblance to the original cabins which were little more than dirty, disease-ridden log shacks (see Figure 67).

When Mason's good antislavery friend, Thomas Jefferson, designed Monticello on a mountain overlooking Charlottesville and his beloved University of Virginia, he decided to make an exception. He eliminated all such dependencies as sheds, smoke houses, stables, wash houses, and slave cabins. Jefferson believed that outbuildings were unsightly on a plantation, and he rendered the service quarters as inconspicuous as possible by placing them in the cellar and beneath long terraces adjacent to the mansion. Although Monticello was one of few southern plantations devoid of slave cabins, Jefferson was not unaware of the physical advantages of log houses properly built as the following quotation indicates:

The private buildings [of Virginia] are rarely constructed of stone or brick; much the greatest portion being of scantling and boards, plaistered with lime. It is impossible to devise things more ugly, uncomfortable, and happily more perishable. There are two or three plans, on one of which, according to its size, most of the houses in the state are built. The poorest people build huts of logs, laid horizontally in *pens*, stopping the interstices

Figure 67. A restored slave cabin on Andrew Jackson's "Hermitage" estate near Nashville, Tennessee, bearing little resemblance to the disease-ridden log shacks which the Negroes actually occupied.

with mud. These are warmer in winter, and cooler in summer, than the more expensive construction of scantling and plank.[47]

Jefferson's use of the word *pens* brings to mind another word used to describe a log cabin, which has also fallen into disuse, namely, *crib*. In 1749, Joshua Hemstead of New London, Connecticut, journeyed on horseback to Cecil County, Maryland, to visit his sister, Lucy H. Hartshorne. In a diary recounting his experiences on the trip he makes references to the numerous "Irish cribb houses" he saw in Delaware and Maryland, leaving no doubt that the Scotch-Irish who landed at New Castle quickly became cabin builders. At Nottingham, where there was a Presbyterian church and a Scotch-Irish congregation, he found "the minister & people here are very modist in their apparel & in their houses mostly Log Houses Cribb fashion." [48] Of the dialect of these Scotch-Irish families, he wrote that their "Tongues Run like mill clocks & haveing an Irish brogue on their Tongue I could understand but little they said."

At Ogletown, Delaware, Hemstead said he "oated" his horse at a corner tavern. He observed that "here are mostly wooden houses Cribb fashion & old, and those that are newly built the logs hewed & thick as hog neck or thereabouts." [49] The inference to be drawn is that the older Swedish log houses in the neighborhood were of round logs whereas the newer dwellings built by the Scotch-Irish were of hewn logs.

Crib is an early English word used to describe a mean cottage or hovel, and it is found in *Henry IV*, Part 2, Act III, Scene I:

> Why rather, sleep, best thou in smoky crib
> Upon uneasy pallets stretching thee
> And hush'd with buzzing night-flies to thy slumber
> Than in the perfum'd chambers of the great.

Entirely apart from the southern planter aristocracy like Jefferson, Mason, and Washington, there was a class of poor farmers, lower on the social scale, who also owned colored slaves. Although some occupied frame houses, the majority lived in log cabins, and it may come as a surprise to some readers, that these log cabin dwellers owned colored slaves who occupied smaller log cabins of even cruder construction. Olmsted's three southern trips as a newspaper correspondent, beginning in 1852, brought him into intimate contact with a number of these farmers as he wandered through the rural parts of Virginia, the Carolinas, Georgia, Alabama, Kentucky, and Mississippi. Of Alabama, for example, he wrote, "Much of the larger proportion of the planters of the state live in log-houses some of them very neat and comfortable, but frequently rude in construction, not chinked, with windows unglazed, and wanting in many of the commonest conveniences possessed by the poorest class of Northern farmers and laborers of the older States." [50]

These unchinked dwellings, which were seen in all the southern states, were usually built of hewn logs, and the absence of daubing left wide open spaces in the walls. "Through the chinks," Olmsted

wrote, "as you pass along the road you may often see all that is going on in the house; and, at night, the light of the fire shines brightly
out on all sides." [51]

Tyrone Power, in his American visit in 1833–1835, also observed
unchinked cabins in Alabama "the interstices between the logs were
unfilled, through these the wind and rain had both free ingress." [52]
The absence of chinking was a matter of choice, not necessity, since
there was plenty of mud and straw in the areas where these cabins
were built. This negative trait is a further example of how certain
builders modified the log cabin to suit their own needs, in this case
the heat of summer.

Olmsted was astonished to see these roughly-built dwellings
flanked by two, three, or more even meaner cabins occupied by
the owner's colored slaves who worked the fields. He had difficulty
reconciling himself to the sight of an aged Negro woman cutting
and carrying wood to her owners, a poor white family living in an
unchinked log cabin. He stopped for supper at a log cabin somewhere in the Carolina backwoods, the structure appearing much
neater than many others he had passed during the day. "There was
no glass in the windows," he wrote,

but drapery of white muslin restrained the currents of air, and during the
day would let in sufficient light, while a blazing wood-fire warmed and
lighted the room by night.
A rifle and powder-horn hung near the fire-place, and the master of the
house, a fine, hearty, companionable fellow, said that he had lately shot
three deer, and that there were plenty of cats, and foxes, as well as turkeys,
hares, squirrels, and other small game in the vicinity. It was a perfectly
charming little backwoods farm-house—good wife, supper, and all; but
one disagreeable blot darkened the otherwise most agreeable picture of
rustic civilization—we were waited on at table by two excessively dirty,
slovenly-dressed negro girls. In the rear of the cabin were two hovels,
each lighted by large fires, and apparently crowded with other slaves
belonging to the family. [53]

Twenty years earlier de Tocqueville was also astounded to find
that poor log cabin dwellers in Kentucky and Tennessee were slave
owners. Compare his remarks with Olmsted's:

One is scarcely better protected than one would be in a shelter made of leafy boughs. Nothing would be easier than to protect ones-self against bad weather and stop the cracks, but the master of the place is incapable of taking such trouble.

The interior of these dwellings show up the master's laziness even more than his poverty—the walls are so open to the day that the outside air comes in on every side.

After passing over a fence of roughly shaped wood, not without the risk of being devoured by the owner's dogs, one reaches a cabin through whose walls a fire can be seen crackling on the hearth; one pushes open a door hung on leather thongs and having no lock; one enters a sort of savage hut which seems the refuge of every misery; there one finds a poor family living with the leisure of the rich. As you come in, the master of the house gets up, and receives you with pressing hospitality, but he is careful not to go himself to get what you need; in his mind it would be degrading to him to serve you. It is the slave who pokes the fire to warm the traveller; it is a slave who gets his clothes dried and brings him the food he needs. The master watches and his gestures direct his servants' work: he does nothing himself. If he opens his mouth, it is to call his dogs or to tell of some of their bold feats. There is no farmer in Kentucky or Tennessee so poor but can represent a fine example of the country gentleman of old Europe.[54]

The cabins occupied by the slaves ranged from simple log structures on the small farms, having one room twelve feet square "with no windows—no opening at all except the doorway, with a chimney of sticks and mud," to those described on a large James River, Virginia, farm where the slaves lived in log cabins twenty by thirty feet, with lofts and shingled roofs, "each divided in the middle and having a brick chimney outside the wall at each end was intended to be occupied by two families." [55]

On the larger, more prosperous farms, where the master and his family lived in comfortable frame dwellings, the white overseer employed by the owner generally lived in the slave quarters, usually occupying a whitewashed log cabin, larger and better built than those occupied by the black slaves he supervised. Olmsted's account of the brutality of some of these overseers in their treatment of the slaves, and the squalor in which Negroes lived, must have appalled his northern readers and probably contained some exaggeration. However, his descriptions of the log dwellings were accurate and are corroborated in the writings of de Tocqueville and others.

No account of the log cabin in America would be complete without reference to the outstanding figure in American history associated with the Kentucky rifle, log cabins, and the rugged life of the frontier woodsman—Daniel Boone. It is appropriate to deal with him in this chapter treating primarily of Pennsylvania and its influence, although it is not widely known that he was a Pennsylvanian by birth.

When the Boone family left Pennsylvania in the spring of 1750, pausing first in the Shenandoah Valley, and then moving on like many others to settle in the valley of the Yadkin River in North Carolina, their English and Welsh forebears would have been astonished at how quickly young Daniel, then aged sixteen, and raised a Quaker, adapted to a wilderness environment. But his participation as a waggoner in the Braddock expedition against Fort Duquesne in his coonskin cap and buckskin leggings, his part in the Cherokee War, his travels into Kentucky with John Finley, his capture by the Shawnee, and his later role as a commander in Spanish territory west of St. Louis are not as memorable as the story of the inscription he carved on a tree in the Tennessee backwoods: "D Boon cilled A BAR on this tree 1760."

Daniel Boone's spelling, like his ciphering and reading, was mostly self-taught, as was his knowledge of building log cabins, a skill he learned in the first place from observing the cabins of the German farmers in Berks County, Pennsylvania. Today, about one mile north of Baumstown in Berks County, the site of the log cabin where Daniel Boone was born has been memorialized in a state park. After marrying Rebecca Bryan he built a log cabin on the Yadkin River and started planting a crop, but Boone's restless nature would not allow him to settle down to the humdrum life of a dirt farmer. During a lifetime of wandering, fighting, and pursuing game, which included a period of residence at Boonesboro on the Kentucky

Figure 68. An old-time artist relied entirely on his imagination when he made this pencil sketch entitled "Daniel Boone Alone in the Wilderness." (Reproduced from *Our Western Border* by Charles McKnight, Phila., 1875)

River where all the occupants then lived in log cabins; sojourns at Maysville on the Ohio; Boone's Station in Kentucky; Point Pleasant in West Virginia; and finally in the Ozarks about sixty miles from the mouth of the Missouri, he built a succession of log cabins. Nobody knows—nor is there any way of ascertaining—the exact number of log cabins erected by this almost legendary character whose name still symbolizes the American frontiersman (see Figure 68). Unknowingly Boone made an important contribution in the diffusion of log cabin technology to an expanding South, and the Daniel Boone-log cabin traditions have made a deep imprint in American lore. Today's parents can purchase for their children a prefabricated

Figure 69. Prefabricated miniature Daniel Boone Cabin made of cedar slabs keeps log cabin traditions alive with the younger generation of Americans. (Courtesy Creative Playthings, Inc., Princeton, New Jersey, and Los Angeles, California)

playhouse of cedar slabs simulating logs, offered by a toy manufacturer under the name of "Daniel Boone's Cabin" (see Figure 69).

Boone's adopted Kentucky, birthplace of Kit Carson, Henry
Clay, Abraham Lincoln, and Jefferson Davis, was first explored by
Dr. Thomas Walker who came through the Cumberland Gap in
1750. Near Barbourville is the Dr. Thomas Walker State Park containing what is believed to be a replica of the log cabin built by the
first exploring party. James Harrod of Pennsylvania, leading another
company of adventurers, came into the Kentucky country in 1774,
and there established the state's first permanent white settlement called
Harrodsburg. From an entry in the journal of Nicholas Cresswell
we learn that in 1775 at "Harwoodsburg" there were thirty houses
built of logs and roofed with clapboards "but not a nail in the whole
town." [56] In the Pioneer Memorial State Park at Harrodsburg is a
reconstruction of the log blockhouse built by the first settlers for
their protection against the Indians. Organized as a county of Virginia in 1776, and admitted to the union as the fifteenth state in
1792, Kentucky has a rich log cabin lore, and the surviving structures are also deserving of detailed regional study.

NOTES—CHAPTER 8

1. Philadelphia Quarter Sessions Minutes, 1685–1686, Manuscript, Historical Society of Pennsylvania, Catalog No. AM 3092.

2. Philadelphia County Deed Book E-1-5, 223:24, 2m 1686.

3. H. W. Kriebel, *The Schwenkfelders in Pennsylvania* (Lancaster, Pa.,
1904), reprint of vol. XIII, *Proceedings* of Pennsylvania German Society.
A sketch of the Yeakel cabin appears opposite p. 48.

4. Gottlieb Mittelberger, *Journey to Pennsylvania*, ed. and trans. Oscar
Handlin and John Clive (Cambridge, Mass., 1960), xi; see also Walter
Allen Knittle, *The Early Eighteenth Century Palatine Emigration* (Phila-
delphia, 1936).

5. *The Pennsylvania Germans*, ed. Ralph Wood (Princeton, 1942), 3.
It seems incredible that Nelson Beecher Keyes, *The American Frontier*
(Garden City, N.Y., 1954), 79, could completely overlook the German
influence and naïvely suggest that everyone borrowed the log cabin concept from the Delaware Swedes.

6. Adolph B. Benson and Naboth Hedin, *Americans From Sweden* (Philadelphia, 1950), 161.

7. Dieter Cunz, *The Maryland Germans* (Princeton, 1948), 49.

8. Robert C. Bucher, "The Continental Log House," *Pennsylvania Folklife*, Summer, 1962, XII, No. 4, 14–19. The two and one-half story Schutz house illustrated on p. 15 is an excellent example of a surviving Pennsylvania log dwelling with a central chimney.

9. *The Pennsylvania Barns*, ed. A. L. Shoemaker (Lancaster, Pa., 1955), 29. Eric Sloane in *An Age Of Barns* illustrates several different forms of log barns.

10. *Narratives of Early Pennsylvania, West New Jersey and Delaware*, ed. Albert Cook Myers (New York, 1912), 433; see also Harry M. and Margaret B. Tinkcom, *Historic Germantown*, American Philosophical Society (Philadelphia, 1955); the Heydrick-Yeakle log house illustrated, p. 27.

11. C. Henry Smith, *The Mennonite Immigration To Pennsylvania* (Norristown, Pa., 1929, reprint of Pennsylvania German Society *Proceedings*, XXXV, Oct. 10, 1924, Part 2), 105. Cf. William I. Hull, *William Penn and the Dutch Quaker Migration to Pennsylvania* (New York, 1935); see also Frederick Klees, *The Pennsylvania Dutch* (New York, 1951), 97, 113.

12. A complete description of the buildings at Nazareth and Bethlehem may be found in William J. Murtagh's doctoral dissertation, "Moravian Architecture and City Planning," etc., presented to the Graduate School of Arts and Sciences, University of Pennsylvania, 1963. I consulted the copy on file in the University of Pennsylvania Library, but it has since been published under the title, *Moravian Architecture And Town Planning* (Chapel Hill, 1967). A visitor in Sept. 1779 made note of "the small log house" first erected in Nazareth, which was still standing, J. C. Ogden, *An Excursion Into Bethlehem, Nazareth, etc.* (Philadelphia, 1800), 44.

13. Garth A. Howland, "An Architectural History Of The Moravian Church, Bethlehem, Pa." *Transactions* Moravian Historical Society, XIV, Parts 1 and 2 (1947), Figure 9. The measurements of the *Gemeinhaus* are discussed in another paper by the same author, "Reconstructional Problems Associated with The Moravian Buildings in Bethlehem," *Transactions*, ibid., XIII, Parts 3 and 4, 175–280.

14. Klees, 85. See also G. Edwin Brumbaugh, "Colonial Architecture of the Pennsylvania Germans," Pennsylvania German Society *Proceedings*, XLI (1930), 5–60; William Oliver Stevens, *The Shenandoah and its Byways* (New York, 1941); S. Kercheval, *History of the Valley* (Win-

chester, Va., 1883); John W. Wayland, "The Pennsylvania Germans in the Valley of Virginia," *The Pennsylvania German Quarterly*, X, No. 1 (Jan. 1909), 1–5.

15. Cunz, 58.

16. Herrman Schuricht, *History of the German Element in Virginia* (Baltimore, 1900), II, 13. There are references herein to log churches at Madison and Kernstown, I, 74, 90.

17. Charles A. Hanna, *The Scotch Irish* (New York, 1902), I, 620.

18. James G. Leyburn, *The Scotch-Irish*, Chapel Hill, 1962), 169. Estyn Evans is the author of two excellent papers dealing with cultural influences of the Scotch-Irish, "The Scotch-Irish In The New World: An Atlantic Heritage," *Journal of the Royal Society of Antiquaries of Ireland*, XCV (1965), 39–49, and "Culture and Land Use in the Old West of North America," *Heidelberger Geographische Arbeiten, Studien zur Kulturgeographie*, XV (Wiesbaden, 1966), 72–80.

19. Hanna, II, 63.

20. John W. Christie, "Presbyterianism in Delaware," *Delaware—A History of the First State*, ed. H. Clay Reed (New York, 1947), II, 646–647.

21. *Ibid.*

22. Leyburn, 181.

23. Hanna, I, 501, 519, 520, 524.

24. *Ibid.*, I, 527, 531, 535, 537, 538, 556.

25. *Ibid.*, I, 545.

26. *Ibid.*, II, 64–65.

27. *Ibid.*, II, 27.

28. *Ibid.*, II, 77.

29. *Ibid.*, II, 80.

30. Solon J. Buck and Elizabeth Hawthorn Buck, *The Planting of Civilization in Western Pennsylvania* (Pittsburgh, 1939), 147; cf. John Harpster, *Pen Pictures of Early Western Penna.* (Pittsburgh, 1938), 157.

31. Hanna, II, 89.

32. F. A. Michaux, *Travels to the West of the Allegheny Mountains*, 2nd ed. (London, 1805), 29–30.

33. Henry Bradshaw Fearon, *A Narrative Of A Journey 5000 Miles Through The Eastern And Western States Of America* (London, 1818), 187, 190, 195.

34. Thaddeus Mason Harris, "The Journal Of A Tour Into The Territory Northwest Of The Allegheny Mountains (1803)," *Early Western Travels, 1748–1846*, ed. Reuben G. Thwaites (Cleveland, 1904), 319–322.

35. David Thomas, *Travels Through The Western Country In The Summer Of 1816* (Auburn, N.Y., 1819), 39.

36. Cunz, 57.

37. Leyburn, 169.

38. *Ibid.*, 186.

39. Thomas J. Wertenbaker, *The Founding Of American Civilization: The Middle Colonies* (New York, 1938), 304.

40. Harlan Thatcher, *The Buckeye Country* (New York, 1940), 87–88.

41. John T. Faris, *When America Was Young* (New York, 1925), 27.

42. Buck, 152.

43. *Travels Through The United States of North America, etc.*, Duke De La Rochefoucault Liancourt, 2nd ed. (London, 1800), I, 158.

44. Louise Welles Murray, *The Story of Some French Refugees and Their Azilum, 1793–1800* (Elmira, N.Y., 1917), 35.

45. Francis B. Johnston and Thomas T. Waterman, *The Early Architecture of North Carolina* (Chapel Hill, 1941), 3–4.

46. Harry Toulmin, *The Western Country in 1793*, ed. Marion Tinling, and Godfrey Davis (San Marino, Calif., 1948), 17.

47. *Thomas Jefferson's Notes on the State of Virginia*, ed. William Peden (Chapel Hill, 1955), 152.

48. *Maryland Historical Magazine*, XLIX, No. 4 (Dec. 1954), 349.

49. *Ibid.*, 350.

50. Frederick Law Olmsted, *A Journey in The Seaboard Slave States* (New York, 1856), 575.

51. *Ibid.*, 385–386.

52. Tyrone Power, *Impressions of America During The Years 1833, 1834 And 1835* (Philadelphia, 1836), II, 93.

53. Frederick Law Olmsted, *The Cotton Kingdom*, ed. Arthur M. Schlesinger (New York, 1933), 165–166.

54. Alexis de Tocqueville, *Journey to America*, trans. George Lawrence, ed. J. P. Mayer (New Haven, 1960), 136, 267.

55. Olmsted, *Seaboard Slave States*, 44.

56. *The Journal of Nicholas Cresswell, 1774–1777* (New York, 1924), 106.

III

LOG CABINS IN AMERICAN POLITICS

9   *The Log Cabin Campaign*

A log cabin elected General William Henry Harrison the ninth President of the United States in the most blatant, almost unbelievable political campaign American voters have ever seen. Because this campaign molded America's image of the log cabin, its significance goes much deeper than its political aspects. Modern attitudes toward log cabins were influenced by this campaign that took place more than 125 years ago, and no history of the log cabin in America can be complete without detailed reference to it.

The election took place during young America's first great business depression, the Panic of 1837, which was blamed on the incumbent president, Martin Van Buren. Banks in America's two major financial centers, Philadelphia and New York, were forced to close their doors, and before long, every bank in the country, large and small, stopped paying out gold and silver. Business houses and factories shut down, and the nation's farmers, unable to obtain credit, were hard hit. Millions of persons, thrown out of work, looked to Washington for aid, but nothing was done to help them. President Van Buren considered it wrong for the federal government to give relief to people who had lost their money or their jobs. When the Democrats nominated Van Buren for re-election in 1840, in the face of widespread unemployment, the collapse of cotton prices in the South, and demoralized land prices in the West, a Democratic defeat was almost a foregone conclusion.

The Whig coalition, which nominated General William Henry Harrison as their candidate at a national convention held in a Lutheran Church in Harrisburg, Pennsylvania, in December of 1839, had no agreed platform and no formal policies. They named as the retired general's vice-presidential running mate John Tyler, a state's rights aristocrat and a former governor of Virginia whose views were entirely opposite from those of most of the leaders of the Whig party, an anomaly scarcely calculated to carry enough votes to win a presidential election.

General Harrison was sixty-seven years of age, and he lived on a farm in North Bend, Ohio, where he held a comparatively low-paid job as county recorder of deeds. At any other time in the nation's history no political party would have dared put up a failing old man and as his running mate a contentious Virginian as candidates for the highest offices in the land, but President Van Buren's unpopularity, the business recession, and the log cabin propaganda were destined to sweep Harrison and Tyler to victory.

The log cabin campaign had its genesis in a sarcastic line written by John de Ziska, a Washington correspondent of the Baltimore *Republican*, a newspaper opposed to the Whigs. In a column appearing in the December 11, 1839, issue, this is what he wrote by way of a sneer and reproach directed at the Whig candidate from backwoods Ohio:

"Give him a barrel of hard cider, and settle a pension of $2000 a year on him, and our word for it, he will sit the remainder of his days in his log cabin by the side of the 'sea-coal fire' and study moral philosophy!"

The hard cider-log cabin allusion, which was to be touted in every hamlet, village, town, and city in the land during the ensuing campaign, had reference to the farm sixteen miles down the Ohio River from Cincinnati where the presidential candidate then resided. When Harrison, as a young army lieutenant, following his marriage to Anna Symmes, purchased 160 acres along the Ohio in 1796, there was a four-room frame dwelling on the property built around an original one-room log cabin erected by a pioneer farmer. Harrison and his bride lived at North Bend for only a short time, although he continued to retain ownership of the property during a long and varied political and military career.

Duty called him to Vincennes in Indiana Territory, where he built a handsome brick mansion in the Georgian style, with thirteen rooms, called "Grouseland," and to other locations in the service of the United States government. As a congressman, senator, governor of Indiana, army officer, and minister to Colombia, he lived in a variety of homes, including the American embassy at Bogota, none of which faintly resembled a log cabin. In his twilight years, as a retired general, he came back to North Bend, where he expanded his land holdings to three thousand acres, there intending to spend his remaining days as a plain farmer, augmenting his income in a minor political job. Upon his return he enlarged the frame dwelling, with its log matrix, to accommodate his growing family.

By no stretch of the imagination could Harrison's North Bend house be termed a log cabin after the general turned it into a commodious dwelling. To the original four rooms he added wings on both sides, and laid out a wide ell, which ran back from the center and opened into a parlor, a spacious dining room, and a wide staircase. All in all, there were sixteen rooms in his house, and the exterior was covered with clapboards, and the interior with wainscoting.

So far as hard cider was concerned, General Harrison was not an intemperate man, and he was no more addicted to the fermented juice of Ohio's crushed apples than his running mate, Tyler, or his opponent, Van Buren. But hard cider, like the coonskin cap, the fringed hunting shirt, the Kentucky rifle, and the hand plow, were associated in the popular mind with rugged, unlettered backwoods folks who shot coons and swigged from the brown jug cradled on their shoulders—and Harrison was accorded the full disparaging treatment by the opposition party to discredit his candidacy. But the slur rebounded, and unknowingly the Democrats sowed the bitter seeds for their own decisive defeat.

"Whiggery," a later historian wrote of the period, "was a complex conglomeration of economic, sectional, personal and ideological components." [1] The Whig party included Masons and anti-Masons, tariff men and antitariff men, proslavery planters and abolitionists, advocates and opponents of the National Bank, and it was divided on other issues.

The problem faced by Whig politicians was to solidify these dissimilar elements in the party in order to elect Harrison. Thomas Elder, a Pennsylvania banker, and Richard S. Elliott, a Harrisburg editor, devoted themselves to the development of an acceptable election theme, the cynical Elder insisting that "passion and prejudice, properly aroused and directed, would do about as well as principle and reason in a party contest." [2] In other words, if they could create a great commotion, the Whigs could conceal the dissonance existing in the party. The Democrats in their disparagement of Harrison gave them the theme they badly needed to cause the commotion.

The log cabin campaign really had its beginning at the Ohio state Whig convention on a rainy Friday, February 21, 1840. At the open air meeting at the corner of High and Broad Streets in Columbus, the convention's president and keynote speaker, seventy-one-year old General Reasin Bell, delivered a spirited opening address. He referred modestly to his own military service at the side of the valiant young Lieutenant Harrison under command of General "Mad Anthony" Wayne. He described Harrison's valor at the Battle of Miami Rapids, his bravery at the defense of Fort Meigs, and his heroism at the Battle of Tippecanoe, successively as a captain, major, and colonel, and he referred to Perry's famous note dispatched to General Harrison after the brilliant victory on Lake Erie in the War of 1812: "We have met the enemy, and they are ours— two ships, two brigs, one schooner, and a sloop."

General Bell went on to laud Harrison as a patriot and a loyal companion in arms to whom the Republic owned its very existence. He upbraided the Democrats who were trying to cast aspersions on the character of a noble, courageous, yet humble man. He was followed by other speakers who delivered stirring speeches, resolutions, and motions, each meeting with thunderous applause and shouts of approbation from the crowd.

The parade that followed the next day was the most exciting political event that had ever taken place in the Ohio Valley. Delegates and their families poured into town from the banks of the Scioto, the Miami, and Mad Rivers; from the Muskingum, Licking, Killbuck, Jelloway, Hockhocking, Kokosing, Maumee; and from every other river and creek valley between Lake Erie and the Ohio. They came on horseback, by wagon, by canal boat, and on foot, hundreds upon hundreds, thronging hotels and boarding houses or staying in private homes with friends and relatives who had their latchstrings out. Many of them had been born in log cabins, others were still living in cabins, and all of them were indignant at the scoff given them by the Democrats, now being fanned into the principal campaign issue by the Whigs. It seemed that every log cabin in the state contributed stalwart Buckeye boys to "set the ball rolling for Tippecanoe and Tyler too," and they even constructed a huge ball which was rolled through the streets of Columbus, and later from one Ohio town to another.

"Tippecanoe" was the nickname the Ohioans gave the old general, whose army of less than one thousand men and officers put down the Delaware, Miami, Shawnee, and Potawatomie uprising almost thirty years before in a skirmish along Burnet's Creek near the mouth of the Tippecanoe River in Indiana Territory. Whig publicists, intrigued with the alliteration of Tyler's name with "Tippecanoe," phrased the memorable slogan that still stands unmatched in American political campaigns, notwithstanding "the forgotten man," "a chicken in every pot," "I like Ike," "New Frontiers," and "the Great Society." The word "Tippecanoe" was like a ripe plum, sweet, juicy, and succulent, and it rhymed on the tongue with many other words, and so the Ohioans lustily sang:

> They say that he lived in a cabin
> And lived on old hard cider, too.
> Well, what if he did, I'm certain
> He's the hero of Tippecanoe!

The next day, Washington's Birthday, to the music of fife and drum, and more than twenty brass bands, with mud over their shoe tops, their clothing drenched with rain, "Old Tippecanoe's" supporters marched through the unpaved Columbus streets, singing and shouting their praises for the "Log Cabin and Hard Cider Candidate" imprinted on their banners. Old comrades in arms joined the procession to support the general, including the Zanesville Guards, the Putnam Grays, the Warren Greens, the Jefferson Guards, and the Buckeye Rangers. Every banner they carried, embellished with log cabins, plows, canoes, and hard cider, spoke out in loud rebuke against the slight given the brave old patriot and pioneer who had given his best years protecting their frontiers, and who, in their judgment, was being villified, slandered, and belittled by the big-city rascals holding political office.[3]

The Ohio convention, with its parade of flags, waving handkerchiefs, streamers, and log cabin floats, electrified the nation. It started a movement that made the log cabin a symbol of honesty, wholesomeness, and humility, which no human power could check, and no political power could control. Some 25,000 aroused backwoodsmen, soldiers, mechanics, laborers, and farmers converged on Columbus that rainy February day to launch an exciting campaign that would carry their candidate from North Bend to the White House. "The whole bosom of the mighty west," wrote an observer during the convention, "is literally heavy with emotions of gratitude and love for the modest but gallant old farmer of North Bend."

But Ohio's tribute to the log cabin candidate was only a small sample of what was to follow when the log cabin mania caught on in the East during the Young Men's National Whig Convention held in Baltimore three months later. The parade in Baltimore began at half-past nine, Monday morning, May 4, 1840, with the firing of a cannon to signal the start of the three-day activities, and what a parade it was! In the lead was the chief marshal and his aides on horseback, wearing sashes and appropriate badges, followed by a band playing a martial tune written for the occasion called "Harrison's March." Behind them rolled a cavalcade of barouches on rubber tires carrying the distinguished guests, including Baltimore's mayor,

Sheppard C. Leakin, Senator Daniel Webster, Henry Clay, and a host of other local, state, and federal officials.

Then came the delegations from every one of the twenty-six states then comprising the Union, starting with more than two thousand delegates from New Hampshire and Massachusetts carrying almost as many silk banners, lettered with such slogans as "Hail Columbia And Harrison," "Old Tippecanoe Forever," "He Never Yet Lost A Battle," "Tippecanoe And Tyler Too." Vermont, Connecticut, and Rhode Island followed, in turn, with their bands, banners, and marching delegates. Next came New York and New Jersey, their delegates carrying flags emblazoned with their state seals, and lettered with such slogans as "Harrison And Tyler," and "Hard Cider —Harrison & Reform."

Pennsylvania's Philadelphia delegation carried a full-length canvas portrait of Harrison encircled with the words, "Honor Be To Him Who Defends Our Home And Friends." Behind the Philadelphians came the delegates from York, Cumberland, Schuylkill, and Dauphin Counties, each contingent waving its multicolor banners. Dauphin County's banner of black satin was decorated with a log cabin in gilt, surrounded by thirteen stars, and attached to the cabin was a barrel of cider, also in gilt.

The Fayette County delegation from the Allegheny Mountains of Western Pennsylvania marched behind a log cabin on wheels drawn by six prancing horses. Deer and fox skins adorned the sides and roof of the cabin, and alongside it was a barrel full of hard cider, with a gourd suspended over it. From time to time a delegate would break ranks and refresh himself from the barrel, wiping his mouth on his coat sleeve.

The delegates from Bucks County struggled with a gigantic banner bearing a brief but expressive message, "Huzza For Old Tippecanoe," and the Pittsburgh delegation marched under a colossal silk banner painted with a likeness of the candidate, and on the reverse side Harrison was pictured standing beside a plow, with a log cabin in the background.

The banner carried by members of the state of Delaware's delegation read, "The First To Adopt—The Last To Abandon The Constitution," and they, too, had a special log cabin float, which was pulled by a double team of dappled-gray horses. The cabin was an old one which had been moved from Brandywine Hundred for the occasion.

Maryland's St. Mary's delegation marched behind another log cabin drawn by eight gray horses. Frederick County was represented by still another cabin bearing a sign "Sweep The Augean Stable," with a broom sticking out of the top of the chimney. On the roof rested the limb of a pine tree, on which a live mountain eagle perched. Washington County had its log cabin drawn by eight horses, each wearing a set of Conestoga bells that tinkled as the animals walked. On the roof, a live 'possum clung to one of the branches of a transplanted gum tree. The Carroll County delegation also had a log cabin float.

On they came—from the District of Columbia, Virginia, North Carolina, South Carolina, Georgia, Vermont, Tennessee, and Kentucky—all with floats and banners. Ohio's marchers received the biggest hand from the crowd lining the streets, as the Hamilton County delegation toted a miniature log cabin fashioned from the limbs of a buckeye tree grown on the candidate's North Bend farm, while other Ohioans waved a banner depicting Harrison at the plow in a furrowed field, a log cabin silhouetted in the background against a setting sun.

Marchers by the thousands advanced down the street, six abreast, in cadence to the drums, representing the states of Alabama, Maine, Missouri, Michigan, Arkansas, Louisiana, Indiana, and Mississippi. The Indiana delegation waved a silk banner reading "She Will Teach Palace Slaves To Respect The Log Cabin." Following them was an eighty-year old soldier from Miami County, Ohio, on a white horse carrying a banner, "The Last Of The Life Guards Of General Washington." Behind him followed a riderless black horse, with a standard fluttering on the empty saddle, reading "The Saddle On Which The Illustrious Father Of His Country Rode When Leading His Countrymen To Battle."

The twelve wards of the host city of Baltimore were represented by young men's marching groups from the city's Tippecanoe Clubs, formed to solidify support for the old general. Each of the twelve clubs marched under its own banner—several of them bearing canoes intended by the inference of the pun to symbolize Tippecanoe.

The paraders converged on the convention grounds, the Canton Race Course, under a triumphal flowered arch, where a full-sized log cabin had been erected, its logs well-plastered with clay, a stick chimney on the exterior, and a door provided with a latch and string. The marchers assembled around the speakers' platform, draped in red, white, and blue bunting, where the sea of faces was exhorted by Daniel Webster, Henry Clay, and other political orators.

The final speaker, John Sergeant of Pennsylvania, known far and wide as a silver-tongued orator, put an important rhetorical question to the throng. "What have you come for?" he proclaimed irrelevantly. "I will answer. To bring back to the people, and *through the log cabins of the country*, the neglected and lost Constitution!"

No one paused to examine the logic of the speaker's remarks. They applauded, whistled, and shouted themselves hoarse for their log cabin candidate.

The following morning the delegates gathered in Monument Square, where a rostrum was erected in front of the court house, and the day was filled with wit, sarcasm, logic, and humor as the speakers denigrated Van Buren and lauded Harrison. At one point in the program, a delegate from Ohio rushed to the lectern and shouted in a hoarse voice that Ohio would bet any other delegation a barrel of hard cider that Ohio would give the largest majority of any other state to Harrison in the election. Following this outburst, the convention resolved that Tippecanoe Clubs should be formed in every town, county, and city in the land to marshal support for the old general.

The log cabin theme spread throughout the nation when the Whig delegations returned to their homes from Baltimore and launched local campaigns with carriage processions, brass bands, bonfires, torchlight parades, stump speakers, booming cannon, clanging church bells, and glee clubs. The buckeye tree became a Whig emblem and partisans carried buckeye canes and decorated their hats and horses' bridles with sprigs of buckeye. The log cabin motif appeared on campaign buttons, paper weights, bookends, almanacs, quilts, umbrella heads, and many other articles, some useful, others ornamental. Ladies set their teacups on Sandwich glass plates embossed with log cabins. These mementos of the campaign were to influence other manufacturers long afterwards, as illustrated by penny banks cast in iron as miniature log cabins, and a famous syrup marketed for many years in a tin container shaped like a log cabin. At Glassboro, New Jersey, where more than a century later another president was to hold a summit conference with a Russian leader, whiskey bottles were molded in the form of log cabins, and then filled with liquor supplied by a Philadelphia distiller, E. C. Booze. As late as 1892 a manufacturer of patent medicine was using log cabin bottles labelled "Tippecanoe and Tyler, Too."

Horace Greeley, whose editorials were a powerful force in molding public opinion, started a new weekly newspaper, published simultaneously in New York City and Albany, called *The Log Cabin*. Pro-Harrison in its editorial stance, its masthead bore an illustration of a log cabin, a cider barrel, and a farmer working in the fields behind a hand plow. To fit the image the politicians created for him as a homespun cabin dweller, General Harrison exchanged his tall silk hat for a broad-brimmed one, and he began to wear a plain frock coat, with a black vest and blue pantaloons to make himself indistinguishable from his midwestern constituents.

During the campaign a lady who lived in Rochester went to Cincinnati where she joined a group of Harrison's constituents who took a steamboat trip down the Ohio to visit the candidate's home and present him with a live eagle. In a letter later published in the Rochester *Democrat* she described the visit, the enthusiasm of her associates, and how, after they anchored near his homestead, "General Harrison came from his *Log Cabin*" and addressed the group. Honesty compelled her to add, "The house is large and the logs covered and painted white." [4]

A great "Log Cabin Raising" was held in Albany with Dutch farmers carting to town oak logs from the surrounding woods, which they cut to the proper length, notched, and used to build a log cabin. Some five thousand Whigs joined the festivities and feasted on corn bread, cheese, and hard cider as the shrine was constructed. Similar "Log Cabin Raisings" were held in towns and hamlets elsewhere, many sponsored by Tippecanoe Clubs.

In Utica, a rally was opened by a nine-mile long parade headed by 110 horsemen dressed as farmers and wearing fringed hunting shirts. They were followed by 417 double wagons and a float with an actor portraying Harrison sitting in front of a log cabin swigging hard cider from a jug.

At Bennington a "Log Cabin Rally" was arranged with one hundred ladies dressed in their finery and riding aboard farm wagons drawn by twenty-five yoke of oxen. The Harrison-Van Buren campaign was one of the first in which American women, not yet legally entitled to vote, actively participated in parades, rallies, and other election festivities. Behind the ladies came a contingent of singing Vermont mountaineers riding a log cabin moved from its original site and transferred bodily to a specially constructed wagon bed.

The Tippecanoe Clubs and the Log Cabin Committee of St. Louis staged a mammoth rally with a parade of canoes, log cabins, and the *pièce de résistance* was a caravan of drays loaded with barrels of hard cider.

At Dayton, in a mass meeting held in a log cabin built for the occasion, a tethered live wolf was exhibited with a sheepskin draped over his sides, labelled "Van Buren." This symbol of political trickery reinforced De Witt Clinton's characterization of Van Buren as one "not of the race of the lion and tiger, but of the lower order, the fox and the weasel."

From Bangor to New Orleans, and from New York City to Kaskaskia on the banks of the Mississippi, crowds gathered on main streets to rally behind the banner of the people's candidate. Log cabin meetings were held in historic Faneuil Hall in Boston and Independence Hall in Philadelphia. The campaign was a contest, Henry Clay told his rapt listeners at Nashville on August 17, 1840, "between the log cabin and the palace, between hard cider and champagne, and the issue will be that the office-holders will take to their heels with more rapidity than the popping of corks from the necks of their favorite bottles!"

Dozens of songs were written and sung during the Harrison campaign on behalf of log cabins, hard cider, and Old Tippecanoe. They rang in the ears morning, night, and noon. Men, women, and children joined the singing, and their exuberance at first worried, later annoyed, and finally crushed the Democrats. New words were written to the music of the *Marseillaise*, *Auld Lang Syne*, *Old Oaken Bucket*, and other well-known tunes. Two verses from a song called *The Rough Log Cabin* are illustrative of the sentiments expressed:

> I love the rough log cabin
> It tells of olden time
> When a hardy and an honest class
> Of freemen in their prime
> First left their father's peaceful home
> Where all was joy and rest
> With their axes on their shoulders
> And sallied for the West
> I love the old log cabin
> For here, in early days,
> Long dwelt the honest Harrison
> As every *loco** says;
> And when he is our President
> Which one year more will see
> In good hard cider we will toast
> And cheer him three times three!

In a speech at a Whig mass meeting at Saratoga on August 19, 1840, on behalf of General Harrison, Senator Daniel Webster tried

* *Loco Foco* was a term used derisively by the Whigs when referring to certain Democratic factions.

to temper the log cabin mania with reason, by pointing out that it
was the Democrats, not the Whigs, who injected the log cabin into
politics in the first place. Occupancy of a log cabin, he frankly told
his audience, was not in itself proof of qualification for the office of
the presidency, nor did log cabin life necessarily endow its occupants with reputable moral and intellectual qualities. Harrison, he
pointed out, possessed these traits as part of his noble character. But
the great constitutional lawyer, caught in the spell of his own words
and carried away by the excitement of the campaign, couldn't re-
sist the urge to sentimentalize about his own family's connections
with a log cabin in New Hampshire, and he held his listeners spell-
bound as he extemporized as follows:

> I was not myself born in one, but my elder brothers and sisters were—
> in the cabin in which at the close of the Revolutionary War, in the perils
> and sufferings of which he bore his part, my father erected on the extreme
> frontiers of New Hampshire, where, beyond the smoke which curled
> from its chimney, not another stood between it and the walls of Quebec.
> In this humble cabin amid the snow-drifts of New England, that father
> strove, by honest labor, to acquire the means of giving to his children a
> better education, and elevating them to a higher condition than his own.
> That cabin I honor for the sake of the venerable man that dwelt in it. . . .[5]

At this point, according to an eyewitness account, Mr. Webster's
golden voice became "inarticulate from emotion."

The paradox, not only in Webster's speech, but in the theme of
the whole fantastic campaign, was that Harrison wasn't born in a
log cabin either! Webster knew this full well, but he was too cun-
ning a politician to say anything to destroy the illusion his fellow
Whigs had created. Although Harrison never directly claimed in
any of his campaign speeches that he was *born* in a log cabin, he did
nothing to dispel the false impression created by the election publicity. In his first campaign speech, he told his listeners, and I have
italicized the qualifying noun, "It is true that *part* of my dwelling is
a log cabin." Thereafter he no longer felt required to use the word
"part." In a later speech at Fort Greenville, Harrison protested that
he did not seek the nomination, and would have preferred to stay

with his family "in the peace and quiet of *our log cabin* at the Bend!" To this modest disclaimer the audience screamed "No!" "No!"

The truth, not fully publicized to the voters of 1840, is that Harrison was born at "Berkeley," a two and one-half-story red brick mansion, with dormered windows and high, richly embellished pediments, situated on the James River in Virginia in the land of the planter aristocracy. He descended from the proud, wealthy, and politically prominent Harrison family whose roots went as far back as 1632 in the Old Dominion. He was the youngest son of the fifth Benjamin Harrison, signer of the Declaration of Independence, and his grandfather, a military colonel, sheriff, and burgess, owned a dozen plantations on the James and Nottoway Rivers, and married the daughter of Robert Carr, one of the richest American-born men of his day. Although in later years hard cider may have been pressed at "Berkeley," there can be no doubt that during the time of the first Harrisons of Virginia the slaves placed before the family and guests decanters of the finest Madeira wines and French brandies, with which the mahogany sideboards were well stocked.

But when the electoral votes were counted at the close of the raucous 1840 campaign, the log cabin-hard cider theme gave General Harrison 234 votes against his opponent's sixty. Van Buren even lost his home state of New York to the humble, plain-talking backwoods nominee from Ohio! After the smoke of political battle had cleared, the President-elect set about writing his inaugural address, but not in the "log cabin in the Bend." He returned to "Berkeley," and in the room where he was born he composed the words of a long-forgotten speech in which he tried to heal the wounds that party politics had inflicted.

Entirely apart from the part it played in electing a President, the Whig campaign established the clay-caulked log cabin as an institution as typically American as the bald eagle, the stars and stripes, and the silver dollar. In the full span of American history no other form of domestic housing has ever had this political significance. The paradox found so frequently in American political life occurred shortly after Harrison's election. Unable to throw off a severe cold, which developed into pneumonia, the old general died in the White House on April 4, 1841, exactly one month after his election to the presidency. Vice-President John Tyler, Virginia-born aristocrat, son of a state and federal judge, and one-time governor of Virginia, then ascended to the presidency of the United States, the first Vice-President to succeed a deceased President. Tyler wasn't born in a log cabin either, never lived in one, and privately looked down his nose at anyone who did, yet due to the vagaries of politics, the log cabin was also indirectly responsible for elevating him to the highest office in the land!

NOTES—CHAPTER 9

1. Robert Gray Gunderson, *The Log Cabin Campaign* (Lexington, Ky., 1957), 11.

2. *Ibid.*, 75–76.

3. The descriptions of the Columbus and Baltimore parades are largely drawn from A. B. Norton, *Reminiscences of the Log Cabin and Hard Cider Campaign* (Cleveland, 1888), although I also consulted a number of newspaper accounts.

4. The letter is quoted in full in the May 4, 1840, issue of *The Delaware State Journal*. A detailed description of the Baltimore convention is given in the May 8 issue of this newspaper, and the May 4 issue explains how a log cabin was moved from Brandywine Hundred to Wilmington in preparation for the trip to Baltimore.

5. Shurtleff, *The Log Cabin Myth*, 190, quotes at length from another version of Webster's speech.

10 From Log Cabin to White House

Of the eight Presidents who preceded General William Henry Harrison to the White House, the only one who may have qualified as log cabin born, and this still is not conclusively proven, was Andrew Jackson. Prior to Harrison's election campaign, the log cabin had not yet come to the front in American politics, and it was not until after Jackson's death that the question of whether or not he was born in a log cabin became a debatable issue. If it could be established that he was born in a log cabin, then Jackson could take his place in the pages of American history as the *first* log cabin President, and that would be a precedent every state would like to claim!

The problem is that two states claim Jackson as a native son—North Carolina and South Carolina and in the controversy over his birthplace there is obviously disagreement about the house in which he was born. A lank, tempestuous, hot-tempered redhead, Jackson was aptly characterized by Thomas Jefferson when in 1818 President Monroe asked his advice about sending Jackson on a diplomatic mission to Moscow. "Good God," the patriarch of Monticello exclaimed, "he would breed you a quarrel before he had been there a month!" It is fully in keeping with "Old Hickory's" contentious nature that 132 years after his death there is still argument about where he was born.

Jackson's father, the elder Andrew Jackson, an Ulsterman, his wife, the former Elizabeth Hutchinson, and their two small sons,

Hugh and Robert, settled about 1765 on Twelvemile Creek in what was then Mecklenburg County, North Carolina, now Union County. This general area was known as the *Waxhaws*, although it had no designated boundaries nor did the term have political significance. Into the *Waxhaws* before the Revolution came several migrations of Scotch-Irish families, many from Pennsylvania, Maryland, and Virginia, and they settled on the fertile bottom lands, built log cabins and churches, and became farmers. Among these settlers were five of Mrs. Jackson's sisters, all married, and probably one of the reasons the Jacksons came to the *Waxhaws* was to be near these relatives.

The elder Jackson built a log cabin where the family lived and farmed the land, and he died in this cabin in February or March of 1767. At the time of his death his wife was pregnant, her unborn child destined to become the seventh President. At this point the facts become clouded except it is generally agreed that after the death of her husband, the pregnant widow woman and her two young sons packed up some of their possessions, left their cabin, and headed for the home of one of Mrs. Jackson's sisters where the delivery of her infant could be properly attended.

The two sisters who figure prominently in the account were Margaret, the wife of George McCamie, who lived in a log cabin near Waxhaw Creek, North Carolina, and Jane, the wife of James Crawford, who lived on Waxhaw Creek, South Carolina, although the nature of the latter's dwelling house has not yet been authenticated. McCamie was a poor dirt farmer, who could not read or write, whereas Crawford was in much better financial circumstances, and was the owner of slaves. Jackson later wrote that he spent the early days of his boyhood with the Crawfords, but that should not be interpreted to mean that he was necessarily born in their house.

Proponents of Jackson's North Carolina birth claim that Mrs. Jackson either went direct to her sister Margaret's home in North Carolina for the delivery of her baby, or stopped there while en route to her sister Jane's house in South Carolina, because of advanced labor pains, and that Andrew Jackson was born in the McCamie cabin. Those who claim the President was born in South Carolina maintain that Mrs. Jackson went direct to her sister Jane's house, and her son was born in the James Crawford residence in South Carolina.

The clash of opinion still exists as I write, and both states continue to memorialize Andrew Jackson in various ways which may confuse the historian but don't seem to faze the tourist who takes his historical markers in stride. Statuary on the capitol grounds in Raleigh commemorates North Carolina's three Presidents by birth, with Andrew Jackson astride a horse looming over the seated James K. Polk and Andrew Johnson. A marker in Union County, North Carolina, placed where the George McCamie cabin is believed to have stood has a log cabin in bas relief on the stone and the inscription, "Here Was Born March 15, 1767 Andrew Jackson Seventh President of the United States." A roadside historical marker at Waxhaw, North Carolina, reads "Andrew Jackson Seventh President of the United States was born a few miles southwest of this spot, March 15, 1767."

In Lancaster County, South Carolina, a short distance from the North Carolina state line is the Andrew Jackson Memorial Park, a beautiful wooded area surrounded by a snake rail fence, opened to the public in 1954. On the property is a two-story blockhouse-type museum building of hewn logs containing Jackson documents and historical exhibits, as well as a log picnic shelter and toilet facilities in separate structures patterned after Waxhaw's old-time log cabin architecture (see Figure 70). Within the park and approximately one and one-half miles from North Carolina's McCamie marker, is a stone memorial erected on land where James Crawford lived and where South Carolina claims that Jackson was born.

Advocates of South Carolina as the state of Jackson's birth point to evidence in the form of a birth certificate which indicates he was born in "Lancaster County, Twp. of Waxhaws, S.C., March 15, 1767," which North Carolina critics say is not valid because it is not a contemporary document, but was issued in 1962 by the Clerk of the Court of Lancaster County. South Carolina's most convincing documentation is a letter Jackson himself wrote to J. W. Witherspoon stating he was told he was born in South Carolina "at the plantation

Figure 70. Log comfort station, Andrew Jackson State Park near Lancaster, South Carolina, better built and much larger than most one-room pioneer cabins.

whereon James Crawford lived," and a clause in Jackson's will referring to South Carolina as his native state.

On the other hand, North Carolina, who claims that Jackson was mistaken because of the imprecise boundary lines, has turned up a series of depositions of persons contemporary with George McCamie who claimed the President was born in the latter's cabin, and there is other evidence which favors North Carolina.[1]

Nothing I can add will reinforce the claims of either state, which I will leave for the future to settle, but it cannot be disputed that Jackson was born and reared in a rough, backwoods environment. If he was born at McCamie's, his birthplace was a log cabin, but if he was born at Crawfords', the type of dwelling is uncertain, although it may have also been built of logs. At least one writer has gone so far as to introduce a drawing which purports to be the likeness of the cabin where Jackson was born, but this author was a

North Carolinian and on this issue his objectivity is open to question.[2] In the Union County Historical Association Museum in the
Belk House at Monroe, North Carolina, there is a miniature log
cabin made from one of the logs preserved from the McCamie home.

During Jackson's youth, and in the early years of his marriage,
he no doubt lived at one time or another in log dwellings. He is
supposed to have boarded in a two-story log house in Jonesboro
when he began to practice law, and when he bought the Hermitage
property in 1804 there were log cabins on it, and he may have occupied one of them before he built his mansion.

Jackson was defeated in the presidential election of 1824, when
the choice among the candidates was thrown into the House of Representatives because none of them had received a sufficient number
of popular votes to carry the election. Forced to make a choice
from among the first three candidates, Jackson, John Quincy Adams,
and William H. Crawford, the House elected Adams.

When a determined Jackson ran for the presidency again in 1828,
the Democrats touted him as a national hero, a great general who
defeated the English at New Orleans, the only major land battle in
the War of 1812 won by the Americans. Other phases of his military
career were publicized during the campaign to solidify his position
with the voters, but the Democrats had good reason for not making
the circumstances of their candidate's humble birth a major campaign issue. The inoculation of the Harrison log cabin virus was to
come twelve years later, and at this point in time it was not yet considered a political asset to have been born in a log cabin; it might
make the candidate appear unsophisticated to the voters of the urban
North. Moreover, the Democrats faced a touchy issue in refuting
the slander about Jackson's wife, a dark-haired, dark-eyed vivacious
girl, Rachel Robards, who had been married before, and had wed
Jackson unaware that she did not have a legal divorce from Lewis
Robards, her first husband.

In a campaign that set a record for character assassination and
scurrility, Jackson was charged with adultery, seduction, murder,
theft, and treason. Rachel was portrayed by the opposition party as

an immoral woman of low birth, crude in her ways, and lacking the social graces expected of the country's first lady. "Ought a convicted adultress and her paramour husband be placed in the highest offices of this free and Christian land?" wrote a pamphleteer. The daughter of pioneer Tennessee settlers, Rachel was a real frontierswoman, reared in a log cabin. Her father was one of the first settlers in Nashville when practically all the homes were of logs. After her marriage to Jackson, she is once said to have explained a family epidemic by saying, "The General kicked the kivers off and we all cotch cold." [3]

Despite the stigma of Rachel's backwoods crudity and her alleged immorality (even though she and Jackson went through a second legal marriage ceremony), Jackson was elected by 56 percent of the popular vote, and he carried the electoral college with 178 votes against eighty-three for John Quincy Adams. Rachel saw Jackson elected, but, as fate would have it, died before her husband's inauguration, fulfilling her expressed wish that she would "rather be a doorkeeper in the house of God than to live in *that* palace." She lost her opportunity to go down in history as one of the nation's first log cabin ladies, but escaped the anguish that White House life might have brought her.

Van Buren succeeded Jackson, and after him came General Harrison and the fanfare of the log cabin campaign. Fortunate indeed was the candidate thereafter who could furnish the orators of his party with a bona fide log cabin background in case it was needed. The first President following Harrison and Jackson who could qualify as log cabin-born was James Knox Polk, and North Carolina stands unchallenged as the place of his birth. The Polks, like the Jacksons, were swept into North Carolina with the Scotch-Irish migrations, and Samuel Polk, James's father, a plain but enterprising farmer, settled in Mecklenburg County near present Pineville where James was born.

As I write (July 8, 1967), I have just returned from a trip to Pineville where, on Route 521 south of the town, I examined the James K. Polk memorial cabin under reconstruction by the North

Carolina Department of Archives and History. The original birth-place of the eleventh President has long since disappeared, and the state authorities are intent on constructing a reasonably accurate facsimile. The reconstruction is a two room, one and one-half story dwelling of hewn logs, measuring sixteen by thirty-two feet, with an outside brick chimney on one end. Although there is little question about Polk's birth on November 2, 1795, in a log dwelling on or near the site of the reconstruction, opinions differ about its size and shape and such details as the number of doors and windows, which become important when one is attempting to duplicate a historic building.

The same writer who introduced a drawing of the log cabin where Andrew Jackson is purported to have been born illustrated the Polk birthplace depicting it as a small one-room cabin of round logs with one door on the front but no windows.[4]

One of Polk's later biographers states, "The Polks lived in a log cabin, as did most of the frontier people, but it was a double log cabin of a type called 'saddlebag.' It consisted of two complete log houses connected by a covered passageway with big fireplaces at each end of the double building."[5] Another Polk biographer agrees essentially with this description, but adds that the house was of hewn logs having mud-chinked chimneys of split logs on either end! [6]

Since none of these three descriptions conforms to the plan of the cabin under reconstruction, I sought clarification from the North Carolina Department of Archives and History, and it appears that they have found accounts of two eyewitnesses. The first described the original Polk cabin as follows:

> The place where President Polk was born was, in 1849 [when he saw it] the property of Nathan Orr. The house pointed out to me, was of logs, had never been weather-boarded and was much dilapidated. It was formed of two pens, one about 20 x 16, the other 12 x 16, making a structure 32 x 16, with a shingle roof, and a brick chimney at the North end, and stood about two hundred yards South of Little Sugar Creek.[7]

This same observer said that there were two doors close together, one for each of the two rooms, "and that there was but a single window to each room." [8]

An account written by the second observer, who also visited the
Polk cabin before it was destroyed, reads in part as follows, to which
I have added the italic:

At this house he lived for twelve years, and then removed with his
father, in 1806, to Tennessee. The building is made of immense logs. *It
has three narrow doors, but no windows.* It stood within two hundred
yards of Little Sugar Creek, but has been removed into a lot near by, and
used, until this Spring, as a cowhouse. In the neighborhood the writer
called on a venerable lady—Mrs. Hargrove—near ninety years of age, who
went to school with James J. Polk, and who slept in the old building
during the Polk residence in Mecklenburg.[9]

The reconstructed cabin has two doors and two windows on the
front, the North Carolina authorities apparently holding to the opinion that the first eyewitness account is more reliable than the second.
However, the reconstruction has two additional windows on the
end of the house opposite the chimney end, and a back door, which
were not mentioned by either observer. The question as to whether
the "immense logs" which formed the walls were round logs, or
were hewn, as they now appear in the reconstruction, still requires
confirmation, and it is unlikely that this can be easily settled. In any
event, the Polk Cabin now takes its place among the nation's ever-
increasing log cabin memorials (see Figure 71).

When James Polk was eleven years old, his family moved to Tennessee where the future President entered a law office, practiced
law in due time, was later elected a Congressman, and still later
Governor of the state. He was a Democratic dark horse candidate
for the presidency in the 1844–1845 campaign, and was elected
largely on the issue of the "Re-annexation of Texas and the Re-
occupation of Oregon," both of which he strongly favored. The
log cabin played no significant part in Polk's election campaign, and
North Carolina voters thought so little of their native son, whose
log cabin birthplace they have since memorialized, that he did not
even carry his home state!

James Buchanan, the nation's fifteenth chief executive, was born
in 1791 in a log cabin in the Alleghenies near Mercersburg, Pennsylvania, built by one John Tom, who operated a mountain trading

Figure 71. James K. Polk birthplace, November 2, 1795, near Pineville, North Carolina, under reconstruction by North Carolina Department of Archives and History when photographed by the writer in 1967.

post at Cove Gap called "The Stony Batter." Buchanan's Scotch-Irish father, who came from Donegal, bought the cabin along with one hundred acres of land for £142 and commenced business on his own as a trader in 1788. The property included "*several* log cabins, some barns and stables, a storehouse and stone building, cleared fields and an orchard." [10] A Pennsylvania historian writing in 1843 said the ruins of *two* log cabins were then still in evidence at Cove Gap, and that James Buchanan was born in one of them. [11] A writer in 1856 said the remains of one of the Buchanan cabins was still to be seen "although little is left but the chimney." [12]

It is a matter of record that the Buchanans moved to Mercersburg when the future President was about six years old, thus severing family ties with Cove Gap. Since the elder Buchanan apparently had no sentimental attachments to the log cabins he had owned, and since he did not suspect that his son would become prominent in his country's political life, he had no reason to bother about them. In

fact, he had been very successful in business, and was in good financial circumstances when he built a two-story red brick house
in Mercersburg, which was to be James Buchanan's home during
his early school days. Not until many years later did the question
of Buchanan's birthplace take on any importance, and by that time
his father, mother, and anyone else who might have been present
at his birth were all dead.[13]

There is a story handed down in one of the old families in nearby
Chambersburg for which no documentation exists, but as it was told
to me, the Buchanans were not poor log cabin dwellers, but lived
in a comfortable manse at "The Stony Batter." It seems that the
manse caught fire during the period of Buchanan's mother's
pregnancy, and she sought temporary haven in one of the small
log outbuildings where her son was born. The story goes that Buchanan himself was amused later when, as a sophisticated politician,
reference was made to his humble log cabin birthplace since he spent
very little of his youth at Cove Gap. According to the story, Buchanan was reported saying that if it made his constituents happy to
refer to his lowly log cabin origin it was agreeable to him!

One of the cabins that stood at Cove Gap—or the remnants of
one of them—was moved to Mercersburg after Buchanan had become
famous, and there re-erected and publicized as the President's birthplace. In 1866 the cabin came into the possession of the Reverend
R. Lewis Mc Cune who bought a second log structure known as the
old Mercersburg "Latin School," which James Buchanan attended,
and he moved the school and joined it to the Buchanan cabin. This
addition was later destroyed by fire, although the supposed Buchanan
birthplace was not damaged.

In 1905 the log cabin was occupied by a Negro family according
to a letter written October 11 of that year by Dr. William Mann
Irvine, president of the Mercersburg Academy, now in possession
of the Coyle Free Library in Chambersburg. In 1925 the cabin was
owned by a Mercersburg barber, Charles Grove, according to a
story in the Chambersburg *Public Opinion*, who sold it that year to
several prominent citizens of Chambersburg for about $1000. The

cabin was then dismantled, moved some twenty miles from Mercersburg to Chambersburg, where it was reassembled on North Second Street and modified for use as an antique shop by the owners who formed a corporation called Stony Batter Antique Exchange, Inc. As time went on this commercial effort was discontinued, and from 1943 to 1947, the cabin was used as the headquarters of the Chambersburg Girl Scouts.

In 1947 the owners sold the cabin to Arthur V. Rock who operated a sandwich shop next door, and he, in turn, leased it to a Gettysburg entrepreneur who converted it to a gift shop and Buchanan Museum. This venture was also discontinued in due time, and for a while the cabin was used as the headquarters of the Chambersburg Democratic party. According to an article which appeared in the Chambersburg *Public Opinion* in 1951, a resident raised the question as to whether the cabin was the genuine Buchanan birthplace, and the owner produced a framed affidavit made by a deceased Mercersburg resident, Mrs. Crist Fendrick, stating that the cabin was, indeed, genuine, and a statement by Charles Grove who maintained everything was original except the roof.

In 1953, the headmaster of Mercersburg Academy, Dr. Charles S. Tippetts, started a movement to return the Buchanan cabin to Mercersburg, and aided by contributions of the parents of several students, he raised funds to purchase it and move it back to Mercersburg where it was reconstructed. This was done at a cost estimated at $5000, and the restored cabin of hewn logs, with V-notched corner timbering and a new chimney and fireplace of stone, now stands in a grove of trees on the campus of the Mercersburg Academy (see Figure 72). In the restoration it is claimed that about three-quarters of the original logs were preserved, and although new logs were substituted for those that were rotted they were carefully patterned after the dimensions and notchings on the original. As a result of its shuttling back and forth, with modifications made by its successive owners and tenants, it is difficult to ascertain how closely this memorial resembles the log cabin where Buchanan was born 178 years ago. Furthermore, if there were, in fact, *two* log

Figure 72. The James Buchanan Log Cabin reconstructed on the campus of the Mercersburg Academy, Mercersburg, Pennsylvania.

cabins at "The Stony Batter," in 1843, one wonders if the remains of the right one were moved to Mercersburg in the first place.

After a successful career as Secretary of State under President Polk, Minister to Russia, United States Senator, and Minister to the Court of St. James's where he was socially popular, Buchanan retired from government service and settled down to practice law in Lancaster, Pennsylvania. His house called "Wheatland" was a stately brick mansion built along certain southern styles, and when he ran for President, lithographs of his dwelling were distributed in the South to leave the inference that he, a Democrat, was a gentleman of the southern school. During the campaign he made a number of political speeches from the front porch of "Wheatland."

Buchanan was a bachelor, having been rejected a number of years before by Ann Caroline Coleman, who died shortly thereafter at the age of twenty-four from an overdose of laudanum, but it was never established whether this was deliberate or accidental. Although Buchanan grieved over her death, it did not blight his life as deeply as some writers would have us believe, for he later sought the company of other females. Although some tried, no one could ever get the eligible bachelor President to the altar. Buchanan's constituents would have had difficulty reconciling the worldly character of their candidate with his humble birth in a dwelling hewn from the trees of the Pennsylvania forests, which would have negated the "Wheatland" propaganda. As a result the log cabin was kept in the background during a compaign wherein the sectional feelings between North and South on the slavery question constituted a major issue.

Buchanan and his running mate, John C. Breckenridge, were elected on a "Buch and Breck" states' rights ticket, the alliteration lending itself to banners and broadsides. The log cabin did not come prominently into Buchanan's life until long after his death when Pennsylvania felt impelled to show the world that its only son who reached the White House was also a log cabin President. The association of the log cabin with Buchanan's successor, Abraham Lincoln, probably had a lot to do with awakening interest in the Buchanan cabin. The Lincoln log-cabin propaganda reinforced the Harrison lore.

Lincoln is by far the best known of all the log cabin Presidents, and even today, the log cabin continues to figure prominently in Lincoln Day exercises conducted in American schools and in other public celebrations held in his memory. Lincoln has been associated with the log cabin in American literature for several generations, and a writer of exciting stories for youth, William M. Thayer, was among the first American authors to romanticize Lincoln's log cabin birth. It would be an exaggeration to say that Thayer deliberately launched a one-man campaign in the 1870's and 1880's to make American boys and girls aware that a number of Presidents were products of the lowly log cabin, but his books had that effect. In his volume, *The Pioneer Boy And How He Became President*, Thayer pictured in painstaking detail the one-room log cabin on the South Fork of Nolin Creek near present Hodgenville, Kentucky, where

"Honest Abe" was born in 1809. Later writers, including Lincoln's best known biographer, Carl Sandburg, all gave emphasis to Lincoln's modest birthplace.

A memorial log cabin commemorating Lincoln's birthplace is enshrined in the Memorial Building crowning an eminence in the 116-acre Abraham Lincoln Birthplace Historical Site near Hodgenville (see Figure 73). Although the many thousands of tourists who visit this memorial return to their homes with the impression that they have seen the cabin where the great emancipator was born, the truth is that the original Lincoln cabin was apparently torn down many years before Lincoln became a national figure. If the testimony

Figure 73. Alleged Abraham Lincoln birthplace, February 12, 1809, housed in Memorial Building near Hodgenville, Kentucky. Proof is lacking that any of the logs were present in the real birthplace cabin nor that the dimensions of this "traditional structure" are accurate.

of an eighty-four-year old Kentuckian given in 1903 can be believed, the logs in the Lincoln birthplace were all destroyed some-
time previous to 1840. "We lived in the house in which Lincoln
was born," Jacob Brothers told J. T. Hobson, author of *The Foot-
steps of Abraham Lincoln,* published in 1909. "After some years,
my father built another house, almost like the first house, and, to
my knowledge, the logs were burned for firewood. Later he built
a hewed log house." [14]

Even if the logs were not destroyed by fire, no log cabin remained
on the former Lincoln farm in 1865, a fact that has been well documented by several eye witnesses. It is possible, but by no means
a certainty, that some of the logs used in the cabin where Lincoln
was born may have been salvaged and used by a neighbor in the
construction of a two-story log dwelling built about one mile north
of the site of the original Lincoln cabin. This latter structure was
subsequently knocked down and re-erected on the former Lincoln
property as a one-room cabin which was represented by the owner,
John Davenport, as the bona fide Lincoln birthplace and sold to
Alfred W. Dennett. Dennett and an associate conceived the idea
of displaying at the Tennessee Centennial Exposition held in Nashville in 1897 the log cabin birthplaces of Abraham Lincoln and Jefferson Davis. It was a stroke of showmanship worthy of Phineas
T. Barnum—the humble homes of a former President of the United
States and his Kentucky-born contemporary, the President of the
Confederate States of America, as a feature of the exposition.

The birthplace of Jefferson Davis had long before been removed,
but this did not deter the promoters. They merely bought some
old notched logs from an unidentified cabin and reassembled them!

Following the Tennessee Exposition, Dennett disassembled both
cabins, and the meanderings of the logs between then and when
they found haven in the Lincoln Memorial more than twenty-five
years later is a strange and unusual tale. For a while the logs were
stored in a mission Dennett operated on the Bowery in New York
City. Then they were sent to the Buffalo Exposition in 1901 where
the alleged Lincoln birthplace was again assembled, but when the

logs were returned to New York some of them are believed to have been lost in transit. They were later moved to Coney Island and there stored for a while, and in 1904, they were in storage in the basement of a Long Island mansion.

Eventually a group of public-spirited citizens raised money to buy the logs and acquire land at Hodgenville for a park, which was dedicated by President Taft on November 9, 1911. A number of years later it was transferred to the control of the Department of the Interior. When the Lincoln cabin was displayed at Nashville and Buffalo it measured sixteen by eighteen feet, but it was reduced to twelve by seventeen feet when it was re-erected in the Memorial Building, but this is of little consequence in view of the doubt existing about the authenticity of the cabin in the first place. In fact, the Department of the Interior summed everything up in admirable restraint in this statement found in one of its publications, "The log cabin in the Memorial Building is the *traditional* birthplace cabin. It is impossible to say with certainty that it is the original cabin. . . . Its history prior to 1861 is a matter of controversy and doubt."

Although the evidence is circumstantial it would appear that Lincoln's log cabin birthplace may have been less crude and of better quality than the cabins built by most of their neighbors. Lincoln's ancestors, like the Boones, came from Berks County, Pennsylvania, where they had been exposed to German log housing and they settled in Virginia at a time when hundreds of mobile families were building log dwellings. The President's grandfather, an earlier Abraham Lincoln, of good yeoman stock, came to Kentucky from Virginia bringing a knowledge of log cabin techniques which was handed down to his son Thomas, Abraham Lincoln's father. Although Thomas Lincoln was poor and uneducated, a hunter by preference, and a farmer through necessity, he had also learned the carpenter trade and managed to assemble a good assortment of tools. It was his skill with the axe that was passed down to his son, and from all accounts Abraham Lincoln became very proficient in the use of this important tool.

After his marriage to Nancy Hanks, Thomas Lincoln built a log cabin home for his bride prior to raising the one on Nolin Creek where Abraham Lincoln was born, and he was no novice in cabin-building. Abraham Lincoln himself had no recollection of the log cabin where he was born, because when he was only two years old his parents moved to a farm on Knob Creek about ten miles from his birthplace where Thomas Lincoln built another cabin. "My earliest recollection," Lincoln later wrote, "is of the Knob Creek place." Unfortunately, the President neglected to describe his boy-hood home which was removed many years ago. Today on Knob Creek between Hodgenville and Bardstown stands a reproduction of this cabin where the Lincolns lived from 1811 to 1816, but how closely this dwelling resembles the original cabin is not known. The

Figure 74. Replica of Lincoln's second cabin home reconstructed on Knob Creek near Hodgenville, Kentucky, where the Lincolns lived from 1811 to 1816. The original structure had long since disappeared when this memorial cabin was built.

Figure 75. Lincoln log cabin traditions are kept alive in the Francis Berry Log House, Lincoln Homestead State Park, Springfield, Kentucky, girlhood home of Nancy Hanks, Lincoln's mother.

best that can be said for it is that it, too, is a traditional structure (see Figure 74).

Since the sixteenth President was born in Kentucky, spent fourteen years of his youth in Indiana, and was eventually elected to the presidency from Illinois, three states feel that each has valid reasons to memorialize log structures having Lincoln associations, no matter how remote. Visitors to Kentucky, for example, may see, in addition to the two Lincoln memorial cabins mentioned above, what is purported to be the hewn log girlhood home of Nancy Hanks, Lincoln's mother, in the Lincoln Homestead State Park near Springfield (Figure 75). In the same park, the Bathsheba Lincoln Cabin, named in honor of Lincoln's paternal grandmother, stands on the site where she supposedly lived (Figure 76). In the Pioneer Memorial State

Figure 76. Replica of cabin where Lincoln's grandmother, Bathsheba Lincoln, is supposed to have lived after the death of her husband, now in Lincoln Homestead State Park, Springfield, Kentucky.

Park at Harrodsburg, Kentucky, there is a restored log cabin in which Lincoln's parents are said to have been married, June 12, 1806.

I cannot vouch for either the historical or architectural authenticity of these log memorials—or of others in the same state which I have probably overlooked—but history is clear that after his family left the Knob Creek farm in the autumn of 1816, Abraham Lincoln lived in, at least, two more log cabins.

In late November, with winter coming on, Thomas Lincoln, then aged thirty-eight, arrived with his family, a sled, and two borrowed oxen on Little Pigeon Creek in Spencer County, Indiana. The move from Kentucky, where· life had been deplorable, was intended to better the family's situation, although all his life Thomas Lincoln had an itching foot and always seemed to want to be moving on.

Thomas, Nancy, their nine-year old daughter Sally, and seven-year old Abe spent their first winter in what Nancy's cousin Dennis Hanks called a "pole shed," a simple lean-to, open at the front, with a roof of poles, slabs, and leaves.[15] Day and night a wood fire burned at the open front, not only for warmth and cooking, but to frighten off wolves and panthers lurking and howling in the woods that surrounded the shed. The family soon ran out of the corn meal they had brought with them from Kentucky, and their food that hard, miserable winter consisted almost entirely of game—turkeys, deer, squirrels, and rabbits—which were plentiful in the woods.[16]

When spring came, Thomas Lincoln, assisted by his son, cleared some of the land by girdling the largest trees, allowing them to stand and die, and by felling others. Nancy and her daughter planted corn and pumpkin seeds which they had brought from Kentucky between the stumps and trunks wherever they could grub out the roots with an axe and hoe. Thomas, assisted by Abe, set about notching logs and raising another cabin, the largest the Lincolns had ever lived in, twenty by eighteen feet, made of round logs, with one room, a loft, a stick-clay chimney, and a roof of poles and slabs. Initially there were no windows or floor—they would come later.

Near present Gentryville, Indiana, and adjoining Lincoln City, is the Lincoln State Park, site of the Lincoln cabin, marked by a low rectangular wall in which the Lincoln fireplace, supposedly the original stones, is set in position. In the Lincoln Pioneer Village at Rockport, Indiana, is a reconstructed log building called "Judge John Pitcher's Law Office" to which Lincoln is said to have walked twenty-two miles to borrow a book.

Nancy Hanks became ill with the mysterious disease known as "milk sick," and there was no doctor closer than thirty miles from the Lincoln cabin. Even if they could have called him it would have been useless because there was no cure for the ailment, and after seven days of suffering Nancy died. Thomas Lincoln, assisted by Dennis Hanks, made a box in which to bury her, and young Abe whittled out the pegs that held the whipsawed planks together. They dug a hole with axe and wooden shovel on a knoll in the woods, and quietly buried her without the benefit of a preacher to read a service or say a prayer. Not until a year later did a traveling preacher conduct a brief service at her grave.

Little Sally did the cooking, such as it was, after her mother's death, and there was great loneliness in the little cabin for the widower and the two children. In the winter of 1819, Thomas Lincoln went back to Kentucky and returned with a second wife, Sarah Bush Johnston, a widow woman with three small children. There were then eight people living in the cabin, and Sarah, who could manage her indolent husband better than his first wife, persuaded him to improve the cabin by laying a puncheon floor, adding windows, and building new furniture. She had brought with her a bed, bureau, cooking utensils, as well as knives, forks, and dishware—niceties that Thomas's children had not been accustomed to using. Dennis Hanks later explained why the Lincoln family had lived so long with nothing but a dirt floor in their cabin home, "Choppin' trees an' grubbin' roots an' splittin' rails an' huntin' an' trappin' didn't leave Tom no time to put a puncheon floor in his cabin."

Tom planed the new floor smooth, and Sarah, who believed that cleanliness was next to godliness, kept it spotlessly scoured with sand and soft soap. She made Tom get some lime and whitewash both the exterior and interior log walls. Since he had built at least three cabins while he lived in Kentucky, we can assume that Thomas Lincoln's Indiana cabin was in no way inferior to the cabins of his neighbors, and we have Dennis Hanks's testimony that, "Purty soon, we had the best house in the kentry."

In the fall of 1829, Thomas Lincoln decided to pull up stakes again, and with several other families traveling in wagons pulled by oxen, they moved to Macon County, Illinois. There the Lincolns settled on the north side of the Sangamon River about ten miles west of present Decatur, then a county seat of a few log cabins, a store, a tavern, and a courthouse. Thomas Lincoln, assisted by the future President, again cleared the land for a farm, erected another log cabin, and split walnut rails to fence in the property.

Here in the fourth log house that he had known as the family home, Abraham Lincoln, a young man of twenty-one, said goodbye to his father and stepmother, and took off for New Salem to seek fame and fortune. Following his son's departure Thomas Lincoln moved again, finally settling in Cole County, Illinois, where he occupied still another log house, one that he bought and then added to it.

Today in Decatur's Fairview Park stands the restored Macon County log courthouse, one and one-half stories high, twenty feet square, where the first court was held in May of 1830. Today it is popularly called the "Lincoln Log Cabin Courthouse," and it really stands as a memorial to the former President because it is said that he appeared here as a young lawyer. Another claim to Lincoln fame is the fact that the logs were chinked and daubed by John Hanks, a cousin of Lincoln's mother, whose wages for the job, according to the documentation, was $9.87.

In Morton Park near Charleston, Illinois, is the Sally Lincoln Chapter House of the D.A.R., a two-story log memorial named in honor of Lincoln's stepmother; and in the Lincoln Log Cabin State Park near Campbell, Illinois, is a reconstruction of one of the cabins Thomas Lincoln built.

As though these numerous log cabin memorials were insufficient to preserve Lincoln log cabin traditions, one may also visit the recreated pioneer village of New Salem, Illinois, on a hill overlooking the Sangamon valley where Lincoln lived from 1831 to 1837, and there find log cabins galore. Here in New Salem, at the age of twenty-two, Lincoln's first job was as a clerk in a store built of logs owned by Denton Offut, and although the original disappeared many years ago, a replica was constructed as part of a restoration program that was started in New Salem in 1932. The numerous other restored houses of logs are intended to illustrate the typical dwellings in a pioneer village, but they are, in fact, tributes to Lincoln's memory. The only original log building remaining is the Onstot Cooper Shop constructed in 1835, where Lincoln studied law books and read other literature by the light of a wood fire.

Can there be any doubt that Americans have been well indoctrinated in Lincoln log cabin lore?

During the presidential campaign of 1860, Lincoln's Republican supporters touted him as a rugged backwoodsman, a rail splitter, a man of the common people born and reared in a log cabin, as the Whigs had publicized General Harrison in the election campaign twenty years before. It was highly effective campaign propaganda, and in Lincoln's case, it was all literally true and the candidate talked and looked like a backwoodsman. It was also true that during Lincoln's boyhood it would have been next to impossible to find any poor family in the backwoods country of Kentucky, Indiana, or Illinois who didn't live in a log cabin and split rails to build their farm fences. Lincoln's parents were no better or worse off than most of them. The schools, which Lincoln intermittently attended, were also built of logs, as was the Pigeon Creek Church in Indiana, a mile across the fields from the Lincoln cabin.

The fact that Lincoln, one among thousands of his contemporaries born in log cabins and educated in log schools, was elevated by his countrymen to the highest office in the land was, indeed, unusual and an accomplishment worthy of utmost respect and admiration. But there was nothing unique about his being born in a log cabin. Considering the time, place, and circumstances of his birth, it would have been unusual if he had been born in any other kind of house.

Lincoln's Vice-President, Andrew Johnson, who became President after the assassination, was born in Raleigh, North Carolina, also of poor parents. One of his biographers claimed that he was born in a log shack [17] and the 1965 edition of *Encyclopedia Americana* (XVI, 167) states he was born in a one-story log house. A similar contention is made in other sources, but the truth is that he was born in a small frame house, with a shingled gambrel roof, having an outside stone and brick chimney. The house formerly stood on Fayetteville Street in Raleigh, and was purchased in 1904 by the Colonial Dames and presented to the city. It was later restored and removed to the campus of the State University in Raleigh as a Johnson memorial where it may still be seen.

Johnson was left a penniless orphan at the age of four after the death of his father, a handyman in a tavern, and as a young man he

practiced tailoring at Laurens, South Carolina, and later at Greenville, Tennessee. He became interested in politics in Tennessee, and
when he ran for the vice-presidency of the United States, references
were made in political speeches to his diligence and industry while
tailoring in a log cabin. I have found no evidence to support this
contention, but it would not have been unusual, because many stores
and shops in both South Carolina and Tennessee during Johnson's
youth were modified log houses.

Ulysses S. Grant, who succeeded Johnson to the White House,
has been accredited in a number of accounts as having been born in
a log cabin, an error that may have had its origin in Hamlin Garland's biography of Grant published in 1898 where in author stated
that the eighteenth president was born "in a small two-room *cabin*"
at Point Pleasant, Clermont County, Ohio.[18] Elsewhere in the same
volume Garland also referred to Grant's birthplace as a "cabin home"
and although he did not use the word "log" the missing adjective
was inferred by some readers who were more than willing to accept
another log cabin President.

Grant's birthplace, as Garland well knew, was a small, one-story
frame dwelling which was still standing at its original location at
Point Pleasant in 1868 when Henry C. Deming published an earlier
biography of Grant.[19] Grant was born there on April 27, 1822, but
in the fall of 1823, while he was still a babe in arms, his parents moved
to Georgetown, Ohio, the seat of Brown County, where they resided in a modest brick house. Grant in his memoirs said of the
Georgetown house, "This place remained my home until at the age
of seventeen in 1839, I went to West Point."

Many years ago, after Grant's death, his birthplace was transported
around the country as a commercial exhibit, after which it was purchased by a private citizen and returned to the state of Ohio for
permanent preservation as a historic shrine. From about 1896 to
1936, it reposed in a glass enclosure on the Ohio State Fair grounds
at Columbus, but it has since been returned to its original site in
Point Pleasant, the task of removal and restoration entrusted to the
Ohio State Archeological and Historical Society.

It is apparent that Grant had no direct log cabin associations in his youth, a fact that was misinterpreted in 1922 when the U.S. government issued a memorial half dollar (as well as two varieties of gold dollars) to commemorate the former President's one hundredth anniversary. The obverse has a profile of the head of Grant and the reverse a one-room cottage surrounded by a rail fence centered in a cluster of trees (see Figure 77). The artist's rendition of the frame cottage can readily be mistaken as a log cabin, and a description of the coin in literature circulated among collectors stated it depicted the "log cabin" where Grant was born.

Of the first issue 95,055 coins were minted of which 67,215 were sold at one dollar each, and since 27,650 remained unsold they were returned to the Mint and remelted. But not to be undone by previous commemorative issues, a *second* issue of the "log cabin" half dollar was struck of the identical design, the only exception being a small five pointed star incised above the name Grant. Only 5006 of the second issue half dollars were minted, and all but 750 were sold, and these were returned and remelted. Grant coins from the second issue bring a much higher price than those of the first in the world of coin collectors.

In recent correspondence with the U.S. Mint I was told that the Director does not undertake the research on the background of designs on commemorative coins unless Mint artists execute them. In the instance of the Grant coins the Grant Memorial Centenary Association was the sponsoring agency who employed a free-lance artist to prepare the design, in this case a frame cottage that to the ordinary eye resembled a log cabin, and was so described in coin collector's literature!

Following his graduation from West Point and several years of military service, Grant decided to settle his family on a farm, and he resigned his captain's commission. Upon leaving the Army he was quoted as saying, "Whoever hears of me in ten years will hear of a well-to-do Missouri farmer," unaware that destiny would carry him back into the Army and later into the White House.

He settled on unimproved land in St. Louis County, Missouri,

Figure 77. Grant Centennial half dollar illustrating his frame birthplace which has been mistaken as a log cabin. (Permission of Don Taxay, *An Illustrated History of U.S. Commemorative Coinage*, N.Y., 1967)

which his wife's father had given her, and there he cut and notched trees for a log house which his neighbors helped him raise and which he called "Hardscrabble." Grant and his family lived in this log dwelling from 1854 to 1859, clearing and cultivating the sixty-acre farm and planting and raising crops in the manner of the Missouri pioneers who had preceded him. He even hauled wood from the property to peddle in the streets of St. Louis. One of his sons, Jesse R. Grant, was born in the log house.[20] In 1859, Grant gave up the struggle, sold the farm, and found a job in St. Louis. Lincoln's call for volunteers took him back into the Army, and after several promotions, he was elevated to the rank of major general following the siege at Vicksburg. Later he was placed in command of the Union armies, and his military successes helped mold a political career, leading to his election to the presidency.

Grant was not born in a log cabin, nor did he live in one in his youth, but, as the builder of "Hardscrabble," he had authentic log cabin associations. Missouri had no log cabin Presidents, but the state can at least lay claim to the *son* of a President having been born in a Missouri log dwelling which a President built! Today, the Grant Cabin, moved about one and one-half miles from its original site, has been restored as a memorial and may been seen along Gravois Road in a park in the southeastern outskirts of St. Louis (see Figure 78).

Perhaps by 1972, the sesquicentennial year of Grant's birth, someone may be sufficiently perceptive to suggest that his Missouri log dwelling might be considered an appropriate subject for another memorial coin. If so, the depiction of "Hardscrabble" on the coin could be honestly justified on historical grounds—the only surviving log house built by a United States President.

The aforementioned Thayer was the author of a biography of James A. Garfield, called *Log Cabin To White House*, published in 1881, which described in minute detail President Garfield's log cabin birthplace at Orange in rural Cuyahoga County, Ohio. Garfield's parents, Abram Garfield of Massachusetts and Eliza Ballou of Rhode Island, were among the Yankees who straggled to the

Figure 78. Double-pen cabin built by Ulysses S. Grant near St. Louis, Missouri, before it was restored as a memorial. Breezeway was originally open, but a later resident boarded it over to form an extra room. (Reproduced from the collections of the Library of Congress)

several Ohio tracts in the days of the great westward expansion. According to Thayer's volume, their cabin, where the twentieth President was born in 1831, measured twenty by thirty feet, having an outside chimney on one end made of sticks and mud. He wrote that the roof of wood slabs was held in place by long weight poles cut from saplings laid across the slabs, and that the corner ladder in the one-room dwelling led to a loft where the children slept on beds of hay. The cabin's only door, he added, was made of rough planks, and the three windows were covered with greased paper.

Although no one could find fault with this description of a prevailing type of pioneer cabin, one is naturally curious about Thayer's source of information. The cabin was no longer standing when he wrote his book, and there is no reason to believe that he ever saw it, nor is there any record of what it looked like. A memorial log cabin, purporting to resemble the dwelling where Garfield was born, was erected as a historic shrine many years after his death at "Lawnfield," his later home at Mentor, a village near Cleveland. This reconstruction is somewhat at variance with Thayer's description, and it would be difficult to decide which more nearly approximates the original —and there is probably more than a soupçon of imagination in both.

Garfield was felled by an assassin's bullet four months after his election, and it is an interesting coincident that the three most widely publicized log cabin Presidents—Harrison, Lincoln, and Garfield —all died in office.

By the time General Harrison's grandson, Benjamin, was born (he became the twenty-third President), the Harrisons were then living in a large red brick manse at North Bend, which had replaced the older residence as the newer family homestead. In his political speeches, Ben Harrison often made references to his grandfather's former log cabin "at the Bend," especially when he was seeking votes up and down the Ohio Valley. His nomination for the presidency came after James G. Blaine, a more influential political figure, refused to run because he was bitter about his defeat four years before. During the campaign the Republicans exploited the candidate's blood relationship with General William Henry Harrison, and to the extent that this contributed to his victory, it may be said that the log cabin indirectly helped sweep Ben Harrison into the White House on his grandfather's coattails. Ben, like his grandfather, was not born in a log cabin either, but like his neighbors and cousins, he attended the old country school at North Bend, which was constructed of logs.

Principally as a result of the publicity of national election campaigns, aided and abetted by such writers as Thayer, and enhanced by dozens of memorial structures, the log cabin became associated in the public mind as an attribute of greatness. In no other country in the world did the log dwelling become so politically distinguished as in the United States where it was seized upon to illustrate how the opportunity to attain the highest office in the land was within the grasp of every man regardless of his lowly beginning. It became, so to speak, a symbol of democracy, and American youth, captivated by the image, grew up in the belief that a log cabin represented everything good and nothing bad in the "rags to riches" land of golden opportunity. The concept that "all men are created equal" has been rationalized through the examples of log cabin Presidents and other prominent men born in log cabins. In many instances, even when the great man was not born in a log cabin, it would seem that devious ways have been found to make the association.

In one instance even a President born to well-to-do parents has found a place in American log cabin lore. Theodore Roosevelt, whose birthplace was a brownstone front on East 20th Street in New York City, went west at the age of twenty-five to settle on the Chimney Butte Ranch in the badlands of Dakota Territory along the Little Missouri River. During the following winter, two of Roosevelt's ranchers built a cabin on Roosevelt's property near present Medora, North Dakota, of ponderosa pine logs that had been stranded on the riverbank and sandbars after a period of high water. The logs are believed to have come from many miles upstream where they had been originally cut, hand-hewed, and floated down the river for use as railroad ties. For a time, Roosevelt occupied the cabin, which later became known as the Maltese Cross Cabin from the name of the brand, during the period he rode the range, hunted buffalo, and, incidentally, lost money as a rancher.

In one of his books, Roosevelt made note of the dwelling in the following line, "The story-high house of hewn logs is neat and clean, with many rooms, so that one can be alone if he wishes to."

In 1899, the cabin became the property of a local cowboy who removed the high-pitched shingled roof and replaced it with a lower and flatter board roof which he covered with dirt. Like the Lincoln and Buchanan cabins, the Theodore Roosevelt cabin has had more than its share of travel. Shortly after Roosevelt became President, the state of North Dakota acquired the cabin; in 1904 it was dismantled, shipped to St. Louis and there reconstructed as an exhibit at the Louisiana Purchase Exposition. It was such an attraction that the next year it was again dismantled and shipped to Portland, Oregon, for the Lewis and Clark Exposition. In 1906, it was exhibited at the North Dakota State Fair in Fargo, and then rebuilt for display on the capitol grounds at Bismarck. After the Theodore Roosevelt National Memorial was established near Medora, the cabin was finally moved to its present location in the park and restored to simulate its original appearance (Figure 79). A visitor, pointing out the cabin to his small son, was overheard saying, "That's the log cabin where 'Teddy' Roosevelt was born."

Even today the log cabin continues to play a part in politics—the ex-governor of Arkansas, Orval Faubus, was touted by his constituents as the poor boy from Greasy Creek in the Ozarks born in a log cabin.

One of the well-known Protestant ministers of our times, Norman

Figure 79. Theodore Roosevelt's "Maltese Cross Cabin," near Medora, N.D., built 1883-1884, and restored to its original appearance as a feature in the Theodore Roosevelt National Memorial Park. (Courtesy Arthur L. Sullivan, National Park Service)

Vincent Peale, made the following comparisons in a sermon he preached in 1967, later reprinted and widely distributed:

God knows how to do things. When, for example, He wanted to bring up the greatest man in all the long history of the American people, where did He have him born? In one of the great and wealthy homes of the nation? Not at all! He had him born in Kentucky, in a mud-plastered, windowless cabin, the beams of which were hewn out of the forest. And when He wanted to bring the Prince of Peace to earth, where did He give Him birth? In some glittering palace on the Tiber? Not at all! He had Him first see the light of day not in a dwelling made by hands, but in a cave where were kept the cattle and the sheep. The first sound the Babe heard, probably, was the bleating of lambs or the soft nuzzling of the cattle. Nobody but God would think of that!

When I first read a reprint of this sermon, I was tempted to write the author and tell him that the great humorist Will Rogers was born in 1879 near Nowata, Oklahoma, in a modified log cabin built by his father, Clem V. Rogers, a blood citizen of the Cherokee Indian Nation, and that the American poet Ambrose Bierce was born in a Kentucky log cabin. Perhaps this, too, could be included among the wonders that God hath wrought.

In objectively reviewing log cabin life, it is apparent that some log cabin families lived in dire poverty, and that log cabins, like any other form of family residence, were also scenes of violence and crimes of passion. Thayer, Norman Vincent Peale, and other writers chose to ignore the plain facts that lawbreakers, as well as men of upright character, were born in log cabins. Among the unsavory individuals of log cabin origin were John Wilkes Booth and the infamous outlaw, Jesse James. Then there was Henry Plummer and his gang of road agents whose hangout was a two-story log structure north of Laurin, Montana, known as "Robber's Roost"; other unwholesome characters who held up stage coaches and robbed un suspecting travellers used the house as a rendezvous.

John Wilkes Booth's birthplace, a log cabin in what was then wooded country north of Baltimore, was purchased by his actor-father Junius Brutus Booth in 1824. Theater audiences in Boston, New York, Philadelphia, and other American cities probably never knew that their favorite portrayer of Richard III, Iago, and King Lear lived in a log house, and that his actor-son Edwin Booth was also born there.

The birthplace of the outlaw, Jesse James, a one-room log cabin, with a two story frame addition built by his brother Frank, is still standing about ten miles west of Excelsior Springs, Missouri. Like Deadwood Dick's log cabin near Deadwood, South Dakota, the Jesse James cabin has become a tourist attraction. Deadwood Dick was, of course, a dime-novel character, strictly fictional, and a colorful frontiersman, Richard W. Clarke, who allowed his hair to grow long, and wore a fringed buckskin coat and high-top boots, was one of several impostors who adopted the name. Clarke's log cabin retreat on the pine-shaded slope of Sunrise Mountain, where he died in 1930 at the age of eighty-five, stands as a memorial to the former prospector and Indian scout. The anomaly is that this particular Deadwood Dick was born in England.[21]

The radical American abolitionist, John Brown, who was considered a criminal by most southerners, lived for a while in a log cabin at Osawatomie, Kansas, which belonged to his brother-in-law, the Reverend Samuel Lyle Adair. Brown himself was born in Torrington, Connecticut, and had no birthplace associations with log cabins, but the American obsession to link cabins with famous people has resulted in moving the Osawatomie cabin to the John Brown Battleground Memorial Park in Kansas where "his soul goes marching on!"

Although John Brown was an insurrectionist convicted of treason and hanged, his latter and tenuous association with a log cabin has tended to make him appear as a national hero. Americans want to hear no evil and see no evil so far as log cabins are concerned, and they are intent upon relating this specific structure, to the disadvantage of brick, frame, stone, and other kinds of dwellings, with good deeds and admirable people. In this misapprehension lies the real myth of the log cabin. The popular point of view is reflected in the following doggerel entitled "Log Cabin Boys" written by John Kenton Carter under the pseudonym Commodore Rollingpin, and published in St. Louis in 1897 in a book entitled *Log Cabin Poems:*

> Where'd you get Lincoln—and say who
> Sent you Grant, and Sheridan, too:
> Corwin and Old Tippecanoe
> General Jackson, who pulled through
> At New Orleans, the Boys in Blue
> When all those red-coat British flew?
> And Tecumseh, who led the crew
> That cut the brave old South in two
> And hoisted the old flag anew?
>
> And Whitelaw Reid and John Hay grew
> Up the same way. The same is true
> Of Garfield the assassin slew.
> And, cracky! There's Mc Kinley, whew!
> Well, these are only just a few
> *Log Cabin Boys* (but guess they'll do)
> Who helped to pull the country through
> And leave it unimpaired to you!

The inclusion of President William Mc Kinley's name among these illustrious "log cabin boys" is not the only hyperbole in this verse —actually he was born in a two-story frame house at Niles, Ohio.

The versifier chose to ignore the names of two famous Negroes born in log cabins. George Washington Carver, born of slave parents in Missouri, was honored by the United States Government, 1946–1951, in the issuance of a memorial half dollar bearing an unmistakable illustration of a log cabin and the inscription "From Slave Cabin to Hall of Fame." Booker T. Washington, born a slave in Franklin County, Virginia, in 1856, was the subject of a United States three-cent stamp, engraved with a log cabin, issued to commemorate the centennial of his birth. Needless to say, stamps and coins are excellent media to perpetuate the log cabin image, and Americans will probably see more of them in the future. Currier and Ives contributed to log cabin lore with at least half a dozen prints on which the log cabin is featured bearing such titles as *Among the Pines, The Arkansas Traveller, A Home in the Wilderness,* etc.

Log cabins may have held appeal to American voters once the propaganda became widespread, but the record shows that log cabin Presidents were no better nor worse administrators than those born and raised in other kinds of houses. It also goes without saying that the reality of life in a log cabin was less glamorous than the politicians suggested in their flowery speeches. Although I do not intend to contradict statements made in the first chapter of this volume relative to the contributions of the log cabin to the American home, there are certain facts which should be apparent to the reader. A one-room cabin where the family ate, worked, played, slept, and bred could not be designated as the ideal environment in which to nurture a future President. Even though the log cabin may have strengthened family ties under the prevailing circumstances of frontier life, it had many disadvantages as a family residence. I would be guilty of bias if I did not introduce some of these disadvantages.

The open fireplace was a constant hazard, and the danger of flying sparks causing a fire was of real and continual concern to a mother raising small children. Furthermore, no matter how tightly the interstices between the logs were caulked, the clay crumbled in time, and if it were not promptly replaced, cold winds found cracks to cause drafts, and even snow and rain seeped through. Amos Powers, born to a pioneer family who moved westward to Kansas about 1854, recalled that during his boyhood, snow piled up on the floor of the family log cabin, and when it melted it made the earth so muddy that his parents covered the floor with straw.[22]

In a journey to the Arkansas Territory in 1818–1819, Thomas Nuttall and a companion were paddling down the Ohio in a skiff they bought for six dollars when, about nineteen miles south of Pittsburgh, they ran into a rainstorm. They found overnight shelter in a log cabin "containing a large family of both sexes, all housed in one room, and that not proof against the pouring rain." [23]

Ventilation was also a problem in a log cabin, because there were no window sashes to be raised or lowered, and the interior temperature was usually too hot or too cold. The air was stuffy with the odors from cooking, churning, washing, and the smell of people in an age when there was no interior plumbing. Carrying water and bringing in firewood was a nuisance, to say nothing of the inconvenience of going out on cold winter nights to the latrine or the necessary house. The only illumination at night was from the dim rays of candles (later oil lamps), and the light from the flames of the open fireplace. The picture of the boy Lincoln lying on his stomach on the cabin floor in front of the fireplace to study his lessons, and scribbling his ciphers in charcoal on the back of a wooden shovel, may make a sentimental scene for the artist, but anyone who has strained his eyes while reading by candlelight or the flames of a flickering wood fire can fully recognize the drawbacks.

"We wusn't much better off 'n Indians," said Dennis Hanks of the Lincoln log cabin home in Indiana, "except 't we tuk an interest in religion and polyticks."

It was that interest in politics and religion, and the determination of its occupants to rise above the adversity of their times, that made the log cabin a great American social institution. For the Lincolns, the Garfields, the Polks, the Jacksons, and thousands of others, the log cabin and the farm on which it stood were the tangible accomplishments of a hard life of seemingly never-ending labor. Thrown into contact with woods, plains, and mountains, the log cabin families started life anew at elementary levels, and they made the best of it within their limitations. The physical man counted for everything, and it was muscles, not modern machines, that girdled the trees, made the farm fields, built the fences, planted the crops, rolled and notched the logs, and raised the cabin. Conquering the wilderness was a slow, laborious process requiring strength, patience, and persistence, and, as illustrated in Thomas Lincoln's case, fortitude to face illness and death.

In the frontier expansion, like the roll of an irresistible sea pressing westward, which gave a patina to democratic institutions and hastened Americanization, the log cabin gave the common man a sense of freedom, independence, and spiritual release. He became a property owner beholden to no man, and his children broke away from Old World traditions. The circumstances of pioneer life tended to intensify individualism and personal enterprise, and from among the log cabin families came blacksmiths, wheelwrights, wagonmakers, joiners, coopers, weavers, fullers, tailors, hatters, rope makers, and dozens of other trades, as the nation expanded and a new social order was created.

From Jamestown and Plymouth to the western slope of the Appalachians required 150 years; it took another fifty years for Americans to reach the Mississippi in numbers; and still another fifty to settle the remaining two-thirds of the country. In this great epic of winning a continent—which has no other parallel—the migrating families severed old ties and lost touch with the Atlantic Ocean and the commerce it bore, and the log cabin contributed to making people Americans instead of transplanted Europeans.

Log cabin life also offered collateral advantages that modern man is slowly but surely being denied—the need to be left alone. Although man, to be sure, is a social being and needs the association of his fellow beings, he also yearns at times, and for various reasons, for the therapy of solitude. It was to escape the pressures of his newspaper profession and the restraints of city life that caused Bob Pinkerton and his wife Kathrene to build a sixteen by twenty-four-foot log cabin in the Canadian woods in search of relaxation and privacy.[24]

The Indianapolis Star of October 22, 1967, reported that a group of families had founded an independent communal society at Indian Springs in Martin County, Indiana, in order to return to simple living without the superficial veneer of modern society. A three-story house of round logs was erected as a meeting hall, church, school, and community residence as the members set about their plans to build individual log cabin homes to be lighted by candles and heated by open fireplaces.

Today, electronic surveillance devices invade the privacy of the American home, office, and vehicle; commercial espionage ferrets out business secrets; computers maintain a statistical dossier on the family's buying, eating, sleeping, and sexual habits; credit bureaus keep a close record of its financial status—these and other things tend to deny man his right to aloneness. The outer world seems to be gaining in its persistent invasion of family privacy as the state demands it know more and more about the habits and needs of its citizens in order to deal adequately with them. The birth and death certificates, marriage, deed, and will records are open to scrutiny, and little is hidden from prying eyes.

Our complex lives, in contrast to the simple existence of our log cabin forbears, are being systematically exposed as matters of governmental record. In retrospect, as we reflect on American frontier society, despite its many practical disadvantages in comparison with the conveniences of modern living, we are beginning to have a greater appreciation of its solitude, its separation from the written questionnaire, the telephone survey, the census taker at the front door, the demanding application forms, the punch cards, and the magnetic tape.

One might add that man is busy today poisoning the air he breathes, and so polluting the water that hardly a river remains that he can safely dip a drink from. In log cabin days he did not smother in his own wastes, and although he mastered his environment, his inventiveness had not perfected a technology which, if used recklessly, could terminate his brief history and make the earth uninhabitable.

Notes—Chapter 10

1. The two most complete works wherein the question of Jackson's birthplace is discussed are Elmer Don Herd, Jr., *Andrew Jackson, South Carolinian*, Lancaster County (S.C.) Historical Commission (1963); and Max F. Harris, *The Andrew Jackson Birthplace Problem*, State Department of Archives and History (N.C.) (Raleigh, 1963).

2. D. A. Tompkins, *History Of Mecklenburg County* (Charlotte, N.C., 1903); see illus. following p. 188; *cf.* John and Alice Durant, *Pictorial History Of American Presidents*, 2nd ed. (New York, 1962), 59, where the statement is blandly made that Jackson was born in a log cabin and another illustration of his log birthplace appears!

3. Marquis James, *The Life of Andrew Jackson* (New York, 1938); *cf.* Robert V. Remini, *Andrew Jackson* (New York, 1966).

4. Tompkins.

5. Edwin P. Hoyt, *James Knox Polk* (Chicago, 1965), 5.

6. Charles Grier Sellers, Jr., *James K. Polk, Jacksonian, 1795–1843* (Princeton, 1957), 5.

7. From an account by David Lowry Swain. The excerpt quoted was supplied me by Mrs. Elizabeth W. Wilborn, Staff Historian, Department of Archives and History, Raleigh, N.C.

8. Quotation from a letter written by David Lowry Swain, January 14, 1852, also supplied by Mrs. Wilborn.

9. From an article by Emma Look Scott, *Olympian*, I, No. 5 (May 1903), also supplied by Mrs. Wilborn.

10. Philip S. Klein, *President James Buchanan, A Biography* (University Park, Pa., 1962).

11. Sherman Day, *Historical Collections Of Pennsylvania* (Philadelphia, 1843), 355. This author states that the Buchanans lived in one of the log cabins and had a store in the other where the elder Buchanan "drove a small but profitable traffic with the Indians."

12. R. G. Horton, *The Life and Public Services Of James Buchanan* (New York, 1856), 14.

13. I am indebted to Professor Philip S. Klein for transcripts of several newspaper clippings which he obtained from the scrapbooks of informants when he was writing his biography of Buchanan. Among these data was an excerpt from a letter written by a Buchanan descendant, Reginald B. Henry of Roanoke, Virginia, to R. F. Nichols, March 12, 1937. Mr. Henry wrote that his father, J. Buchanan Henry, was in total ignorance about the James Buchanan birthplace cabin, and that his cousin, Annie Buchanan, told him "she did not have any belief in the genuineness of this cabin as the birthplace, though she thought it might possible have been an outhouse of the place."

14. "The Authenticity of Lincoln's Birthplace Cabin," *Lincoln Lore* (Fort Wayne, Ind.), No. 1016, September 27, 1948; see also *ibid.*, No. 1019, October 18, 1948. Much of my data relative to the Lincoln cabin were taken from Roy Hays, "Is The Lincoln Birthplace Cabin Authentic?" *The Abraham Lincoln Quarterly*, V, No. 3 (September 1948), 127–163.

15. Eleanor Atkinson, "Lincoln's Boyhood," *The American Magazine*, February 1908, 36–369; for a more detailed account of her interview with Dennis Hanks see her *The Boyhood Of Lincoln* (New York, 1908).

16. William E. Wilson, *Indiana, A History* (Bloomington, Ind., 1966), 153–159.

17. Claude G. Bowers, *The Tragic Era* (New York, 1929).

18. Hamlin Garland, *Ulysses S. Grant* (New York, 1898), 1. Franklin Spencer Edmonds, *Ulysses S. Grant* (Philadelphia, 1915), says correctly that Grant's small, frame cottage birthplace was removed and preserved at Columbus; W. E. Woodward, *Meet General Grant* (New York, 1928), 12, states categorically and correctly that Grant's birthplace was not a log cabin.

19. Henry C. Deming, *The Life of Ulysses S. Grant* (Hartford, 1868), 24.

20. Jesse R. Grant, *In the Days of My Father, General Grant* (New York, 1925).

21. John Drury, *Historic Midwest Houses* (Minneapolis, 1947), 242.

22. *Log Cabin Days* (Riley Historical Society, Kansas, 1929), 37.

23. "A Journal of Travels into the Arkansas Territory, Thomas Nuttall's Journey, 1819," *Early Western Travels, 1748–1846*, ed. Reuben Gold Thwaites (Cleveland, 1904), XIII, 48.

24. Kathrene Pinkerton, *Wilderness Wife* (New York, 1939).

11 Conclusion

In the log complex that characterized American frontier society, which persisted in the southern states up to the eve of the Civil War, and continued in the Midwest and Far West even later, the reader can readily recognize a distinctive expression of *folk architecture*. The American pioneer family not only adapted to a sylvan environment (and there were about six hundred species of trees native to the United States), but utilized the trees as an integral part of its folkways. The frontiersman lived in a log dwelling, kept his livestock in a log stable, cured his meats in a log smokehouse, stored his farm implements in a log shed, sent his children to a log schoolhouse, worshipped in a log church, served on a jury in a log courthouse, and sentenced the law infractors of his society to terms in a log jail. He split logs and set them up in a zig-zag configuration to build what he called worm or snake rail fences around his property, and he adapted the whole log for a number of domestic uses ranging from stools, tables and benches, to chopping blocks, corn mortars (Figure 12), pirogues, corduroy roads, and even cradles made by troughing the logs.

Where there was a wide variety of timber available on or near his property, as in western Pennsylvania, for example, the settler learned to make selective use of each of the different kinds of wood. White oak afforded the best material for building log cabins and farm wagons; chestnut, black walnut, and locust were strong and durable and excellent for fence posts and rails; black walnut went into the stocks of the famous Kentucky rifle, actually made by Pennsylvania

German gunsmiths; the more elastic hickory and the light-weight black, white, and red ash were ideally suited for scythe handles, ox yokes, and other farming implements and tools; red maple made fine spinning wheels, saddletrees, bureaus, bedsteads, and chairs; and white pine was commonly used in frame buildings and for timber and siding. Hickory was the preferred fireplace fuel because it was slow-burning and gave out intense heat without throwing sparks across the room. The bark of the red, scarlet, and black oaks were much used in tanning, although other barks were also used.

Men and women split oak and ash and wove the splints into baskets for measuring, toting, or storing, and craftsmen learned to make durable chairs without nails or glue by inserting seasoned rounds of hickory in holes drilled in green wood, which, in drying, shrank to an everlastingly tight joint. Fiddlers made violins of curly maple to play at frolics, and ballad singers made their guitars of black gum or cedar. It was a period not of stone, bronze, and iron, but one of wood, and there was a wide variation in preference in the selection of trees, depending upon regional ecology, and experience became the best teacher.

Like folk speech or folk songs, the residential log cabin and associated log housing, products of cultural tradition and natural conditions, were created by common people to suit their own needs. Like other forms of folk architecture, log housing was a simple, direct expression of a fundamental human need transmitted orally from one generation to another, or from one man to his neighbor, without written direction or professional counsel. I have referred throughout this volume to the American log cabin, admittedly a loose term, because it must be conceded that every feature employed in the construction of a log dwelling, large or small, had ample precedents in Old World folk architecture. Nevertheless, one can travel today through southern Germany, Switzerland, Russia, and the rural parts of the Scandinavian countries examining old log dwellings that have survived the attrition of time without finding a single example that is identical in all respects with the American log cabin.

What happened in the acculturative processes in the New World was that particular architectural features found in older lands, some having distinct national or ethnic individuality, were brought together in a new combination, and the American log cabin emerged. Even so, and after all that has been said in this volume, it is difficult to phrase a precise definition of an American log cabin in contrast to a log dwelling of European provenience. As the little girl said when asked to describe a giraffe, "I can show you one, but I can't tell you what it is." To describe an American log cabin requires an explanation as lengthy as de Crêvecoeur's answer to his own question, "What is an American?" There are obviously different variations of American log cabins, but these characteristics have not yet been isolated definitively and formal types established. When this task is finally completed, it can be assumed that folk cultural regions can be delineated, but this remains a task for the future.

An interesting example of the folk extension of log house techniques in America was in the log corn crib to which incidental reference has already been made. Here we have an example of a utilitarian log structure that has no Old World traditions because corn was strictly a New World product unknown on the European continent before the discovery of America. Built to accommodate an indigenous product, the corn crib represented, as in other types of log construction, European antecedents that blossomed forth as a pseudoinnovative New World architectural form (see Figure 80).

John Woods, whose account of log cabins in the English settlement in Illinois was quoted in Chapter 3, also wrote a detailed description of the log corn crib and its functionality. This is what he said:

Corn-cribs are built the same as cabins, except that they are placed on logs, so as to stand hollow for some distance from the earth; the bottom is made of cleft pieces, laid pretty close. They are built of different lengths and widths, but about six feet on the inside is deemed wide enough, as corn will dry in them better than if wider. The roof is only drawn in on one side, which two lengths of boards will cover. As they lay the top pretty flat, they most times take off the greater part, or the whole of the boards, when filling them with Indian corn ears, as they only gather the ears.

When full, or the whole growth of the year is put in, the boards are put

Figure 80. A contemporary round log corn crib on Fouracre Farm near Smyrna, Delaware, built along traditional lines.

on, and the weight poles again laid on. Should a heavy shower, or even a set rain, come on whilst the corn-crib is filling, as the bottom and sides are not close, not being mudded, it will soon dry out again without damaging the corn. I had one built for 15 dollars, that will hold upwards of 600 bushels of corn in the ear. I suppose it would hold near 1000 bushels of cleared corn. The Americans never shell theirs till it is wanted for use or market; but most of what is sold, is in the cob or ear.[1]

Of equal interest as another example of American folk architecture are the log tobacco barns, and since tobacco, like corn, was also unknown in Europe before the discovery of America, these structures also have certain innovative qualities. Built both of round and hewn logs, old tobacco barns can still be seen today in many parts of the South, many abandoned, others still in use. Their longevity has been greater than that of the log dwellings constructed by their builders, whose descendants now live primarily in frame houses. The chimneys or appended stacks distinguish the tobacco barns from conventional farm barns or stables, inasmuch as heat was required in the curing process. Slow-burning wood fires circulated the heat around the tobacco leaves hung on racks to age and mellow. The log tobacco barn, some constructed in double pens, was the predecessor of the modern tobacco curing barn with its kilns, thermostats, and sheet-iron flues, built either of wood or brick. Some of the old structures have been redaubed with cement to replace the crumbled clay caulking, and some have been completely covered with red, black, or even green tar paper, and still others with tin siding to protect the weather-worn log sides against further erosion.

On a recent motor trip, without getting out of my car, I counted more than twenty old tobacco barns along the highway between Raleigh, North Carolina, and Myrtle Beach, South Carolina, the logs still exposed. There were doubtless many others covered with tar paper or tin. Between Reidsville, North Carolina, and Danville, Virginia, I saw at least fifty of different sizes, also with the logs exposed; see Figures 81, 82. I have not been able to document the date when the first log tobacco barns were built in the South, but one can infer they were an invention of the people who built the first log dwellings. A treatise on tobacco published in London in 1800 contains an illustration of a tobacco barn of round logs.[2]

Since the distribution of tobacco barns is highly sectional, they are insignificant in numbers compared to extant log dwellings found throughout the United States. In March 1939, the United States Department of Agriculture published *The Farm-Housing Survey* (Misc. Publication No. 323), the only study of its kind that has ever been made. It was conducted under the direction of the Bureau of Home Economics, whose investigators called on 595,855 occupied farmhouses in 308 counties of forty-six states. (Pennsylvania and New York were omitted, which is regrettable, because of the large number of log dwellings still standing in these states.)

Figure 81. Abandoned tobacco barn of round logs, Route 29 north of Reidsville, North Carolina.

The sampling purported to be a valid representation of the 7,360,212 occupied farm dwellings in the United States revealed by the 1935 census, although to my mind this is questionable because of the uneven distribution of log dwellings. For example, only Burlington and Middlesex Counties of New Jersey were included in the survey, and since no log houses were found in these two counties, none were recorded for the state. This leads to incorrect inferences since it is common knowledge that there are still log houses in other farm parts of New Jersey. In Delaware only one county, Sussex, was surveyed, where the incidence of log buildings is known to be much smaller than in New Castle County, which also has a number of farms.

The survey figures, which would appear to be on the low side, indicated that 3.7 percent of the occupied farm houses in the United States were of logs, and if this percentage is extended to the national farm house total, an estimate of 270,000 log farmhouses has

Figure 82. Hewn log tobacco barn west of Route 29, between Greensboro and Reidsville, North Carolina.

been projected. This does not take into account the log dwellings in cities, towns, and suburbs, nor the log barns, stables, sheds, etc., in the farm areas which run into additional thousands.

Although the basic concept of notched log construction diffused westward from Europe to America, and continued in a southerly and westerly flow over the Appalachians and through the Rockies as the frontier advanced, there was another cultural wave to North America which should not be overlooked. This influence came from the opposite direction—the same route that brought the Paleo-Indian huntsman from Asia to America in prehistoric times and also brought horizontal log construction to the Eskimo. The log dwelling entered Alaska from the east carried by Russians to what they called Russian America at the same time the concept was spreading across the continent to the Pacific.

Okhotsk in Siberia was a settlement of a log fort, a log church, and log houses in 1727 when the Danish-born navigator, Captain Vitus Bering, serving in the Russian navy, departed for Kamchatka on his first voyage to seek an answer to a puzzling question. This question raised by Peter the Great, and after his death in 1725 by his widow, Empress Catherine I, was whether or not the Asian and American mainlands were connected. Bering found the answer during a second voyage in 1741 which took him into Alaska across the straits now bearing his name. It was commercial, not geographical motives, that prompted the Russian curiosity because they were primarily interested in accumulating the wealth represented by the pelts of the seal, the sea otter, and other fur-bearing animals. Following Bering's voyage, the Russians built trading posts in Alaska to exploit the fur trade.

The *promyshlenniki*, rugged, boisterous hunters and trappers, were the first Russian frontiersmen in Alaska, and their adventures led to the organization of a Russian American Fur Company. Kodiak, or *Paulofski*, was the company's first headquarters where a number of log buildings were erected. In 1800, the company's activity was centered at present Sitka, then called *Novo Arkhangelsk* (New Archangel), where additional log structures were built. By 1861, New Archangel was the busiest port on the Pacific Ocean, not excluding San Francisco, and its population of 2500 people had built schools, hospitals, and even a public library. Alexander Baranof, governor of the Russian American Fur Company, ruled like a czar at Sitka and over the other scattered Russian communities in Alaska where a number of churches and chapels had been built.

When Secretary of State William H. Seward negotiated the purchase of Alaska in 1867, Americans, not fully aware of how well the Russians had developed the commerce during their 126-year ownership, called it "Seward's Folly" and "Seward's Frog Pond." Few Americans were conscious of the fact that Alaska, as Russia's eastern frontier, had undergone a pattern of log cabin building similar to that which characterized American pioneer life.

Trading posts, blockhouses, churches and chapels used to Christianize Alaska's Eskimo and Indian population were built by the

Russians of both round and hewn logs, and residences ranged from small one-room cabins to multifamily log dwellings. In Sitka in 1865 there were a number of large apartments 150 feet long by fifty to eighty feet wide, three stories high built of dovetailed, hewn spruce logs. They had whipsawed wooden floors tongue and grooved by hand, and the roofs were covered with sheet iron. The logs were painted a lemon-yellow and the roofs red.[3]

Some of Sitka's log structures were built under the direction of Adolf Karlovich Etolin, born in Alaska of a Finnish father and an Aleut mother. His father was a sea captain in the employ of the Russian American Company and he sent the boy to Finland to be educated. In 1840, Etolin was appointed chief manager of Russian

Figure 83. Hewn log cabin with dovetailed corners built by a Finn at Tenakee Springs, Alaska, in the 1920's resembles old Russian cabins. Original roof has been replaced with corrugated aluminum.

America and he imported a number of Finns to assist in the reconstruction of the chief Sitka buildings where hewn logs were widely used (see Figure 83).

There are still standing in Alaska a number of log structures built by Russians, or Finns in their employ. At Kenai, a fishing port southeast of Anchorage, there is a vacant hand-hewn log chapel dating back to the era of Russian ownership. As one might imagine, the Russians and Finns, who had been constructing log dwellings in their homelands for hundreds of years, would have developed sophisticated notchings and architectural embellishments different in appearance from the American log cabin. The chapel at Kenai (Figure 84), is of hewn logs, tightly fitted, with a gabled roof topped with a wooden spire and having an onion-like dome, characteristic of the Greek Orthodox Church. An old Russian-built blockhouse at Sitka, no longer standing, further illustrated the sophisticated log architecture of Russian America (see Figure 86).

The Russians carried on trade with California, importing among other commodities redwood siding which they nailed on the exterior walls of many of their log buildings. In the coastal areas of Petaluma County, California, one sees aged stumps of giant redwoods, some of which doubtless resulted from the forest activities of the Russians. As in other parts of the United States, there are still standing in Alaska old log buildings effectively concealed beneath exterior layers of board siding. In 1921 a frame building in Sitka that had formerly been used as the United States District Court House was torn down. It had previously been used as an Army barracks, and prior to 1867 it had been the barracks for Russian soldiers and workmen. When the redwood siding was stripped away, a Russian-built hewn-log structure was uncovered, with some of the redwood logs measuring eighty feet in length!

During the gold rush to Alaska in the late nineteenth century, which brought an influx of American prospectors, the log cabin influences from the west met those from the east. Hundreds of log cabins (as well as shanties, shacks, tents, and nondescript frame shelters) were thrown up by the gold miners, and some of these

Figure 84. Abandoned chapel at Kenai, Alaska, built 1846, shelters grave of founder, Egumen Nicolais, a Russian monk who brought Christianity to the area.

Figure 85. Russian church, built at Archangelsk in 1690 and later moved to Moscow, the kind of log architecture that was traditional with the Russians who settled Alaska. (From Martin Hürlimann, *Moscow and Leningrad*, London, 1958)

log structures are still standing, some enlarged and modified. Examples may be seen in Circle City, the oldest town in the Yukon, which could boast between 1895 and 1897 that it was the largest log cabin town in the world!

An American visitor to Fairbanks in 1939 wrote:

> Probably there are more log than frame houses; one story log dwellings, often with tin roofs; lots of log mansions, low and cozy and homelike and obviously snug and warm in winter. Nearly every little log house has a huge front window; all have electric lights (meters or transformers decorating the front porch) most of them have radios, many have telephones. . . .
> Flowers and bright weeds enliven earth-covered roofs of old log cabins. In Alaska, by the way, a log house is a "cabin," a frame dwelling, a house.[4]

In 1935 a United States emergency relief agency transported two hundred families to Alaska to establish a colony at Matanuska where, even at this late date, a number of log houses were erected for the newcomers. In 1941, when an American newlywed couple went to live at Anchorage they rented a log cabin, and the bride noted in a book she wrote telling of their Alaskan experiences that many of their neighbors were living in "sagging, hastily built log cabins." [5]

Many years before Americans built log cabins in Alaska, California, or the Oregon Territory, the Russians carried the concept of log housing down the Pacific coast to California. It began in 1808 when Ivan Kuskov set sail from Sitka on an exploration and sea otter hunting expedition and dropped anchor in Bodega Bay on the California coast north of present San Francisco. This territory was then claimed by Spain, but the Spaniards had made no serious effort at colonization. In August of 1809, Kuskov returned to Sitka with more than one thousand sea otter pelts taken in California waters and confirmation that this coastal area was not occupied by Europeans.

The Russians, under the auspices of the Russian American Company, returned to establish a port at Bodega, which they called *Port Rumiantzof*, and there they built a warehouse, a four room log residence, and a bathhouse. They also established four large ranches in

Figure 86. Russian blockhouse, part of stockade defense of Sitka, Alaska, against the Thlingets, which stood until about 1920, built in late eighteenth or early nineteenth century. Dozens of cannon balls were unearthed when it was torn down.

the area of present Freestone, Jenner, and Russian Gulch, and among their other activities planted an orchard of 260 trees which produced apples, peaches, pears, quince, and cherries. In 1812 they built a coastal fort and palisaded settlement called the Colony Ross (derived either from the Russian word *Rus* or *Rossiya*, a poetic name for the Russian state), which later became known as Fort Ross. Kuskov was the company's first manager or commandant at this settlement intended as a base for sea otter hunting, to grow food for the Alaskan settlement, and to extend Russian commercial influence.

On opposite corners of the palisades Kuskov built two two-story blockhouses or bastions of dovetailed hewn redwood logs, one with seven sides twenty-five feet in diameter, and the other with eight sides, twenty-eight feet in diameter, both having windows, doors, and cannon ports. The commandant's house constructed in the west corner of the palisaded area, containing six rooms, fireplace, and glass windows, was made of round redwood logs, hewn square at the ends to permit full dovetail notching and flush corners. A total of fifty-nine different structures were erected to accommodate the two hundred to four hundred inhabitants that eventually peopled the settlement, expanding from the original party brought by Kruskov of ninety-five *promyshlenniki* and eighty Aleut hunters and their skin bidarkas. Although the exact number is not known, it is certain that many of the buildings were of notched logs and Fort Ross was described by a contemporary French visitor as resembling a Muscovite village.

The structures at Fort Ross included a warehouse, blacksmith shop, tannery, coopers shop, carpenter shop, flour mill, stable, sheep cote, etc., as well as twenty-four log cabins built to house the Aleuts. A ten-room house known to have been constructed of horizontal redwood logs was built for the commissioned officers, and an eight room barracks, also of horizontally-laid notched redwood logs, accommodated some of the other men. Thus, through the extension of their commercial enterprise the Russians carried their log house technology into California, hundreds of miles south of their main settlement at Sitka. If their efforts had not been interrupted the

Figure 87. Juneau, Alaska, cabin, erected by Americans in 1882 as a dwelling; became first public school in 1885; in 1890 when picture was taken, it was being used as a church, with new bell tower under construction; torn down in 1914.

Russian log house would presumably have advanced farther down the California coastline to meet the northern movement of the stone and adobe architecture of the Spanish Franciscans. What happened was that the Russians, and Aleut hunters in their employ, carried on such a ruthless slaughter of the sea otter, storing the pelts at Fort Ross and Bodega for later shipment to China, Manchuria, Siberia, and Europe, that the animal practically disappeared from California waters. Although the Russians maintained more than three thousand head of cattle, horses, mules, and sheep, they were not successful as ranchers, and their attempt at agriculture also failed because of the absence of experienced farmers in the colony. By 1841 the settlement had become such an expensive burden that the Russians sold the property to Captain John A. Sutter for $30,000 and abandoned the settlement.[6]

As time went on the site of the fort became the center of a large American ranch, and the buildings were used for various purposes, although eventually they were mostly destroyed. The Russian Orthodox Chapel, with its six-sided wood tower, was successively used as a stable, grain storehouse, hay barn, and milk house, but it finally collapsed in the 1906 earthquake. Fortunately, enough of the wood was preserved to permit rebuilding the chapel as a feature of the Fort Ross Historic Park now operated as a memorial by the state of California. The two log bastions were used as pigstys until they fell apart, and they, too, have now been restored along with a replica of the original stockade which was torn down in 1893.

The commandant's house (covered with siding and modified for use as a hotel some years after the Russians left) is the only original log building remaining at Fort Ross. The roof and flooring were added after the siding was stripped off to expose the original redwood timber walls as they were originally notched and fitted together. As one examines these sturdy timbers today it is difficult to realize that they were raised in place more than 150 years ago by hardy *promyshlenniki* in accord with the folk housing practices in old Russia (see Figure 88).

Originally it was my hope that the several methods of corner notchings found on the American log cabin, and possibly other constructional features, could be neatly classified in terms of a chronology, if not by specific date, at least by different time periods. Once in a bold moment I made an attempt to do so, an ambition inspired by an account of the typology of log structures in Sweden published by Professor Sigurd Erixon in which he gave special emphasis to the corner joint or *knut* as a diagnostic trait for certain time periods.[7] I also discussed this subject with Dr. Gerda Boëthius, another Swedish log house authority, when she visited Wilmington, Delaware, in 1955. Dr. Boëthius thoroughly covered the subject in

Figure 88. Russian commandant's house, Fort Ross, California, built 1812, showing original west wall with round logs hewn square at the corners. Redwood
logs on front and other two sides were evened off when American owners
later affixed siding on the structure. (Courtesy Department of Parks and
Recreation, State of California)

a monumental volume on Swedish log construction.[8] The Swedish
scholars were in agreement that round logs, with curved notching
either on the top or bottom side of the log, are illustrative of the
very earliest *knut* in Sweden, whereas logs hewed square, with more
complicated corner notchings (of which there are a number of methods found on Swedish log structures), evolved later.

In 1953, I had an exchange of correspondence with Professor
Erixon, and I told him I was attempting to arrive at a dating system
for American log houses, and, in fact, he quoted a letter I wrote

him on September 20, 1953, in an article published in *Folk-Liv* in which I compared certain notchings on American cabins with illustrations of Swedish notchings he had published previously.[9]

Since that time I am less convinced that this is a valid approach, and after additional study, and so far as American log cabins are concerned, it has become evident to me that I am incapable of even approximately dating a log structure on the sole basis of the method of corner notching used in its construction. It is a different story in Sweden because an evolutionary process took place over several centuries by a relatively homogeneous ethnic group resulting in modifications of the *knut* and other associated architectural features. This may also be true of log houses in Finland, Russia, Poland, Switzerland, Germany,[10] and elsewhere, although the evidence is not available to the extent that it has been compiled in Sweden.

The Swedish cultural historian is permitted to view the evolution of the corner notching of the archaic round log dwelling from 800 or 1000 A.D. to the more sophisticated structures of hewn logs being built five hundred years later. Furthermore, in Sweden a mature method ultimately evolved in which the individual logs were hewn with six or eight sides, and notched with a finesse and variety totally absent on the American log cabin. Some of these Swedish dwellings and farmsteads have gable and roof adornments, spacious wings, and other features missing on American log structures.

The whole constructional process in America appears to have lacked orderly development, and instead of an early form undergoing gradual modification over a period of centuries, the time span was telescoped. Builders of differing cultural backgrounds were thrown together in a new environment with a resultant acceleration of what otherwise would have been a slow process of change. The different methods of corner notching characteristic of the American log cabin, discussed below, while representing Old World importations, were used contemporaneously in the postpioneer American settlements depending upon the skill, the whims, the available tools and materials, and the previous experience of the builder. I do not discount individual adherence to the local practices of a

cultural group, but this, too, is difficult to evaluate because log construction has been highly vulnerable to destructive forces, and we
have little data relative to dwellings that are no longer standing.
Furthermore, a cohesive body of traditions embraced by the European ethnic groups could not be expected to remain undiluted in
America where a mixture of racial stocks, a variety of religions,
diverse climatic and geographical conditions, and dissimilar economic
interests characterized the population growth. Consequently, folk
housing represented by the log cabin became, in time, a coalescence
of many influences.

Shurtleff wrote thirty years ago, "Investigators using the well-
developed technique of Dr. Sigurd Erixon should take measured
drawings of surviving log houses and cabins in every part of the
older states and the forested West and South, sketch and photograph
their notchings, and attempt to date them from documentary evidence." The sketching and photographing of the notches is not
difficult, and has been accomplished by a number of regional scholars, as I have done, but there are complications which Shurtleff did
not recognize. For instance, it is not unusual to find two different
methods of notching on the same structure, and on one house recorded by the Ohio Historical Society (Mintum-Taylor-Smith house
in Greene County) there are *three* different methods of notching.
Moreover, attempting to relate existing log structures to documentary evidence is another story. Only in rare instances are there deed
references to specific log dwellings, and there is such a paucity of
other recorded data that no accurate dates can be assigned to the
majority of log cabins from documentary sources, and this is particularly true of those built in the seventeenth and eighteenth centuries.

Up to the present writing I have been unable to discern any tem-
poral sequences in the several methods of corner notchings, because
in the New World, cabins of round logs, those of hewn logs, cabins
expertly built, and those crudely thrown up, some with simple, and
others with more complicated notchings, were all being erected
within a relatively narrow time span. I have seen structures of round

logs built in the present century (restaurant, taverns, residences, etc.) having notchings of the archaic type found on early log dwellings in Sweden. Conversely, as I indicated in an earlier chapter, some of the early cabins in the Delaware Valley are expertly hewn and dovetailed and far superior in construction to many cabins in the South and West which were built a century or more later.

In offering these comments, I am not in disagreement that it is still possible in the eastern United States to distinguish initial occupance patterns established by migrants from seaboard source areas. There is no question that, culturally speaking, the major source area for log housing on the Atlantic seaboard centered in southeastern Pennsylvania, but also included, as I have previously suggested, are the northern parts of the state of Delaware and southwestern New Jersey. Whereas one scholar inclines to exclude the Swedes as having been "lost in a sea of alien culture," [11] I submit that their early influence on tidewater Maryland before the beginning of the German emigration, added to their imprint on the Scotch-Irish who entered at New Castle, qualifies their inclusion. Therefore, I incline to credit the Germans of Pennsylvania, and the Scotch-Irish under the influence of *both* Germans and Swede-Finns, for being the prime disseminators of log construction methods, not only in the area east of the Mississippi, but through others, in turn influenced by them, to the Far West.

My observation of the most common kinds of corner notchings found on log cabins east of the Mississippi (and some of the same styles were taken farther west by eastern builders) coincides with those enumerated in a technical paper published in 1966 by Professors Fred Kniffen and Henry Glassie.[12] As a step in the direction of standardization, I have also borrowed the descriptive terms they used for the six most common methods: *saddle notching, V notching, diamond notching, full dovetailing, half dovetailing,* and *square notching.*

Saddle notching, the simplest method, is almost always used on round logs, which for maximum tightness of the corner joints, must extend beyond the plane of the wall. There are three forms of this

a. Saddle notch—top only

b. Saddle notch—bottom only

c. Saddle notch—top and bottom

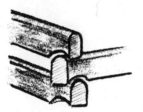

d. Hewn logs, saddle notched

e. Indented V-notch

f. Regular V-notch

g. Round log, V-notched

h. Adze for hewing log

Figure 89

method of curved notching, the double notch in which the notches are made on both sides of the log; the single notch on the top of the log; and the single notch on the bottom of the log; see Figure 89a, b, c. As noted earlier, the oldest European forms of log construction used the round log, and the saddle notch appears to be the most ancient method of corner timbering.

In contrast to the round saddle notch is the V-shaped cut of the V notch made in the bottom of the top log into which the chamfered head of the lower log fits. If the log is left in the round, the crown is usually cut pear-shaped, the pointed top of the lower log fitting the notch of the top log. When the log is hewn, the crown is cut with a top like that of the gable end of a house. Where V notching is used, the ends of the log are usually, but not always, flush (see Figure 89e, f, g).

When the diamond notch is used, the top and bottom ends of the log are chamfered to make a diamond-shaped crown. The logs must also be notched both top and bottom to support each other fully (see Figure 90).

Full dovetailing is one of the most complicated methods of corner timbering, requiring considerable skill in the use of an axe. This method locks the logs in both directions, produces a box corner, and slopes downward on every face of the notch so that the rain water will drain away from the joint. The full dovetail is usually confined to hewn logs although there are known examples of it being used on round log buildings (see Figure 90a, j).

The half dovetail is, in fact, half of a V notch, although it seems to have developed from the full dovetail; hence its name. The head of the notch slopes upward, but the bottom is flat, and the joint is easier to construct than the full dovetail (see Figure 90).

The square notch is a very simple form, but it lacks the quality of effectively interlocking the logs as in the other methods (see Figure 90n). It is found on logs that are square or rectangular in cross section, but never on round logs. Its basic weakness is sometimes strengthened by drilling and pegging, a corrective measure not required on the other five methods of corner notching. Although other

i. Full dovetailing

l. V-notch, log
ends tapered

n. Square notch

j. Full dovetailing

m. Half notch

o. Diamond notch

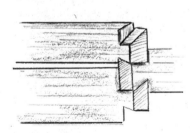

k. Half dovetail

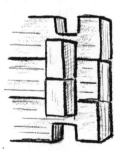

p. Double notch

Figure 90

methods of notching are sometimes encountered in the United States, such as the so-called "half-notch" and "quarter-notch," which I have observed in Texas, and the double-notch, a prevailing method in northern New Mexico, the five methods described above have the widest distribution in America.

On the old cabins in southeastern Pennsylvania, Delaware, and New Jersey, *i.e.*, the territory comprising the original New Sweden, the three predominant methods are saddle notching (usually single notching on the bottom of the log), V notching, and full dovetailing.

Figure 91. "A day is rapidly coming when the American log cabin, except for memorial structures, will be extinct." The seasoned logs from this frontier cabin at the foot of the Alleghenies, near Connellsville, Pennsylvania, have mostly been hauled away to be burned in modern fireplaces.

All three methods were known in Germany, Finland, and Sweden, and were used in America in the seventeenth century by builders from these Old World countries. Therefore, in a region known to be occupied by peoples of both German and Scandinavian origin, such as New Jersey, the method of corner notching observed on an old structure cannot with certainty be attributed to German, Swedish, or Finnish craft culture on the basis of typology alone, and in the absence of other evidence.

Kniffen and Glassie made an attempt to catalog the distribution of the differing methods of corner notching in the states east of the Mississippi, and the reader interested in pursuing the technical aspects of log housing will do well to consult their paper. A number of other geographers have been investigating the subject of settlement housing and doubtless further contributions will be made in the area of log buildings.

Geographers have come to recognize that there is an important difference between the *natural landscape* and the *cultural landscape*, in that the latter, which is the basis of cultural geography, reflects the alterations introduced by man such as dwelling houses, farm buildings, villages, towns, roads, mines, quarries, etc. The structure and forms of housing is one of the outstanding features of the cultural landscape, and is generally the first cultural phenomenon introduced into a region although it is inevitably subject to change. Future research may be expected to reveal additional data about the log cabin, particularly the associations of different methods of corner notchings with different cultural groups and why certain preferences resulted in the domination of one method over another in certain areas. This I will leave to others better qualified to investigate, but time is growing short. A day is rapidly coming when the American log cabin, except for memorial structures, will be extinct.

Notes—Chapter 11

1. "Two Years Residence in the Settlements on the English Prairie," *Early Western Travels, 1748–1846,* ed. Reuben Gold Thwaites (Cleveland, 1904), X, 279.

2. William Tatum, *An Historical and Practical Essay On The Culture And Commerce Of Tobacco* (London, 1800).

3. Henry W. Elliott, *Our Arctic Province* (New York, 1887), 32.

4. Henry A. Franck, *The Lure of Alaska* (New York, 1939), 112.

5. Constance Helmericks, *We Live in Alaska* (Boston, 1944).

6. An account of Fort Ross occurs in an unpublished thesis for the Master of Arts Degree, submitted to the faculty of the University of California (Berkeley) in 1949 by Ynez Haase entitled "The Russian American Company In California." A full account of Russian California penetration is found in *The Russians In California*, Special Publication No. 7, reprinted from the *Quarterly* of the California Historical Society, XI, No. 3, 1933; see also Clarence John DuFour, "The Russian Withdrawal From California," 133–146 of Morgan B. Sherwood, *Alaska And Its History* (Seattle, 1967). While I was investigating in the Fort Ross area I learned that there are a number of Russian families still living in the environs of Guerneville, California, who continue to speak their native language. It would appear that this group should constitute an interesting subject worthy of ethnic investigation.

7. Sigurd Erixon, "The North-European Technique Of Corner Timbering," *Folk-Liv*, Stockholm, 1937, 13–60.

8. Gerda Boëthius, *Den Nordiska Timmerbyggnadkonsten, etc.* (Stockholm, 1927).

9. Sigurd Erixon, "Är Den Nordamerikanska Timringstekniken Överförd Från Sverige," *Folk-Liv*, Stockholm, 1955–1956, 56–68.

10. One of the most interesting volumes published in Germany on wood architecture containing log house data is Herman Phleps, *Der Blockbau* (Karlsruhe, 1942).

11. Fred Kniffen, "Folk Housing: Key to Diffusion," *Annals of the Association of American Geographers*, LV, No. 4, Dec. 1965, 549–577.

12. Fred Kniffen and Henry Glassie, "Building in Wood in the Eastern United States," *Geographical Review*, Jan. 1966, 40–66. Mr. Glassie's appendix, "The Types of the Southern Mountain Cabin," to *The Study of American Folklore* (New York, 1968), also deals with the typology of log residences in the mountain area of Virginia, North Carolina, South Carolina, and Georgia.

APPENDIX

Appendix

John Woods' Description of Building a Log Cabin, 1820[*]

The buildings round us being chiefly of logs, I will give the best description in my power of a log-cabin; as I could form no idea of it till I saw one, that was at all like it. They are of various widths, lengths, and heights, but generally only one story high. The usual shape a long square, some are made of round, and others of hewn logs. In building a cabin, suppose 30 feet long and 20 wide; first, two logs, 30 feet long, are placed on the ground on a level, and about 18 feet from each other, these two logs are then notched in, near their ends, for a few inches; and then two more logs of 20 feet long, having their undersides also notched, are laid on the two first, forming [167] a long square of the following figure, about 26 feet long, and 16 feet wide on the inside. One square being thus formed, they next proceed to place on two more of the longest logs on the sides, notched as before, and then two of the shortest, as before; this they continue till the building is nine or ten logs high on each side, when the two last cross-logs are laid on three or four feet longer than the other cross ones; this is to form a sort of eaves to drip the logs; two more of the longest logs are then laid on, and this completes

* "Two Years Residence In The Settlements On The English Prairie," *Early Western Travels, 1748–1846,* ed. Reuben Gold Thwaites (Cleveland, 1904), X, 274–279.

the upright of the building. Two cross-logs, cut slanting at the ends, are next placed on, just the length of the width of the building, and then two more of the side-logs on the cross-logs, but not to the end of them by some distance; then two more, cut slanting at the ends, are placed just to reach to the last side-logs; thus drawing in the sides, till the side-logs meet in a point at the top of the building. [168] A cleft piece of a tree is next placed on the outer end of the long cross-logs, and pegged on to prevent the cleft boards from sliding off, this is done on each side of the building. The whole is then covered with cleft-boards, (here called clap-boards;) they are about four feet long and six inches wide, laid on nearly double, so as to cover the joints; the boards at the top of the cabin on one side come a little over those on the other. When the roof is thus covered, some poles are laid along the building to keep the boards on; these poles are kept at about three feet distance from each other, by some short pieces of wood placed on the boards, to keep up the weight-poles as they are called. When they have done thus far, they call the cabin "raised." But no door-place, window, fire-place, floor, or ceiling is yet made, nor is the house very close on the sides, but looks something like a bird-cage. Next a door-place, of the usual size, is cut through the logs, and two pieces of wood are nailed or pegged up to the ends of the sawed logs, to keep them in [169] their places, and to serve for door-posts; frequently two doors are made opposite to each other. The windows are made in the same manner as the door-places. The chimney is generally placed at the end of the building, and is made as follows: First, four or five logs are cut out the same as for a door-place, of what width people chuse, and then some logs are cleft and placed in the following form on the outside, ⌐   ⌐ so that the ends of them are let in between the ends of the end-logs of the cabin that were sawed. The cleft-logs are thus continued, till they rise as high as the logs that were sawed out. The chimney is then carried up thus, ⊤   ⊤ exactly in the form of the cabin, but of much smaller logs, till it rises above the roof of the building; it is drawn in and made smaller from the bottom to the top. It is then chunked, that is, cleft pieces of wood are driven in between the logs, to fill up the open places. The next thing to be done, is to mud the cabin on the outside [170] between the logs; that is, it is plastered with loam or clay: this is sometimes done on the inside also, but more frequently cleft boards are pegged on to cover the joints on the inside. A few pieces of timber are next laid to lay the floor on, which is most commonly made of cleft-logs, hewn smooth on one side, and notched a little on the under side to lie level on the sleepers or joists. A ceiling is then made; some small saplings are cut and put in between the side-logs of the building, just under the roof, about three feet apart; and these ceiling joists are then covered with cleft boards, beginning at one end of the cabin, and laying a line across the end on the two joists, and then another row with their ends just resting on the first; and this is continued till the whole is covered. Most times the chimney is walled up several feet on the inside, the stones are laid in loam or clay instead of mortar; and above the wall it is plastered on the inside, and sometimes on the outside to the top of the chimney. The hearth is [171] made of stone or clay. The doors are generally made of cleft boards, nailed or pegged on some ledges, with wooden hinges, made in the following manner. A piece in the back part of the door is left longer than the door, and enters a hole in the sill; and at the top of the door a piece is also left to rest against the top of the door-place, which is covered with a piece of wood, either nailed or pegged over it. The windows are always sash ones; the usual size of the glass is eight inches by ten; the windows are sometimes made to open with hinges, and others to slide backwards and forwards, while others take out and in. When the doors are made of sawed boards they have eight or ten panes of glass in them, and then it is seldom there is any other window in the cabin. A porch is often made before the cabin, the whole length of it, and covered with cleft boards; which cost seventy-five cents a hundred, cutting the trees and cleaving out; they are always made from large trees, mostly the black [172] oak. Cabins are frequently made double; that is, two are built from 10 to 20 feet a-part, with a roof laid over the space between them. A shelter like this is very convenient, and, in the summer, it is more comfortable than a close room in so warm a country.

Many cabins, belonging to the Americans, have no ceiling nor windows, and some of them have no floor, nothing but the bare earth; and some are not mudded, but open on all sides. Locks to doors are nearly unknown, but wooden bolts are common with the English: many of the American houses have only a latch, and some have not even that.

A double cabin, with a 20-feet porch between, with floor and ceiling, finished as above described, may be built for the sum of 150 dollars, 33*l*. 15*s*., or something less. But with ceiling, floor, and doors, made of sawed boards, will come, I suppose, to near 50*l*. Sawing comes very high, being 9*s*. per hundred feet; but the sawyers cut [173] down the trees and go with the horses that draw them to the pit.

The cabin I inhabit first consisted of a double one, with a porch 20 feet wide between them: this I have since converted into two rooms; the end rooms are of logs, the centre ones of frame and board, with a brick chimney. At the back of the cabin I have added a cellar, &c. Smoke-houses are very common, and built much as dwelling-houses, only slighter, and not often mudded. Some cross-pieces are put on the joists to hang the bacon on. I have built one; it cost 23 dollars; it is about eighteen feet square and nine feet high. We are obliged to cut our flitches asunder, as we have not sufficient height above the fire. Old wood, nearly rotten, is best for drying bacon, as it makes much smoke and but little strong fire. The fires are kept burning a considerable length of time, as bacon, in this warm climate, requires to be well dried, to keep. The Americans, do not, in general, I think, allow sufficient [174] salt. The average price of salt near three pence per pound; bacon from eight to twelve and a half cents per pound; in summer it is sometimes rather higher; now (August) from ten to twelve and a half cents.

A Birthplace of America *

You go in by a little door in a brick annex to the Delaware State Museum, in Dover, and there, inside, is a veritable log cabin, with hewn logs showing the marks of the adze, and buff-colored chinking of clay. The shingles of the pitched roof are not original—roofs wear out—but they are very old.

You enter the front door and find yourself in the single room, very small, that was home to a Delaware family at least 200 and maybe 250 years ago. The walls are simply the inside of the single thickness of logs and mud daubing. The little glass-paned window may replace a wooden slide shutter of the wilderness days, and the boards of the sleeping shelf (like an open attic) form the kind of bedtime nook reserved for children or guests. There's a fireplace. The table, chairs, and benches are certified of the early 18th century.

That's what the museum had to show visitors last night, and we warmly congratulate the Archives Commission, its Archivist Leon de Valinger, Jr., (who discovered the house) and the museum staff on a salient job of conservation. For what is now preserved for future generations is a rare survival of America's log-cabin days and all they suggest of the earliest American tradition of courage in tackling a great wilderness. This little house is tangible history.

The State Museum could not better mark its fifth anniversary than by offering this example of the type of house-building that the Swedes introduced to America via Delaware and New Jersey. Sweden was (and still is) a forested land, with straight evergreens fit for easy notching and laying up as walls. From the shores of the Delaware the log houses went west and south with the pioneers. This house is of white oak logs. Oak doesn't grow as straight as fir or hemlock, but whoever built the tiny house now rescued from the side of the highway near State Road Junction wished to build for keeps.

As well as to Mr. deValinger, public thanks can go to C. A.

* Wilmington (Delaware) *Journal*, Feb. 15, 1955.

Weslager, the historian and skilled archaeologist who led the Delaware Archaelogical Society's careful excavation of the site. The soil was rich in things like coins, buttons, and tobacco-pipes over a span of centuries of domesticity. And thanks are due, also, to the State Highway Department for help in moving the house to Dover.

Index

Abbottstown, Pennsylvania, 233
Abraham the Finn, 140, 152
Abraham Lincoln Birthplace Historical Site, Hodgenville, Kentucky, 289, 291
Absecon, New Jersey, 174
Acadia, Canada, 81
Acrelius, Israel, quoted, 160
Adair, Samuel Lyle, 308
Adams, Clement, quoted, 88
Adams, John Quincy, 280, 281
Addison Township, Vermont, 121
"Adena," Ohio, 241
Adobe, 35, 36, 38, 112, 331; caulking, 39; Indians and, 51
Agriculture, 22, 25, 39, 316; California, 330, 331; Delaware, 154, 162, 165, 226; Dutch, 128, 131; English farmhouses, 103, 139; farmhouse census (1939), 320–22; German, 85–86, 211, 216, 217, 235; Grant and, 300, 302; Harrison farms, 262, 263; implements, 317; Indian, 47, 50, 52, 62, 65, 136, 235; Lincoln family and, 291, 295; Maryland, 136, 138; New Jersey, 176; Panic of 1837 and, 261; ranching, 35–36, 305, 328, 330, 331, 332; Scotch-Irish, 227, 234–35, 277; slavery and, 246, 247, 249–52; Virginia, 99, 249
Alabama, 33, 76, 115*n*15, 268; slavery in, 249, 250

Alaska, *xiv*, 58, 153, 322–30
Albany, New York, 127, 128, 129–30, 131, 133; Harrison campaign and, 270, 271
Albion, Illinois, 71, 75
Albrecht, Josephine, *xxi*
Aleuts, 324, 330, 331
Algonkian Indians, 47, 48, 49; place-names, 200; wigwams, 51, 52, 53, 120, 127, 128, 136
Allegheny County, Maryland, 144
Allegheny County, Pennsylvania, *xii*
Allegheny Mountains, 4, 70, 80, 267; Bradshaw in, 233; Buchanan in, 283; Dickens in, 78; as frontier, 6, 32, 38, 235, 237, 239; McMillan in, 230; Simpleton in, 126
Allegheny River, *xii*, 6, 61
Alloway Creek, New Jersey, 170, 171, 172
Alricks, Jacob, 159
Alsace, 208, 212
Altenburg, Missouri, 34
Ambridge, Pennsylvania, 60
America (vessel), 208
American Notes (Dickens), 78
American Revolution, xvii, xxiv, 5, 31, 42, 199, 213, 224, 225; Indians and, 62; Ohio partition after, 239; Scotch-Irish in, 226, 277; Valley Forge camp, 81–82
Amish, 211

351